The Preachers' Teacher

The meaning and message of the Sermon on the Mount

COVENANT
PUBLISHING

STUDIES IN HONOR OF
DR. MARION W. HENDERSON

Edited by Danny D. Clymer

www.covenantpublishing.com

P.O. Box 390 Webb City, Missouri 64870
Call toll free at 877.673.1015

Library of Congress Cataloging-in-Publication Data
The preachers' teacher : the meaning and the message of the Sermon on
the mount ; studies in honor of Dr. Marion W. Henderson / Danny D.
Clymer, Editor.
    p. cm.
Includes bibliographical references.
  ISBN 1-892435-40-3 (pbk.)
  1. Sermon on the mount. I. Henderson, Marion W., 1922- II. Clymer,
Danny Drewry, 1948- . III. Title.
  BT380.3.P74 2003
  226.9'077—dc21

                              2003002397

Acknowledgments

I am blessed that so many Christian friends wanted to help make this book possible. The obvious are those who wrote the chapters. The diversity of gifts and ministries of these men are reflected in the different styles of writing, testimony to the breadth of Dr. Henderson's influence over the span of fifty plus years of ministry.

For an edited work of this nature there are more Christlike servants needed to proofread, correct, check references, and type the final copy. I want to thank Linda Clymer, Ron and Nicole Gagnon, Paula Harrison, Curt and Linda Nordhielm, Sue Rogers, and Leslie Starasta who served with excellence when needed. John Hunter from Covenant Publishing encouraged and supported me throughout the whole process, from contract to finished book.

Foreword

Marion Wright Henderson was born on December 22, 1922, near Hillsboro, Illinois. Graduating from high school in 1941, Marion was drafted into the Army in 1943. During his two years of military duty he served as a surgical technician. He married his high school sweetheart, Vera Elaine Martin, on March 28, 1943, in Abilene, Texas.

He enrolled in Lincoln Bible Institute, Lincoln, Illinois, in June 1945 and graduated three years later. He spent the summers of 1948-1950 attending Greenville College standardizing his LBI degree. He and Vera moved to Scottsburg, Indiana, in the fall of 1948 to minister with the Zoah Christian Church and to further his education with Southern Baptist Theological Seminary in Louisville, Kentucky.

In the fall of 1951 (and continuing through 1976) he taught at LBI (now Lincoln Christian College), while also beginning a 25-year ministry with the South Fork Church of Christ near Rochester, Illinois. Those who heard him on special occasions and in numerous revivals came away challenged, inspired, and with a deeper understanding of the Word of God. He received his Ph.D. in 1966, and soon thereafter became known as "Doc."

When he became "Coach," he extended his teaching pulpit from the classroom to the basketball court in what is now called Henderson Hall. That setting allowed him to shape a whole generation of preachers. While they practiced the skills connected with getting the ball through the hoop, they learned discipline, endurance, and character. Several alumni admit that they came to Lincoln Christian College primarily to play basketball and left to preach the gospel because of Coach Henderson's influence.

The summer of 1976 he was called to serve as the Chairman of the Biblical Department for Central Florida Bible College, now Florida Christian College. He then served as President of that college from 1980-1986.

Dr. Henderson returned to LCC in 1986 to work as "Special Assistant to the President" so that he and Vera could be closer to their daughters: Jane, Jill, and Judy, their sons-in-law, and their six grandchildren. He remained as professor with the college until his retirement in the spring of 2003.

For over fifty years, he has embodied the words of Earl C. Hargrove's inaugural theme: "The Preachers Are Coming." Hundreds of students can testify that Dr. Henderson preaches when he teaches and teaches when he preaches. Many freshmen would say that his Gospels class not only taught them the life of Christ, it also challenged them to a deeper commitment to Christ and persuaded them for the first time to consider Christian leadership ministry. His passion for preaching and teaching and his love for word studies in the Greek New Testament have furnished insights and illustrations for his many lectures in third-year Greek.

Thank you, Dr. Henderson, for a life well lived as a preaching teacher and for the rich legacy you are leaving through the lives of your students who are preaching and teaching the Good News all over the world.

Ben Merold
Harvester Christian Church
St. Charles, Missouri

Contents

Introduction to the Sermon on the Mount

Matthew 5:1-2

Knofel Staton

*¹Now when he saw the crowds, he went up on a
mountainside and sat down. His disciples came to him,
²and he began to teach them, saying:*

Augustine was the first person to call Matthew 5–7 The Sermon on the Mount. The Sermon on the Mount has received more attention than any other single section of Jesus' teaching. It has been viewed as the Magna Charta of the kingdom; the compendium of Christ's doctrine; the ordination address to the twelve (Barclay 78-9); Jesus' preventive medicine (Bruner 133); Jesus' design for living in the new age (Neil 156); an inaugural address (Shephard 176); the manifesto of the king (Morgan 41); and the most searching and powerful utterance we possess concerning moral life (Hunter 9).

The Sermon on the Mount is the most quoted section of the New Testament by the Ante-Nicene Fathers during the first three centuries of Christianity (Allen 245) and throughout the 20th century has been the stimulus for more entire books than any other passage of the New Testament.[1] Hunter noted that, "after nineteen hundred years, the Sermon on the Mount still haunts men . . . some may praise it while others curse it, but they cannot ignore it. This Sermon continues like some mighty magnetic mountain" (9). Stott describes it as the best known of Jesus' teachings, but also both the least understood and obeyed (15). Bauman views it as "the most important and most controversial biblical test" (3).

Several scholars believe this section is not one sermon, but a collection of Jesus' teachings[2]; however, others believe Jesus spoke the Sermon on the Mount in one setting.[3] The rationale for this being a collection of sayings is weak. Plummer is correct, "There is too much order . . . and too much coherence. . . . Could anything so orderly and coherent be constructed out of short extracts from the Epistles of St. Paul?" (56). It would be inappropriate for people to suggest I did not write this specific chapter because they found similar or identical statements in some of the thirty-five books and over two hundred articles I have written. It seems more likely that Jesus spoke this Sermon in one setting as a preview of His holistic relational teachings, some of which He would repeat at different times and to different audiences, which is normal for popular speakers to do.

The more important question is, "How does the Sermon on the Mount fit into the big picture (purpose) of Matthew's Gospel?" It is clear that Matthew was writing to a Jewish audience for the following reasons: (1) Jesus' family tree is traced no further than to Abraham, while Luke traces it to Adam; (2) Matthew repeatedly quotes Old Testament prophets to affirm Jesus as the Messiah; (3) Matthew patterns Jesus' early life after some of Israel's key experiences—life threatened as an infant, going to Egypt for the continuation of His life, after leaving Egypt being baptized (Israel's crossing the Red Sea was considered their baptism, 1 Cor. 10:2), being tempted forty days (Israel for forty years), and Jesus going to a mount to give instructions (Israel at Mt. Sinai to receive God's instructions).

However, this does not mean that Jesus is God's new Moses, as some suggest, for not once is Jesus referred to as the new or second Moses anywhere in the New Testament, although God had the opportune time to do so in the mount of transfiguration experience (Matt. 17:1-8). Matthew is the only Gospel that mentions the church (16:18; 18:17). The church is to fulfill God's original intention for Israel by keeping God's call of privilege and purpose in proper balance, which He first issued in Genesis 12:2-3.[4] Paul wrote that the purpose side of that call was "the gospel preached in advance" (Gal. 3:8), and Peter announced that the church inherited that purpose (Acts 3:24-25). On the one hand, Matthew clearly revealed Israel's failure to keep privilege and purpose balanced (the parables in Matt. 22:28–23:14), while on the other hand revealed Jesus as the designer of the ones who would—His disciples, the church (16:18).

Keeping privilege and purpose balanced is essential for the church to advance the kingdom (will, rulership, kingship, charactership) of heaven (of God), which is a major theme in Matthew.[5] This Sermon illustrates the kind of life necessary to keep privilege and purpose balanced and thus to advance God's kingdom. The Sermon on the Mount demonstrates that Christianity does not fulfill God's will by ritualism, but by relationships; not by legalism, but by lovalism[6]; and not by being coldly correct, but by being warmly compassionate. That is the only way righteousness (proper relationships—God's kind) can surpass that of the Pharisees and teachers of the Law—the major issue in the Sermon on the Mount (5:20). This Sermon issues the call for each Christian to be different "from both the nominal church and the secular world" (Stott 19).

There are many different suggested ways to view the contents of this Sermon.[7] Some of them include seeing it as a handbook for the early church's teaching, with the Sermon on the Mount being an interim ethic (Trites 181), or an impossible ideal (Tasker 60). However, the way to interpret the Sermon on the Mount must come from the identity of both the contents and the first, intended audience. Here are some of the ways the content has been described: (1) the lifestyle all Christians are to follow which will make our world a better place (Dumais 316-26); (2) the messages Jesus' disciples are to take to the world (Barclay 78); (3) a summary of Christian morality (Lambrecht 20); (4) the character of kingdom people with moral principles that surpass all human standards as Christ's ideal righteousness (Shephard 76-7); (5) a summary of the repentant lifestyle (Keener 55); (6) a charter of what it means to be like Christ (Piga 491-3); (7) an assault on pharisaic reading of the Torah (Donelson 43-53); (8) community living taken seriously (Bailey 85-94); (9) the relational theology of the oldest church in Christianity (Betz 74-80); (10) ways to demonstrate the transformed life (Williams 89-112); (11) ways to build the kind of community God desires (Bailey and Saunders); (12) ways to demonstrate radical pastoral care (Lischer); (13) the ethical goal of every Christian (Hagner 83); (14) the ideal Christian life (Plummer 57); (15) Jesus' way to live when facing relational issues (Thurneysen 14); (16) counter-cultural living (Stott; and Barth IV. 2 188); (17) practical demonstrations of being impelled by the Holy Spirit (Barth II.2 699); (18) a counterpart to the address on the last judgment in Matthew 25:31-46 (Lenski 179-80); (19) not a complete set of regulations, but "situations and responses to show what it means when Christ's presence enters a perverted world" (Jeremias 33). Perhaps the finest description is Willard's, "a curriculum for Christlikeness" (311).

While all the above use different descriptions, they converge on describing the empowered characteristics of Christian living. Jesus preached the Sermon on the Mount shortly after He called His first disciples, who soon afterwards witnessed His healing powers. So perhaps Jesus' disciples may have asked or pondered this question, "Is our ministry as disciples to be demonstrated first of all and best of all by doing miracles of healing?" To that question, Jesus would have answered, "No," by the content in the Sermon on the Mount.

But how will the new movement Jesus will build (the church) succeed with the kinds of shady leaders He had already chosen and will continue to choose? All were from Galilee, which produced people with a speech impediment. These men were uneducated (Acts 4:13); some smelled like fish; a couple had quick tempers (James and John, whom Jesus nicknamed "sons of thunder"); one kept putting his foot into his mouth (Peter); one exploited people's money for taxes and for his own personal wealth (Matthew); and one probably carried a hidden sword to start or join a potential revolution against Rome (Simon the Zealot). How could such characters be channels for transforming the character and destiny of the world (Staton 69-70)?

To that question the Sermon on the Mount gives the only answer that will work—righteousness (proper relationships) that surpasses the Pharisees and teachers of the Law—the focus of the Sermon (5:20). Consequently, in this Sermon Jesus introduces what will be expected of His disciples by prioritizing the characteristics His disciples would have to develop in their relationships to self, God, others, rituals, and things. And that is the organizational flow of the Sermon.

The Sermon begins with the internal characteristics (beatitudes), moves to the influence those characteristics have (salt and light), and flows through the kinds of exterior conducts that spring from the interior characteristics. The Sermon then concludes by describing the destiny of those who will and will not live the relational activities described in the Sermon. Every external relational fruit mentioned in this Sermon is rooted in and comes out of one or more of the beatitudes.

The Sermon on the Mount is not so much a contradiction to the old way in Judaism as it is the completion and transcendence of it (Neil 160). Proper relationships have been God's intention for individuals and the community from the first creation in Genesis (humans created in the image and likeness of God, Gen. 1:26) and from the new creation in Christ.[8] This Sermon provides the disciples (the church) with objective ways to assess how well their spiritual formation into Christlikeness is going. The entire Sermon gives examples of how to live "Thy kingdom come, Thy will be done on earth as it is in heaven." The Sermon describes transformational relationships that are Christlike. It reveals how to be authentically human in an awfully inhuman world. Its unified purpose is to:

> help people come to hopeful and realistic terms with their lives here on earth, by clarifying in concrete terms, the nature of the kingdom into which they are now invited by Jesus' call to repentance, because the kingdom of heaven/God is now available (Willard 133).

Jesus set this up by introducing certain relational problems and then bringing correct solutions to them (Barth II.2 688).

But who in this world can live this Sermon? That becomes the incarnational question. Jeremias ties the possibility of living this Sermon to forgiveness:

> It is as if to every saying of the Sermon on the Mount, we must supply the protasis, "your sins are forgiven". . . . Thus because we are forgiven, we can relate according to the Sermon on the Mount. *The Gospel preceded the demand.* To each saying belongs the message of a transformed person—this is what the new life is like (30-1).

Others agree. Lloyd-Jones states, "all Christians are meant to manifest all of these characteristics" (34). Windisch correctly noted that neither Jesus nor Matthew considered feasibility a problem. "The idea of impracticality appears absolutely senseless within the framework of a correct understanding of the Sermon on the Mount. . . . Being in Christ and Christ in us is the natural and normal response" (96) to living the Sermon on the Mount. Barth suggested that apart from Jesus, the Father, and the Spirit, the new person would be no more than the Pharisees on the one hand and heathens on the other hand (II.2 696). He further observed that the new life of the new community would be fulfilled only by the outpouring of the Spirit and by people living under the control of that Spirit (699).

No one can live this Sermon on the Mount simply by rolling up the sleeves, flexing the muscles, and going after it as if mastering some kind of Olympic feat. This message can be lived only as the Holy Spirit—the extended earthly presence of God (Ps. 51:11; 139:7; Eph. 2:22)—lives in us and we in Him (1 John 3:24). Paul expressed the "how of the what" when he confessed ". . . I no longer live, but Christ lives in me . . ." (Gal. 2:20) and when he declared: "which is Christ in you, the hope of glory" (Col. 1:27). Usually the word "glory" would be better translated "character." Christ in us is God's only hope of His character being where we are—at work, home, behind the vehicle wheel, at play, etc. It was easy for Christ to live this Sermon. He lived it before and after He lipped it. And as we increasingly integrate the Holy Spirit—the ongoing presence of Christ—into our inner feelings, thoughts, attitudes, and plans, we will in Willard's words "increasingly take on the substance of the eternal and living the Sermon on the Mount becomes increasingly easy" (82). Biblical information is for our formation, and the content is for our character development.

Of course, this does not mean that new Christians will immediately do all the external conducts mentioned in this Sermon. Living out the practicalities of the Sermon on the Mount calls for a commitment to grow up and not just to grow old. Paul referred to that when he wrote, "My dear children, for whom I am again in the pains of childbirth until Christ is formed in you. . . ." (Gal. 4:19).

While the Sermon does not begin until verse 3, the first two verses introduce the intended audience for the Sermon: "Now when he saw the crowds, he went up on a mountainside and sat down. His disciples came to him, and he began to teach them saying. . . ." (5:1-2).

Jesus had just selected some of His disciples and then went throughout Galilee teaching and healing all kinds of diseases (4:18-23). In 5:1, Jesus saw the crowds that were following Him in 4:23-25. Then He went up on a mountain not to escape the crowds, but to be more visible and audible (Strecker 20). There is no support for McKenzie's position that the use of a mountain was meant to introduce Jesus as the new Moses with a new revelation on a new Mt. Sinai (69). However, several times in Matthew significant things happened on mountain settings.[9] Davis and Allison link going up to a higher place to fit Jesus' weighty words. That is, the revelational character of what He was about to say calls for a site consistent with its quality (423). However, that is reading more into the text then the text suggests, for Jesus spoke from many different kinds of places in Matthew; and everything He said was quality.

When Jesus saw the crowds, He would not have seen just masses of population, but individuals with hurts, addictions, feelings, oppressions—people who were helpless and hopeless in all kinds of relational predicaments. Later we read, "When he saw the crowds, he had compassion on them, because they were harassed and helpless, like sheep without a shepherd." So He took on a shepherd's role with the crowds and told His disciples, "The harvest is plentiful but the workers are few. Ask the Lord of the harvest, therefore, to send out workers into his harvest field" (9:36-38). But how could the workers be few with at least twenty thousand priests and six thousand Pharisees around? It was the presence of committed compassionate workers that were few, and perhaps still is—those who would look at the crowds with sensitive care. As Jesus saw the crowds in 5:1, He modeled His relational compassion in this Sermon, which He had and would continue to live Himself.

It is clear that the crowds heard the Sermon (7:28-29), but it is not clear whether or not Jesus directed it to the crowds, to the disciples, or to both. The Greek grammar does not clarify that for us. Guelich believes Jesus spoke to both groups, with the crowds representing people who will eventually respond to Christ's mission—the church (59). Barclay believed this was the ordination address for Jesus' disciples (84). Strecker seems to opt for both, since for Strecker the possibility of living it excludes no one (26). Lenski believed Jesus spoke to the disciples, but in such a way the crowds could hear, so Jesus could invite those outside the circle of disciples to join those inside (189). Keener agrees—Jesus wanted both to hear in order to invite others from the crowd to become disciples (103-4).

On that elevated spot, Jesus took the position of a teacher as He sat down (Tasker 59), which He did five times in Matthew. But perhaps sitting down had no significance other than the fact that Jesus intended to speak for quite a while (Plummer 54), or that He was tired from the teaching/healing ministry He had just concluded.

The inner circle of the crowds, Jesus' disciples, came to Him. It is probably accurate to view the disciples as representatives of the church (Boring 175), for the church is to live out the stipulations of this Sermon.

But what did it mean to be a disciple in Jesus' day, and how does that square with being a Christian today? The Greek word for disciple appears seventy-one times in Matthew, with the first appearance being in 5:1. It then appears in every subsequent chapter except chapters 6–7 (but the Sermon on the Mount includes those chapters) and chapter 25 (but the contents of that chapter continues Jesus' answer to His disciples in 24:3). The point is that two collateral foci in Matthew are "disciples" and "the kingdom."[10]

The basic description of a disciple is "a student—a learner." But a disciple in Jesus' day was far different from today's concepts about students and learners. A disciple in Jesus' day referred to someone who bonded himself to another person for the purpose of becoming just like that other one. The disciple was committed to assimilate the attitudes and actions of the mentor. In short, to imitate—to mimic—the teacher. To be a disciple called for unconditionally surrendering his independent lifestyle to the lifestyle of the bonded person. It was a call to service by being fanatically devoted to the other one. It was such a relational bonding that the disciple realized he could be a recipient of how others would treat the mentor, positively or negatively (Muller 480-92). Willard captured it well, ". . . someone who has decided to be with another person, under appropriate conditions, in order to become capable of doing what that person does or to become like who that person is" (282). Becoming capable is the key. It is too easy to forget that the Holy Spirit, who conceived Jesus and equipped Him to live God's character (glory) on earth, is the same Spirit who conceived our new creation (John 3:5-8; Acts 2:38; Rom. 8:9-11; 1 Cor. 12:13) and equips us to live God's character on earth. His eternal life enters from the outside to our inside so we will live from the inside—His inner presence empowering us—to the outer practices, extending Him to the world around us.

Being a disciple of Christ calls for us to habitually be changing into His likeness. And that assimilation calls for applying the Sermon on the Mount to our daily lives—at work, at home, in leisure, on the freeway, with friends, when separated from whom might know, when alone, etc. A contemporary business word that parallels a disciple is an apprentice. However, the biblical word that parallels a disciple is a Christian. In Greek, that word is Christ with an *ianos* ending—*Christianos*. Those letters attached to a person, such as to Caesar, meant that whoever was called by that name belonged to that other person, such as to Caesar, and was totally devoted to live for that other one as his cheerleading representative. So, those so devoted to Jesus came out of the crowd to sit under His feet.

The NIV deleted "and opening his mouth," which is found in the Greek. Some might see no reason to include those words when the text reads, "he began to teach them." However, "opening his mouth" intentionally introduces a teaching of Jesus with words, not works—a telling ministry, not a touching one—from a mouth, not from a miracle. "Opening the mouth" was a Semitic idiom in that day to report the beginning of a public speech (Hagner 86), which would be a solemn, grave, and dignified speech (Barclay 81).

The content in the Sermon on the Mount presents us with a challenge. Do we really want to be so bonded to Jesus that we become His loyal, devoted, fantastic cheerleading representatives—His ambassadors on earth (2 Cor. 5:18-19) who practice the principles in this Sermon? Do we really want to live a counter-cultural life, to be viewed as different and odd? Do we really want to be identified with the minority instead of with the majority (7:13-14)? Our eternal destiny is determined not just by our answer, but also by our application of this Sermon to the totality of our life. This is more than a Sermon to hear, but a lifestyle to do. It is a spiritual lifetime course, which is neither to be argued nor audited, but assimilated (7:21-27).

An essential concluding question penned by Barth remains:

> The only question now is whether the Church will live or not live in the fullness of the life already granted to it, in recognition or non-recognition, gratitude or ingratitude in face of what God has finally and once for all accomplished for man, in the freedom which God has decisively accorded to man, or the bondage from which he has finally and conclusively released, and which has now become a complete anachronism (II.2 688).

The first people who heard this Sermon were amazed and recognized that Jesus spoke as One with authority (7:28-29). How about those who hear it today? His disciples back then eventually left everything to follow Jesus (19:27). How about His disciples today? This is not an easy Sermon to live, but it is an essential one.

NOTES

[1]Some of the authors are H.D. Betz, Gene Davenport, W.D. Davies, D. Dockery and Garland, Robert Guelich, Herman Hendricks, A.M. Hunter, Joachim Jeremias, E. Stanley Jones, Jan Lambrecht, John MacArthur, Daniel Patte, Rudolf Schnackenberg, John Stott, George Strecker, E.T. Thompson, W.J. Townsend, Eduard Thurneysen, and Hans Windisch.

[2]See Albright and Mann, 45; Barclay, 9; Filson, 75; Hagner, 83; Hill, 108; Keener, 103; Jeremias, 17; Marshall, 25; Mounce, 36; Neil, 160-1; Songer, 165; and White, 20.

[3]See Blomberg, 96; Plummer, 56; Shephard, 176; Stott, 23, and Willard, *The Divine Conspiracy* 132.

[4]The concepts of privilege and purpose were in the original creation of humans. Our privilege is being created in the image and likeness of God. Our purpose is to care for this planet and to reproduce. In Genesis 12:2-3 we see the privilege—"I will make you into a great nation and I will bless you; I will make your name great. . . . I will bless those who bless you, and whoever curses you I will curse." The purpose is ". . . and you will be a blessing . . . and all peoples on earth will be blessed through you." God's divine strategy is to bless all categories of people THROUGH His people. These two aspects of God's call run throughout the entire Bible; however, it is easy to stress the privilege side and to ignore the purpose—especially when considering being a blessing to those kinds of people we do not like. But that is precisely the ministry Jesus came to model as announced in his first hometown sermon in Luke 4:16-30. And for that reason the disciples of Christ—the church—exist on earth. Each congregation must analyze how it is open to all diverse kinds of people in its area.

[5]Matthew uses the term kingdom fifty-six times, with nine times being in this Sermon.

[6]See various passages that reveal how the proper relationship of love fulfills the law system of the Old Testament: Matt. 7:12; 25:37-40; Rom. 13:8-10; Gal. 5:13-14; Jas. 2:8. Every one of the 613 commandments in the Old Testament deal with proper relationships with either self, God, others, things, or the devil.

[7]Connick lists twelve; Greenfield discusses twelve hermeneutical approaches; and Bauman identifies thirty-six different interpretations.

[8]See 2 Cor. 5:17 along with passages that stress being changed into Christ's/God's likeness: Luke 6:40; Rom. 8:29; 2 Cor. 3:17-18; Eph. 4:11-16; 4:22-5:1; and Phil. 2:5-11.

[9]See Matt. 14:23; 17:1; 21:1; 24:3; 28:16.

[10]As seen by the fact that the word disciple(s) is used seventy-one times and kingdom is used fifty-six times in Matthew.

1 ■ Blessings

Matthew 5:3-12

Mark Scott

[3]Blessed are the poor in spirit, for theirs is the kingdom of heaven.
[4]Blessed are those who mourn, for they will be comforted.
[5]Blessed are the meek, for they will inherit the earth.
[6]Blessed are those who hunger and thirst for righteousness,
for they will be filled. [7]Blessed are the merciful, for they will be
shown mercy. [8]Blessed are the pure in heart, for they will see God.
[9]Blessed are the peacemakers, for they will be called sons of God.
[10]Blessed are those who are persecuted because of righteousness,
for theirs is the kingdom of heaven. [11]Blessed are you when people insult
you, persecute you and falsely say all kinds of evil against you because
of me. [12]Rejoice and be glad, because great is your reward in heaven,
for in the same way they persecuted the prophets who were before you.

"Some subjects seem to attract a lot of discussion. Pretty soon so much has been written on the subject that others begin writing just to describe what has been written" (Carson, *God with Us* 33). This statement fits well what we have labeled the Sermon on the Mount, as recorded in Matthew, chapters five through seven. An enormous amount of ink has been spilled on this section of the New Testament. This is the discourse (the first of five major ones in Matthew)[1] that contains the beatitudes, the charge to love one's enemies, the model prayer, the golden rule, and the parable of the wise and foolish builder. We are dealing with familiar material, which is both a blessing and a curse. It is a blessing because familiarity always aids exegesis. It is a curse because familiarity breeds contempt. The temptation is to believe that there is nothing new to be discovered.

Jesus gives this Sermon early during His popular Galilean ministry. It is intended for His disciples,[2] but we know that the crowd[3] overhears this authoritative teaching (Matt. 5:1; 7:28-29). This is why Chouinard says, "The primary recipients of Jesus' teaching are those who have embarked upon a life of discipleship" (93). Without this perspective, the applications will become sticky, to say the least.

The Sermon reflects tremendous unity even though some scholars believe that Matthew pieced it together from fragments of Jesus' preaching. The Sermon gives evidence of the genre we call wisdom literature with themes that flow in and out of each other. But it still hangs together hand-in-glove. The introduction is 5:3-16; the thesis is 5:17-20; the development of that thesis is 5:21–7:12; and the concluding appeal is 7:13-27. The key phrase in the Sermon (and in keeping with the entire Gospel of Matthew) is Law and Prophets. Notice that the phrase occurs in 5:17 and in 7:12. This phrase forms the bookends of the development of the Sermon. Matthew is attempting to prove Jesus' Messiahship from those twin towers.

The key word in the Sermon is righteousness. It means "conforming one's life to God's standard." We should be careful of downloading Pauline thinking about imputed righteousness here. Righteousness means living the way God wants you to live. The Sermon on the Mount is, therefore, a serious call to discipleship and the real, greater, fulfilled righteousness. We could sermonically label it "Live Like a King." In fact, Marion Henderson used to talk about the characteristics of the kingdom person. The Sermon on the Mount describes what that person looks like.

BEGINNING WITH BLESSINGS

The Sermon begins with blessings. No opening joke, no warm and fuzzy illustration, and no personal story. Jesus begins with a word of congratulations.[4] The kingdom person, who is a committed disciple of Jesus Christ, is applauded.[5] The word blessed originally meant "to be free from daily cares." Therefore, it was a condition of the supposed gods. It became a formal way of saying "happy." It conjures up the idea of divine or inner joy and perfect happiness regardless of the circumstances.

Sometimes people will say that their favorite passage of Scripture is the beatitudes in Matthew 5. When they respond that way, it shows they probably have not studied them carefully. The beatitudes are anything but comforting. They frame up a total reversal of the world's values. The people congratulated in heaven are different from those honored by the world. In fact, we have made honoring the wrong kind of people into an art form. No wonder the beatitudes are called "revolutionary aphorisms" (Carson, *God with Us* 35).[6] Heaven congratulates or blesses the kinds of people described in these eight cryptic statements.

Four more items of introduction need mentioned before walking down through these eight descriptions of the kingdom person. First, notice the verb tense in the beatitudes.[7] The first one (3) is present tense (is). The next six beatitudes (4-9) are future tense (will be). The final beatitude (10-12) is present tense again (is). Perhaps the point is that while we enter a state of blessedness in the here and now, some blessedness remains for some day in the future. For instance, there is some comfort from God in this life through the Holy Spirit, but the ultimate comfort comes in heaven. Or, Christians experience mercy in this life, but mercy in the life to come is mercy at an entirely different level.

Secondly, Jesus does put an appendix on the beatitudes. Similar to the appendix that Jesus places on the model prayer (6:14-15) about forgiveness, the beatitude that receives an appendix is the one on persecution (5:11-12). Does this say anything about Matthew's audience? Since we shift back to present tense (see the above paragraph), does this mean that Christians are going through rough times during Matthew's life? It probably is appropriate for us that Jesus expounds on the persecution theme, since we just concluded the bloodiest century on record for the church.

Thirdly, what about the issue of progression to the beatitudes? Dr. Henderson often taught that there was a strong sense that these beatitudes progressed. For instance, one had to sense one's need for God (poor in spirit) before one would mourn about one's sin. Indeed, it is not hard to see how these beatitudes feed the ones that surround them. It seems that there may be some sense of progression, but it is not hard and fast. We cheapen the genre of the beatitude itself if we demand that something on the order of a proverb must flow like the logic in an epistle.

Finally, several of the beatitudes deal with huge overlapping concepts. For instance, some of the larger concepts of Jewish life concerned mercy, heart, and peace. Jesus uses these words to address huge areas of life. This may explain why Jesus purposely leaves open whether these beatitudes are to be understood vertically (one's relationship with God) or horizontally (one's relationship with others).

DESCRIPTIONS OF KINGDOM PERSONS

The first cryptic description (3) of the kingdom person is "Congratulations to the person who recognizes his spiritual bankruptcy, because he is open to the reign of God in his life." This spiritual poverty is spoken of in terms of being poor in spirit. It is the opposite of self-congratulations. It is the spirit behind Psalm 51:17, "The sacrifices of God are a broken spirit; a broken and contrite heart, O God, you will not despise." The word translated poor means "to cower down or bow down pitiably." Luke's account[8] (6:20) leaves the beatitude more rustic. It just says, "Blessed are you who are poor." In light of how Luke uses the word poor, probably some kind of financial condition is envisioned. But from Matthew's point of view, poverty of spirit is the necessary starting point of the real, greater, fulfilled righteousness. It is the only approach of an honest person before God. Only when we admit our need for God, can God's government (kingdom)[9] flood our souls.

The second cryptic description (4) of the kingdom person is, "Congratulations to the person who can be touched by the sin and the sorrows of this stained planet, because God will come along side of that person in this life but even more so in the life to come." There is nothing profound about the word cry. It simply means to "mourn." What is surprisingly absent is what the kingdom person is crying about. Is this sadness about personal sin? Is it emotional ownership of the sins and troubles of the world? Is it just the ability to be touched by the human condition? Is it empathy for the oppressed? Jesus did not specify it. Carson says, "It is not enough to acknowledge spiritual bankruptcy with a cold heart" (*Matthew* 133).

Two biblical examples are worthy of mention. Normally one would not think of Nehemiah as one who illustrates this kingdom trait. However, when he heard about the ruined city of Jerusalem, he could do nothing but sit down and weep (Neh. 1:4). Nehemiah was a strong and crusty leader who could get angry enough to tear people's hair out (Neh. 13:25), but He could also cry. Jesus also illustrates this trait in His own ministry. The Bible does not record the laughter of Jesus, but it does record His tears (John 11:35). He had some funny moments, but He also took His mission seriously; and the results of sin in a fallen world brought Him to tears. Someone defined empathy as "your pain in my heart." This is allowing yourself to be touched.

The promise for the person who is thusly touched is comfort. The word comfort means "to be called along side of." It is an expression of companionship. The noun form of this verb is actually a description of the Holy Spirit, i.e., comforter. But notice again the verb tense of the second phrase. This time it is future tense. While people who cry in this life do receive the tender mercies of God through His special Holy Spirit presence, ultimate comfort will come some day in the future. Little wonder that Luke records it, "Blessed are you who weep now, for you will laugh" (Luke 6:21). In the real end, the whole drama we call the Christian life ends as a comedy—or to use biblical language, victory!

The third cryptic description (5) of the kingdom person is "Congratulations to the person who has strength and energy under control, because that person will have peace now and will be postured to enjoy the new heaven and new earth the most some day." The word translated meek or gentle is a word that has a good dose of humility in it, but it does not mean "weak." Kenny Boles, Greek professor at Ozark Christian College, has often said, "Meek is not weak in the Greek." It was a word that was used to talk about a horse that had been broken. Now, instead of running wild and bucking, the horse can be led or ridden with safety because its strength is under control.

The world does not congratulate this type of person. We applaud people who get even, blow stuff up, and blow people away. The little, seemingly insignificant, people count for nothing. Yet, those are the very ones who save the world. Moses said that he was meek (Num. 12:3), and He delivered Israel from Egyptian bondage. Jesus said He was meek (Matt. 11:29), and He delivered the world from sin. Meek people know their place before God and find their place in serving others daily.

The tricky part of this third beatitude is the last phrase. What does inherit the earth mean? If this world is going to melt with a fervent heat (2 Pet. 3:10), why would anyone want to inherit it? The language is that of Psalm 37:11. In that psalm, David is calling Israel to trust in the Lord and commit their ways to Him instead of trusting in evil men. He states that there is coming a day when the wicked will be no more, but the meek will inherit the earth and be at peace. Is this the sense that Jesus intends in the beatitude? Is He promising peace on earth? Is it a promise only to be enjoyed by Israel with regard to the Holy Land? Or, in light of the eschatological feel of Psalm 37, is it a reference to heaven? Maybe Jesus is saying that the meek person will enjoy life on earth the most because he is living unselfishly. And, since heaven is a place of total unselfishness, the person that will be most at home is the meek person who is awestruck by just being there.

The fourth cryptic description (6) of the kingdom person is, "Congratulations to the person who is starved to death and parched of throat for God's standard, because that person will be stuffed like a fattened calf." This description is very upside down as far as the world is concerned. The world says that the blessed person is the one who is filled and has no needs. But Jesus commends the ones who are continually starving and the ones who are continually thirsting. All would agree that the desire for food and drink are two of the strongest desires humans have. Jesus is talking about an intense longing and drive. In fact, one could argue that our real, existential god is "whatever it is of which we cannot get enough." If we cannot get enough food, then food is our god. If we cannot get enough sex, then sex is our god. If we cannot get enough power, then power is our god. Jesus addresses our desires in this beatitude. One could argue that conversion, in many regards, is the changing of desires and affections and, as a result, the changing of behavior.

What is it for which Jesus would have us starve? In a word, righteousness. This word wraps up so much of what the Sermon on the Mount concerns.[10] The word means "conforming to a standard." If I obey the speed limit, then I am righteous in the eyes of the law. If I am faithful to my wife, then I am righteous in the light of my wedding vows. If I am loyal to my job and keep myself above reproach in how I perform my job, then I am righteous in the eyes of my employer.[11] In light of the rest of the Sermon on the Mount, it is obvious that Jesus has in mind something more than just jumping through religious hoops. Jesus wants our sense of capturing God's standard to go all the way to the heart.

When we are starved for God and His way, we will be satisfied. The NIV translates this word "filled." The word carries the idea of a calf being fattened for butchering at a special occasion. Think Thanksgiving table. Notice again that the tense is future. Many days, when the church is really being the church, we have an overwhelming sense of being filled.[12]

Many times, when the beauty in nature of the fallen planet undoes us, we have an overwhelming sense of being filled. But church and creation pale in comparison to the overwhelming sense of being filled when we gather around the throne of God and join our voices to the angelic choir (Rev. 5). Then we shall be filled to overflowing.[13]

The fifth cryptic description (7) of the kingdom person is, "Congratulations to the person who puts hands and feet to his empathy, because that person will receive the kindness of others and be welcomed into heaven by the tender mercies of God." The word mercy goes back to the Old Testament word that is often translated "loving kindness." It highlights compassion and forgiveness. It would have been understood in terms of God's tender covenantal love. It is pity plus action. It is seeing a need and moving to meet it. Perhaps the best illustration of mercy is in Aesop's classic fable, *The Mouse and the Lion*. The mouse has been captured by a huge lion, which is preparing to eat the little mouse for lunch. The mouse pleads with the lion for his life with a promise that he will be willing to help the lion some day. For some strange reason, the lion's tender mercies are released, and he lets the mouse go free. Some time later, the lion is caught in a trap. But before the captors arrive to fetch the prize lion, the mouse hears of it, makes his way to the lion, and chews through the rope, which allows the lion to escape.

In the fable we could add, "And they all lived happily ever after." But that's not how it is in real life. Haddon Robinson taught us to always ask the text, "What are the contraries?" What potential objection lurks ahead? If we show mercy, is it always a guarantee that it will be shown to us? Absolutely not! Being kind to people is, in part, what got Jesus crucified. This is why we must keep in mind two points: first, the beatitudes are very much in the genre of Jewish wisdom literature. That is, they function much like proverbs, which are short pithy statements of general truth. They are not intended to handle all the potential objections. Second, the tense in the latter phrase of the beatitude is once again future. We may not receive mercy in this life. We may receive bigotry and persecution. But, in the grand end, God will show mercy to us.

The sixth cryptic description (8) of the kingdom person is "Congratulations to the person who is clean all the way to his heart, because then he will have clean enough eyes to gaze on the weighty presence and shining brilliance of God." The word pure means "clean, morally upright, and without blemish." It is where we get our English word catharsis. Jesus commends the moral excellence of His followers with this term. Heart is one of the most significant words in the Bible.[14] So to be pure in heart means to live a life of moral excellence from the inside out. In other words, this beatitude describes someone who lives one way all the time. There is no duplicity. This person is the same if he is holding a communion tray or holding a remote of a hotel television.

Rich Mullins tried to capture this idea of single-minded devotion in his song, "One Thing." The song goes back to a supposed quote from the Danish Philosopher, Søren Kierkegaard, when he said that to be pure in heart is "to will one thing." There is something attractive about a person who is consumed by purpose. The Apostle Paul gives evidence of this when he writes, "This one thing I do . . ." (Phil. 3:13).

Seeing God is no small thing. Just ask Moses (Exod. 33:12-23). Just ask Isaiah (Isa. 6:5). Just ask Nathanael (John 1:48-49). Just ask Philip (John 14:8-9). Just ask John (Rev. 1:17). The language of this beatitude takes us back to Psalm 24. How clean do you have to be to come into the presence of God? Well, more clean than you think. You have to have clean hands and a pure heart to really see the King of Glory.

The seventh cryptic description (9) of the kingdom person is, "Congratulations to the person who aggressively works for everyone's well-being, because that person will be marked as being in God's family." Jesus does not put His blessing on the peace-lover, the peace-demonstrator, but rather on the peacemaker. The original hearers would have thought of their traditional greeting (*shalom*). The word has to do with a state of well-being. The focus in this beatitude is on relationships. Jesus develops this theme ever so strongly in the six antitheses later in chapter five (vv. 21-48). But let us not forget the most important relationship, i.e., the one between God and people. To be a peacemaker in the vertical sense means we involve ourselves in evangelism.

Make no mistake about it: being a peacemaker is risky business. Jesus is our peace, and He made peace; but it ended Him up on a cross. More than one neighborhood boy has come over to his friend's house to play only to see his friend and the friend's brother fighting in the backyard. When he tries to separate the fighting brothers, they turn on him. Peacemaking usually involves a risk.

The promise attached to this beatitude is that we are God's sons. This term of family inclusion is precious and to be highly valued (1 John 3:1). We know from the context that we are not God's unique, one-of-a-kind son (Matt. 3:17). But by joining in Jesus' mission of reconciliation, we get to carry the banner of family intimacy.

The eighth cryptic description (10) of the kingdom person is "Congratulations to the person who gets hunted down for living by my standard, because he is open to the reign of God in his life." The parallelism between the final phrase here and the final phrase in the first beatitude is obvious. We both recognize our need for God now (poor in spirit), and we receive persecution now. Other blessings in their final form are reserved for the future.

Notice that this persecution is because of righteousness. There is no virtue in suffering if it is because you have done wrong. Do not blame the policeman for pulling you over for doing eighty m.p.h. in a school zone and think that it is persecution. It is just being stupid on your part. If we suffer for following God's standard, then we are blessed. And, be assured of this:

the text does not encourage us to seek persecution nor to retreat from it.

Of all the beatitudes, Jesus expands this one. Maybe Matthew's listeners needed that. Maybe we need that. Being a Christian in today's world is no walk in the park. Insults hurt, persecution stings, and being misrepresented always makes one feel cheated. But much like Jesus' brother taught (Jas. 1:2), we are told to actually rejoice. And two things motivate this rejoicing: first, reward in heaven, and second, we join a great company, namely, the prophets. Their lives were full of challenges just like the apostles' lives will be. Occasionally it is good to ask ourselves, "Is no one offended by our message?" If the answer is no, then it might mean that we are no longer a threat for Jesus Christ.

NOTES

[1] The others are Matt. 10, 13, 18, 24–25.

[2] A term that occurs seventy-three times in Matthew and most often applies to the Twelve, though generic followers are sometimes identified with this label (Matt. 8:21) as are John's disciples (Matt. 12:2) and the Pharisees' (Matt. 22:16).

[3] A term that occurs fifty-one times in Matthew and usually indicates some level of curiosity but lacking in commitment.

[4] This may be the best English translation of the Greek word. There are two major words in the Bible for blessed. One means "to speak well of God." The other means "good for you." The one used in the beatitudes is the latter.

[5] See Max Lucado, *The Applause of Heaven*.

[6] "The upshot of the Beatitudes is a complete inversion of the attitude popularly known in our culture as 'machismo.'" (Blomberg 101).

[7] Technically there is no actual verb in the first phrase of each beatitude. For instance, the first one reads, "Blessed, the poor in spirit." The verb is supplied in English. It is the verb in the second phrase of each beatitude that is my emphasis here.

[8] Not all are convinced that Luke's sermon (6:17-49) is the same sermon as Matthew's, but the texts are still too parallel to neglect making some kind of comparison. Luke's account frames half of the beatitudes in terms of positive congratulations and half of the beatitudes in terms of woes. See Blomberg 98, fn. 15, for both nuances of poor.

[9] "Kingdom" occurs 162 times in the New Testament. Most of the occurrences are in the Synoptics, Acts, and Revelation. The word emphasizes more of the reign of God than the realm of God, though both matter. Matthew most often uses the phrase "kingdom of heaven" (except for four times) because, in presenting Jesus as the royal Jewish Messiah, he wants to stress the kingly abode of God. For Matthew "of heaven" is metonymy for "God."

[10] It also appears in the eighth beatitude (5:10) and is the thing for which Christians are persecuted. In 5:20 Jesus says that our righteousness must surpass that of the religious people of the day—a statement that must have shocked the original hearers. In 6:1 we are cautioned against practicing righteousness just to be noticed by them. Finally in 6:33 (a parallel text to the present beatitude) we are told to continually seek first the kingdom of heaven and God's righteousness.

[11] Of course no one is perfect in conforming to God's standard. That is why we need Jesus and the cross. This is the emphasis that Paul picks up in Romans and Galatians. He stresses that since no one is righteous, then we need Jesus to do something for us that we could not do for ourselves. This is imputed righteousness; i.e., righteousness given to us as gift. But the teaching in the Sermon on the Mount was given previous to the cross. Therefore it should come as no surprise that Jesus gives a radical call to obey God. To follow Christ is to obey Christ. This is not antithetical to being saved by grace. It is the only way to

embrace a grace that is not cheap.

[12]Luke's account very much puts the accent on the present reality of being filled (Luke 6:21). [13]The unicorn captures this when he says, "I have come home at last. This is my real country! I belong here. This is the land I have been looking for all my life, though I never knew it till now. The reason why we loved the old Narnia is that it sometimes looked a little like this" (Lewis, *The Last Battle* 171).

[14]It occurs over 850 times in the Bible. Sometimes it refers to the physical organ in the chest that pumps blood. Sometimes the Bible uses it figuratively to describe something deep (e.g., God threw Pharaoh and his army into the heart of the sea). But most often it refers to the center of the inner person. For the Hebrew mind, it embraced the mind, the senses, and the will.

2 ▪ Making a Difference

Matthew 5:13-16

Danny L. Dye

[13]You are the salt of the earth. But if the salt loses its saltiness, how can it be made salty again? It is no longer good for anything, except to be thrown out and trampled by men. [14]You are the light of the world. A city on a hill cannot be hidden. [15]Neither do people light a lamp and put it under a bowl. Instead they put it on its stand, and it gives light to everyone in the house. [16]In the same way, let your light shine before men, that they may see your good deeds and praise your Father in heaven.

Armando Valladares was being held incommunicado in a prison in Cuba under the Castro regime. For twenty-two years he was abused, tortured, and humiliated because he was a believer in Jesus. On one occasion another prisoner, Fernando Lopez del Toro, slit his own jugular vein with a piece of sharp metal and died in a few minutes. Mr. Valladares said that before doing this Mr. Lopez told him in a tone of despair "that what hurt the most, out of all of the torment, was that our sacrifice might be in vain. It was not the pain, but the apparent uselessness of enduring it that was defeating Fernando" (Olasky 42). The church will be ineffective and useless if we believe that we are not making a difference in the world. An old radio preacher used to end each daily broadcast with the words, "It *does* make a difference what you believe."

CHRISTIANS ALWAYS MAKE A DIFFERENCE

Christians always make a difference, although we may never see the difference that we make. We know this is true because Jesus told His disciples, "You are (made emphatic by the use of the pronoun with present tense verb) the salt of the earth and the light of the world." He did not say, "You might be"; "You can be"; or "You will be." He said, "You are!" He reinforced that revelation with the imagery of a city set on a hill. It just cannot be hidden. Perhaps the crowd could see a city's white buildings reflecting the sun.[1] Video from a spacecraft helps us to understand how lights from a city make it visible at night.[2] "He wanted them to realize that they had within themselves the purpose and the power to make other men better" (Thomas 21). God has no other agents for this work. If the followers of Jesus "conform to the norms of verses 3-12, they cannot help but be an influence for good in society" (Carson, *The Sermon on the Mount* 31). What a transformation of our society would occur if every follower of Jesus humbly accepted the responsibility to make a difference.

Being told that they were salt and light must have been a perplexing thought to those listening to Him. Salt was so valuable in Jesus' day that soldiers were paid with salt. They had not been born salt and light. They were nobodies. They were not an organized movement. There was not a large church that influenced city or state government. There was not a network of radio or television stations commanding a following that carried political clout. There was not a church government to which secular governments sent envoys. But once Jesus turned over the saltbox and threw the light switch for His followers, they became difference-makers.

They were to make a difference for the occupying military? Yes, indeed! The first Gentile convert was Cornelius, a Roman centurion (Acts 10). The entire elite Praetorian Guard knew about Jesus from Paul (Phil. 1:13). The Philippian jailer's conversion (Acts 16) was so unique that Luke included it in the second volume of his systematic and accurate account (Luke 1:3) of all that Jesus began to do and teach (Acts 1).

They were to make a difference to the professional religious leaders and zealots of the day? Yes, indeed! Jesus was buried in a tomb donated by a rich member of the Sanhedrin who had become His follower (Mark 15:43). Another council member, Nicodemus, was also His follower (John 3:1; 19:39). Large numbers of priests were converted (Acts 6:7).

CHRISTIANS ARE DIFFERENT FROM THE WORLD

Followers of Jesus make a difference in the world because they are different from the world. They follow a different pattern for life,[3] live by a different standard,[4] and imitate a different hero.[5] Jesus is pointing out this difference all through the Sermon on the Mount. "There is no single paragraph of the Sermon on the Mount in which this contrast between Christian and non-Christian standards is not drawn" (Stott 19). Therefore, the progression of topics that Jesus covers is understandable: a list of characteristics of a follower of His; the persecution of His followers; a command to make a difference in the world; and finally, several examples of how His followers will make a difference.

However, these examples were such a radical departure from the behavioral norm of the day—the Law and its interpretations—that His followers would have stood out like a full moon on a black night. Salt and light included a stricter standard of sexual purity, marital faithfulness, honesty, love, forgiveness, integrity, grace, goals, finances, and obedience to God. Perhaps His followers reacted to this stricter standard like some students of Texas A&M University did when writing short essays about the Sermon on the Mount:

"extremely strict and allows for almost no fun";

"hard to read and made me feel like I had to be perfect";

"the most extreme, stupid, unhuman statement that I have ever heard" (Yancey 130).

Was Jesus' standard so high that His points of light whom He commanded to shine could not shine? Philip Yancey's conclusion provokes an "Oh, I see" response:

For years I had thought of the Sermon on the Mount as a blueprint for human behavior that no one could possibly follow. Reading it again, I found that Jesus gave these words not to cumber us, but to tell us what *God* is like (143).

Jesus' followers are to make a difference by being holy like God is holy (1 Pet. 1:15,16).

The statement that His followers are the salt of the earth has several widely held possible applications (Fisher 49). One is that salt is a necessity of life. Therefore, the disciples of Jesus are necessary for the fact that they carry God's word into the world (49). Another application, perhaps most widely mentioned, is that salt is a preservative. This makes His followers the spiritual preservative against the moral decay of mankind. The application of salt as fertilizer has Jesus' disciples preparing the world for a great harvest from the seed of the gospel (50). Salt adds flavor, which makes Christians being the ones to bring spiritual flavor to the world (MacArthur 242). Whichever application of the use of salt one assumes, salt must make contact to do its work, unlike light that can shine from afar. For example, a New Testament professor and coach can be light through his instruction by pointing out God's deep love for the students and players, Jesus' depth of care seen by His agony of decision in the Garden of Gethsemane, and the urgency that students should feel to tell others of God's love. However, the professor and coach is salt by the way he cares for and counsels his students and players outside of the classroom and off the court and by the way he carries out verses 3-12 in his personal life.

Whichever application one makes, the need for the disciples to be salt for the earth is not in dispute. Some want earth here to be taken literally while taking world in the next verse metaphorically. For example, Fred Fisher states that earth is rarely, if ever, used "in true biblical speech" to be a synonym for "people of the world" (50). However, since Jesus sometimes expressed Himself with Hebrew parallelism (Gaebelein 814) and the context has Jesus' disciples working to influence the godless to be godly, we can see both earth and world referring here to all people who are not worshiping and obeying the true and living God.

The world needs followers of Jesus to make a difference. Can we imagine a world without the influence of Jesus' followers? Imagine a rotted road-kill carcass that you have seen or smelled. Imagine total darkness. Visitors to a famous cavern in the United States experience total blackness when the lights are turned off for a few seconds. Many feel great relief when the lights are turned back on. Surely nothing can be more frightening than to be a diver exploring a cave that loses his way when the light battery goes dead, leaving him in total, and perhaps final, darkness. Now transfer those sights, sounds, smells, and feelings to the spiritual condition of people who do not know Jesus or life acceptable to God.

Without the light of Jesus' followers, the world is lost in darkness. This is a world of selfishness, hate, crime, murder, sexually transmitted diseases, poverty, and anarchy. My brother was in a search party looking for a lost little girl. He was trudging through rugged terrain at night. Suddenly he stopped and shone the light toward his next step. He stood on the edge of a cliff. Taking the next step would have meant disaster. Light meant the difference between life and death. The Apostle Paul explains that Jesus has "destroyed death and has brought life and immortality to light through the gospel" (2 Tim. 1:10). Christians extend that beam of Jesus' light into the world.

TWO WARNINGS

Jesus gives two warnings to His followers. Jesus speaks conditionally about salt that becomes tasteless (*mōrainō*, "loses strength") saying that it is good for nothing (*ouden ischuei*, "no longer having power"). This is the type of conditional sentence in which the speaker believes the statement to be "generally true in the present or probably realizable in the future" (Goetchius 274). Salt that loses its power is useless. Useless salt is thrown out on the street to be trampled under foot. We can only conclude that Jesus is implying that followers who fail to make the attempt to make a difference in society will be thrown out of His presence. This term for throwing out is used elsewhere by Jesus to indicate final judgment.[6] Disciples of Jesus cannot adopt the corruption of the world, losing the power to make a difference, and still be followers of Jesus.

Ministers who have sex sin exposed lose their power to make a difference in the world and diminish the church's ability to make a difference. Churches that split diminish their power to make a difference. Behavior condemned by the Bible but sanctioned by churches diminishes the power of the church to make a difference. Division among the Christian world diminishes its collective power to make a difference. "The only hope the world has is to see God as He really is; the only place they can look for such a vision is to the lives of true Christians" (Conzelmann 423-45).

Jesus also warns that light that is covered does no good against the darkness. Since the world needs light, it must be in darkness. There is a consistent picture in history of darkness metaphorically being used for death and punishment (Fisher 54). Darkness is a reference for the absence of God (Matt. 8:12; 22:13; 25:30). Jesus brought light to the world (Matt. 4:16). Before following Jesus, people are in darkness (Eph. 5:8). However,

Jesus delivers them from it (Col. 1:13).

Powerful lights were brought to the World Trade Center site after the September 11, 2001, attacks on the towers. Those lights made the area as bright as day so the rescue efforts could continue around the clock. The rescuers would never have thought of covering those lights for a while so they could get some rest. Neither did Jesus intend for His followers to turn their lights off for a time so that they could attend parties, be in adulterous relationships, be racists, move up in their companies, sow wild oats before marriage, or be themselves at home when the public was not looking. "The light which Christians have is indispensable to the solution of the problems of mankind" (Thomas 24). The followers of Jesus always need to shine. They cannot cover the light and still be Jesus' followers.

The absence of spiritual light from God may not even be noticed until there is disciple-light shining. "Pardon my French" has become an apology to Christians by those who say words that they themselves believe to be wrong. Until the light was in their midst, they felt no need to apologize. The light of godliness will either bring opposition or change. Darkness wants to be left alone. Light exposes it for what it is (Eph. 5:11-14). Still, there are those who are drawn to the light. They become a part of it—synonymous with being saved (Eph. 5:8).

Shining is not an option. Just as Jesus made the emphatic statement, "You are" salt and light, He also commands (imperative mode) His points of light to shine. Jesus did not ask His followers if they would like to make a difference. He told them they would. He told them they should "Shine!" The imperative in the third person is used.[7] This is the equivalent to "Allow the light to shine." This has caused some to comment that the light shining from the follower of Jesus is a reflected light like the moon reflects the sun's light (Barclay 119). In keeping with the warning not to cover the light, perhaps we need to see this command to be Jesus' ordering His followers to be transparent, not opaque, so that His light shines through.

Even the faintest light in the darkness has an impact. During World War II, blackouts at night were ordered in London, England, when German bombers were detected in the area. Just one light could give away the location of the entire city. Just one light can make a difference in the world. The Christian who refuses to laugh at the dirty jokes at the construction site shines. The one who explains why he does not laugh when asked shines. The family praying before the meal at the restaurant shines. The law firm arguing before the Supreme Court for the right to have Bible study in a schoolroom shines. The Christian teen that says "No" to sexual advances shines. The schoolteacher that says to administrators, "My Bible stays on my desk. Go ahead, fire me," shines.

ULTIMATE GOAL

Jesus commanded His followers to make a difference in the world. The world needs this difference made. However, being salt and light is not the end Jesus sought. It is only a means to the end. The light is to shine for a particular purpose. The ultimate goal is the praise, glory, and honor that God will receive because our lights shine.[8] Instead of getting caught up in our efforts to salt and shine, Jesus' disciples need to be caught up in bringing praise to the heavenly Father. Instead of despairing over whether or not we are making a difference, Jesus' disciples are to keep focused on doing what needs to be done to glorify God.

What needs to be done are good works (*ta kala erga*). The adjective good refers to something "winsome and beautiful and attractive" (Barclay 121). Christians or churches that cloister themselves from the world simply cannot attract the world to God. They only attract themselves to God. The lamp in Jesus' illustration was on the lampstand, not under the grain-measuring basket. Unless we do good works that bring glory to God, we are not lights. We are only unlit wicks. What we are and do does make a difference.

NOTES

[1]"Many of the cities of Judea were placed on the summits or sides of mountains, and could be seen from afar. Perhaps Jesus *pointed* to such a city, and told his disciples that they were like it" (Frew 48).

[2]Picture taken November 27, 2000, April 11, 2002.

[3]*tupos*, Phil. 3:17; 1 Thess. 1:7; 1 Tim. 4:12; Titus 2:7.

[4]*plērōmatos*, Eph. 4:13.

[5]*mimētai*, 1 Cor. 11:1; Eph. 5:1; 1 Thess. 1:6.

[6]Matt. 3:10; 5:29,30; 7:19; 13:42,50; 18:8,9.

[7]Powers points out that the aorist imperative is the one normally used (51).

[8]Peter (1 Pet. 2:9) emphasizes the praise of God when he writes, "But you are a chosen people, a royal priesthood, a holy nation, a people belonging to God, that you may declare praises of him who called you out of darkness into his wonderful life."

3 ■ Righteousness

Matthew 5:17-20

Mark Miller

[17]Do not think that I have come to abolish the Law or the Prophets;
I have not come to abolish them but to fulfill them. [18]I tell you the truth,
until heaven and earth disappear, not the smallest letter, not the least stroke
of a pen, will by any means disappear from the Law until everything is
accomplished. [19]Anyone who breaks one of the least of these commandments
and teaches others to do the same will be called least in the kingdom of heaven,
but whoever practices and teaches these commands will be called great in the
kingdom of heaven. [20]For I tell you that unless your righteousness surpasses
that of the Pharisees and the teachers of the law, you will
certainly not enter the kingdom of heaven.

Having sat down on the mountainside and drawing His disciples around Him, Jesus begins the Sermon with a wonderful and encouraging description of the blessings (i.e., rewards) available to those whose attitudes and actions reflect the perfect character or righteousness of God (5:3-12). In the background are the masses of people who have followed Him to the mountain, including the religious leaders of the day—the scribes (teachers of the Law) and Pharisees. All are striving and straining to catch each and every word. With His audience, the majority of whom are famished for any form of emotional and/or spiritual blessing, held in rapt attention, He promises them immediate blessings of life such as comfort from their grief (v. 4), an earthly inheritance (v. 5), satisfaction of their needs (v. 6), and mercy for their failings (v. 7). More importantly (though they may not have necessarily shared such a sentiment, since our nature is to allow the short-term to overshadow the long-term), He promises them future, eternal blessings of life such as the kingdom of heaven (vv. 3,10), an audience with God (v. 8), a familial identity with God (v. 9), and a heavenly reward (v. 12). With hardly a pause, He progresses quickly to point out that these attitudes and behaviors, while attached to blessings, are empty and meaningless unless and until such a time as they serve to fulfill their inherent God-ordained purpose (v. 13). He proclaims that the authentic purpose of these righteous attitudes and actions is not merely to obtain an immediate or even an eternal benefit, and certainly not for any personal glory that might fall to an individual of earthly decent, but purely and naturally to draw worthy attention to the Holy One for Whom we live—to bring glory and honor to our heavenly Father (vv. 14-16).

A RUMOR

It is at this point in the Sermon that Jesus now turns His attention to a rumor regarding His religious objectives that has been circulating amongst the crowd. Jesus' words in verse 17 seem to indicate that He has had enough public exposure to start both the masses and the religious leaders to wondering as to the scope and authority of His ministry and teachings. Apparently it had been suggested by someone that Jesus was seeking to annul or do away with (lit., "destroy") the observance of the Law. This proposition could have legitimately found its origins either in Jesus' own words or His actions. While the Sermon on the Mount was likely proclaimed relatively early in Jesus' public ministry, a harmony with the Gospel of Mark shows that He had already come into conflict, on at least two separate occasions, with both the scribes and the Pharisees. The encounter with the scribes occurred in Capernaum when He had the audacity to forgive the sins of a paralytic. The minds of the scribes screamed blasphemy so loudly that Jesus heard them in His Spirit. Their contention was that only God Himself[1] could forgive sins. But Jesus silenced and stupefied them when He not only discerned their hearts but also commanded the man to get up and walk (Mark 2:3-12), having healed him of his paralysis. His next altercation with the religious leaders, this time the Pharisees, came in Galilee a short time later when Jesus defended His disciples for gathering food on the Sabbath by first declaring that the Sabbath was made for man not vice versa, and then further stating that "the Son of Man is Lord even of the Sabbath" (Mark 2:23-28). Later that same day, He further embittered the Pharisees by healing a withered hand, again on the Sabbath (Mark 3:1-5). It is not inconceivable that these very incidents had fueled concern and consternation (on the part of the religious leaders) and curiosity (on the part of the masses) pertaining to Jesus' plans and motives.

It is quite likely that both parties (the people on the one hand and the religious leaders on the other) were equally interested in determining the answer to the very same question, but ultimately they had very different concerns in mind. The sincerest of the leaders were experiencing growing apprehension regarding the damage, even destruction, which Jesus' teachings would do to the religious community that, in their mind, was held together by the strict adherence to the Law that they prescribed and administered. But as Jesus will state throughout the remainder of the Sermon, and indeed His entire ministry, most of the scribes and Pharisees were ultimately more concerned that the authority and teachings of Jesus might threaten their position of authority, eroding the age-old influence and control that they wielded over the masses through the Law (or at least their interpretation and application of it). The people, on the other hand, were likely waiting in hopeful anticipation that the yoke or burden of the Law might be lifted, or at the very least, lightened upon their lives. As we can see from Matthew 11:28-30, Jesus Himself acknowledges that the yoke or burden of the Law that the scribes and Pharisees had placed upon the people was over-bearing and exhausting. Jesus spoke these words of comfort and hope: "Come to me, all you who are weary and burdened, and I will give you rest. . . . For my yoke is easy and my burden is light." Between the people and the religious leaders, Jesus has basically two Law issues with which to deal. The first is the limited and/or warped understanding that the people have regarding the nature and purpose of the Law; and the second is the misuse and misrepresentation of Law by the religious leaders (i.e., the scribes and Pharisees), regardless of motive or intent.

DYNAMICS OF TERMS

Before addressing more of the specifics of the rumor, it would seem important that we address the dynamics involved with the use of certain terms in this historical context, specifically related to the use of the term Law. When Jesus used the phrase Law and Prophets, He could have rightly been referring only to the five books of the Pentateuch[2] and Prophets.[3] At the same time, it was not uncommon or even improper for the phrase Law and Prophets to be used as an inclusive term for the entire Old Testament canon. Either way, all involved parties would have had no problem understanding the terms, nor would they have been confused by them. On the other hand, when the term Law is used in the Gospels, it could have any number of meanings depending upon the context and the person(s) who used the term—meanings that, while embraced by one, would have found resistance from another. While Law quite literally referred to the Ten Commandments, it was also regularly used in a more general sense to refer to the five books of the Pentateuch. As with the phrase Law and Prophets, either of these uses would have caused no great confusion or concern. The real confusion and conflict came from the fact that by the time of Jesus, the term Law was commonly used to refer to the Old Testament Law as well as a massive system of man-made rules and regulations known as scribal law[4] that were aimed at defining and clarifying the Mosaic Law for application in everyday life. This scribal law first began as a series of oral transmissions handed down by the scribes over the generations to aid the Jewish people in understanding and obeying the Law during changing times and conditions. But by the time of Jesus, these oral laws were so vast as to extrapolate how much weight amounted to a burden and therefore broke the Sabbath Law of rest.[5] These laws had themselves become a burden. It was these laws for which Jesus had shown such contempt on previous occasions and had consequently riled the religious leaders.

But it was not these laws that Jesus is referring to when He states that He "did not come to abolish the Law or the Prophets but to fulfill[6] them." He is now speaking of the Mosaic Law; and Jesus' words demonstrate that He has the greatest respect for the true Law of God because He understands its source, its nature, and its purpose. Some have suggested, in light of these words, that there was a common belief held in the time of Jesus that when the Messiah came, the old Law would be put aside and a new law would take its place. But this view has been largely discounted, leaving us with the natural conclusion that Jesus was using this rumor as an opportunity to clarify His mission (Carson, *Matthew* 141). The concept of Jesus fulfilling the Law and the Prophets is one that has spurred many a discussion and debate, with the result being three basic positions[7]: 1) that while not abolishing the Law, Jesus' self-revelation eliminated the need for the Law; 2) that Jesus merely brought fuller meaning and understanding to the Law; and 3) that in Jesus we find the fulfillment of the Law in that He was the complete embodiment of the Law. As is almost always the case when sincere people go searching for truth, we can see that there is at least an element of truth in each conclusion. In response to the first proposition of having Jesus as the living Revelator of the character or righteousness of God, one could easily argue that the necessity for a Law (written or oral) no longer existed. Yet if this were the case, what would cause Jesus to go to such great lengths to insure that all understood that until both heaven and earth had ceased to exist, not the smallest letter[8] of the alphabet or even the most insignificant punctuation mark[9] found in the Law would be eliminated until all that God ordained had been accomplished? In responding to the second suggestion, there can be no denying that Jesus, by teaching and example, brought a more complete understanding of the principle and practice of the Law. Yet, to limit His revelation merely to "more" would surely be a travesty to the incarnation. More still implies something less than the whole. The nature of the incarnation is not *fuller* of God, but *the fullness* of God. And finally, in the third conclusion we see that coming to an understanding of Jesus as fulfilling the Law and the Prophets through His living example of perfect righteousness more closely captures the spirit of the Word's intent. Even here, we are still left with the need to insure that readers understand that, while Jesus thought, spoke, and acted as a perfect example of the purpose and intent of the Law and the Prophets, His actions were not born of practiced habits, but of divine character. His thoughts, His words, His actions were not a mere reflection of good choices, but of godly character. What He said and did was an expression not of what He wanted to be or do, but of who He was. It can also rightly be said that Jesus was the fulfillment of the Law in theory and in practice.

DEFENSE OF AUTHORITY

So strong was Jesus' passion for the Law that He begins His defense with a statement of authority (v. 18), "I tell you the truth. . . ."[10] With this simple phrase and the words that follow, Jesus seeks to affirm the authority of the Law and the Prophets; but at the same time He now asserts that He is the lens by which it may now be fully understood. Jesus' words here are much more than merely didactic—they have the impact and authority of prophetic statements. He was making a proclamation of truth, signing His name, and dating it. Jesus used an authoritative formula that no prophet or scribe had ever used before—Himself! And His promise was good until heaven and earth pass away. The promise was that neither the smallest word nor the tiniest mark found in the Law would cease to be in effect until the Law had accomplished its God-intended purpose. With Jesus' declaration of personal authority, one can only conclude that what was true of the Law of Moses is also true of the Law of Jesus. Paul also vindicates the Law and affirms the Law of Jesus in Romans 8 when he writes, "For what the Law could not do, weak as it was through the flesh, God did: sending His own Son. . . ." (8:3 NASB). Paul states that the problem was not with the Law, but with our fleshly nature. Our flesh tends to limit our understanding of the Law to an oppressive list of do's and don'ts whose pursuit always seems to end in failure and frustration. These tendencies prevent the Law from fulfilling its intended purpose, requiring Jesus to fulfill them. Jesus indicates that the Law served a greater purpose that would not be fulfilled until the end of time—such a purpose as could only be found through the fulfillment of the Law. This is not fulfillment as in our perfect compliance, but fulfillment as in Jesus as the Fulfiller of the Law. Assuming this principle to be true, then the Law serves not merely as a list of behaviors to practice or avoid, but more as a reflection of the character of the Lawgiver and His progeny: "for they will be called sons of God" (Matt. 5:9). Not something merely to do, but more importantly someone to be.

He further strengthens and affirms His position by evoking both a blessing and a curse. Jesus begins by declaring a sanction against anyone who would annul (i.e., break)[11] one of even the more insignificant commandments[12] and then teach others the same. A stance that, on the outside, looks as stern and unyielding as that of the scribes and Pharisees; but upon further searching, one discovers Jesus is reflecting His true orthodoxy by showing His knowledge of and commitment to the authority of the Law as seen in Deuteronomy 27:26, "Cursed is the man who does not uphold the words of this law by carrying them out." This thinking is consistent with Jewish religious teachers who, although they distinguished between lighter and heavier law, agreed that punishment and blessing were equal. As stern as the previous words were, at first glance the sanction itself seems relatively inconsequential—"[They] shall be called least in the kingdom of heaven" (5:19).[13] But, through deeper delving, one discovers that Jewish theology had only one kingdom—there was no alternative. Those who were the least in a kingdom often lived outside the gates of the city and, consequently, the protection and provisions that the city provided. Using later Christian thought, one could suggest that being least was better than being nothing at all. But to make such an assertion demonstrates a lack of understanding of the Jewish concept of the afterlife.[14] nothing could be worse than to leave the burdens of this life only to face more of the same in death, except maybe as was the case for the scribes and Pharisees—to leave life of affluence and position to enter death in poverty and obscurity. Furthermore, in contrast to the curse, He offers a blessing to those who both keep (i.e., practice) the commandments and teach others to do the same— he "will be called great in the kingdom of heaven" (v. 19b).

TRUE VS. FALSE RIGHTEOUSNESS

At this point in the Sermon Jesus' teachings have served to neutralize the consternation of the scribes and Pharisees by making statements affirming complete Jewish orthodoxy. In their minds one can be sure they heard Jesus' words as serving to further establish their authority and rule—all was well again in the kingdom! Unfortunately for them, Jesus' next statement lands without warning, like a dead-blow hammer—"unless your righteousness surpasses that of the Pharisees and the teachers of the law, you will certainly not enter the kingdom of heaven." Two thousand years later, it is impossible to ascertain who was more devastated by Jesus' words: the Pharisees, who believed they had all but mastered the right-eousness of the Law, or the masses, who also believed that the Pharisees were the model of righteousness and had to be wondering what hope there might be for them. And yet Jesus has now identified the thesis of the Sermon (true righteousness) and the antithesis (false righteousness). This is the premise of the Sermon[15]: There is a righteousness that is connected to salvation, and the Pharisees do not have it! In the Sermon Jesus identi-fies three forms of righteousness: (1) true righteousness—right behavior, right source; (2) unrighteousness[16]—wrong behavior; (3) false righteous-ness[17]—seemingly right behavior, wrong source. True righteousness is not rooted in behavior as much as it is rooted in God. True righteousness can only be acquired from God as a gift through the sacrifice of His Son. This surpassing righteousness is "both qualitatively[18] and quantitatively[19] dif-ferent from a 'righteousness' grounded in the minutia of Law keeping" (Chouinard 105). Paul further attests to this, distinguishing between the righteousness of moral effort[20] and the righteousness of God that can only be acquired as a gift from God (Rom. 5:17). False righteousness—the righteousness of the Pharisees—has its beginning and its end in the flesh. In fact, later in the Sermon the effect is that the righteousness of the Pharisees is placed on an equal plain with the actions of hypocrites and strivings of the Gentiles. While the righteousness of the Pharisees had a vague connection to the Law of God—His moral character—their view of the Law was translated through the flesh, not through the Spirit of God.

While, in the current context, righteousness at first appears to be some-thing to be practiced and, in its most common use, was a virtue rooted in observance of the Law (Schrenk, Bromiley 171), Jesus teaches that it is something to be desired more than practiced (5:6; 6:33). In fact, it appears that when the focus turns to practice, as in the case of the Pharisees, malevolence begins (6:1). Later, Paul seems to indicate that prior to Christ, the righteousness of God was not evident (manifest) apart from the Law (Rom. 3:21). This is not to say that the Jewish leaders were justified in their righteousness founded upon strict adherence, since Scripture gives ample examples of men and women whose adherence to the Law was bound not by legalism or false righteousness, but by a faith-filled relationship with God.[21] The Law was first a reflection of the righteousness of God. Therefore, those who loved God loved His Law; and in the same way those who loved God's Law loved God. God's very nature, His character, is righteous; therefore, righteousness is first and foremost defined through God. Man, therefore, can be truly righteous only when he reflects the character or righteousness of God. Righteousness is not merely a principle of life; it is the very character of real life. There can be no kingdom people apart from kingdom character. Recognizing that while, by its nature, righteousness will always be demonstrated through behavior, in Christ it is more than just right behavior, because it is rooted in the source and, to an extent, in the motive behind the behavior. Right behavior is not righteous apart from a righteous source. The problem that we face with any discussion of righteousness is that our humanity can identify behavior much more easily than it can source or motive. Recognizing this, Jesus devotes the rest of the Sermon to defining and describing true righteousness so that the captives may come to understand the principles of real life.

NOTES

[1] They were yet to be made aware of the fact that Jesus was born God incarnate.

[2] I.e., Genesis, Exodus, Leviticus, Numbers, and Deuteronomy.

[3] The Prophets was a broad term referring to both the Major (earlier) and Minor (later) prophetical books.

[4] There were 613 laws not to mention many other rules and traditions.

[5] E.g., food of equal weight to a dried fig or the amount of oil required to anoint a finger.

[6] Lit., "complete."

[7] At least three that carry some degree of orthodoxy.

[8] Lit., *iota* in the Greek, relative to the *yod* in Hebrew.

[9] Lit., "stroke" or the serif that distinguished between similar characters in the Hebrew alphabet.

[10] This is the first of thirty-eight times that Jesus evokes this statement of personal authority (in one form or another) throughout the Sermon.

[11] Lit., "free," in this context *luō* carries forth the idea of stepping outside the boundaries.

[12] The Jews distinguished between "light" and "heavy" commandments.

[13] Matthew is unique in his use of the phrase "kingdom of heaven," as the rest of the Gospels defer to the phrase "kingdom of God." Some have suggested that Matthew has a different concept in mind, but it seems more likely that he is following common Jewish practice of avoiding the name of God.

[14] While in no way was the Jewish concept of life after death as developed as the later Christian views of heaven and hell, there was certainly an understanding of having and not having, of being and not being.

[15]Jesus refers to righteousness six times in the Sermon, making this the thread that ties the points together.

[16]See 5:45; while Jesus acknowledges the existence of unrighteousness, His primary focus is to contrast between true righteousness and false righteousness.

[17]The argument could be made that false righteousness is the same as unrighteousness. But, as stated elsewhere, Jesus seems to want to make a distinction in order to question the motives of the scribes and Pharisees.

[18]Its source is the righteousness of God, not in the moral efforts of the flesh—whatever the motives.

[19]As demonstrated by Jesus in the passages that follow—"You have heard that it was said . . . ." "But I tell you. . . ."

[20]Which he calls the righteousness of the Law, Phil. 3:6,9.

[21]E.g., Moses, Joshua, Daniel.

4 ■ Anger

Matthew 5:21-26

Dick Jorgensen

²¹You have heard that it was said to the people long ago, "Do not murder, and anyone who murders will be subject to judgment." ²²But I tell you that anyone who is angry with his brother will be subject to judgment. Again, anyone who says to his brother, "Raca," is answerable to the Sanhedrin. But anyone who says, "You fool!" will be in danger of the fire of hell. ²³Therefore, if you are offering your gift at the altar and there remember that your brother has something against you, ²⁴leave your gift there in front of the altar. First go and be reconciled to your brother; then come and offer your gift. ²⁵Settle matters quickly with your adversary who is taking you to court. Do it while you are still with him on the way, or he may hand you over to the judge, and the judge may hand you over to the officer, and you may be thrown into prison. ²⁶I tell you the truth, you will not get out until you have paid the last penny.

DEFINING CONTEXT

Jesus introduces this section of His Sermon on the Mount with the amazing declaration in 5:20:

"For I tell you [on my own authority] that unless your righteousness [unless you are authentic and obey God from your heart] surpasses that of the Pharisees and teachers of the law [they are not the *sine qua nons* of righteousness because they set the bar of righteousness in the wrong place], you will certainly not [not maybe or possibly, but never] enter the kingdom of heaven."[1]

Whew! Attention: this is important truth coming up!

Jesus proceeds to give six teachings, each of which can stand alone, as examples of a "righteousness that surpasses that of the Pharisees and teachers of the law" (5:20). When these teachings are taken together, they are more powerful and form a unit of teaching on six authentic issues of the heart: managing anger (5:21-26); having sexual purity (5:27-30); keeping marriage whole (5:31-32); speaking truth (5:33-37); giving to the evil (5:38-42); and loving enemies (5:43-48). Jesus raised the bar from Law to grace.[2] Using familiar legalistic terminology, Jesus opens the curtains of grace and introduces the heart of God. Jesus is saying, "I don't want you to be in the prison of anger, or the hell of adultery, or the heartbreak of divorce, or the swamp of deceit, or the cycle of revenge, or the pit of hate."

Fred Craddock correctly says that Jesus' teachings and the Scriptures themselves have already been organized; and if we can discover how and why, both become more powerful.[3] Thus this question: Why did Jesus choose these six subjects and why was managing anger first?[4] Might it be that these six cover the spectrum of lifestyle righteousness and that how one manages anger is a huge part of how the other five heart issues are realized in one's life? The truth is that anger is a God-given and divinely used emotion for healthy righteousness; but it is also a pivotal emotion to every heart issue that humans can easily use in unhealthy ways, which can lead to sin.[5] In this first and primary focus of his six teachings, Jesus shows us the power of unrestrained and unhealthy anger, the results that occur, and then gives two examples of how to manage anger in a righteous way. Jesus uses the pattern of "what," "so what," and the "for instance," that is often found in the New Testament, as Craddock observes.[6]

What is anger? Les Carter insightfully defines anger as the "emotion of self-preservation" (8). What does it preserve? Carter asserts, "Anger is defined as an interest to preserve (1) personal worth, (2) essential needs, and (3) basic convictions" (8). I believe anger is a defense emotion designed by God to preserve these three values essential to every person—including the Godhead Himself.

God displayed anger with the Israelites (Exod. 32:1-14). Likewise, Jesus displayed anger with the Pharisees over healing a man's hand on the Sabbath (Mark 3:1-6). And the Holy Spirit displayed anger when lied to by Ananias and Sapphira (Acts 5:1-11). In these three instances, we see first that God was preserving righteousness based on His own holiness. Secondly, Jesus was preserving a man's personal worth, essential need, and his own convictions. Finally, the Holy Spirit was preserving the basic convictions of truth.

HEALTHY VS. UNHEALTHY ANGER

The Apostle Paul teaches Christ-followers that there is healthy anger, which leads to righteousness and positive change, and unhealthy anger, which leads to sin and destructive change (Eph. 4:25-32). In our text, Jesus deals with the latter as the first of six wrong applications of the Law. The first wrong application is, "You can be angry, just don't kill anybody." The other five wrong applications are: "You can lust, just don't commit sexual sin." "You can divorce without worrying about how it affects your wife." "You can spin your answers if you swear by the right authority." "You can take revenge just as long as it's tit for tat." "You can hate people just as long as they are not as good as you or like you."

Jesus teaches us that bad, unhealthy anger can lead to murdering someone in your heart.[7] And we know from experience that such anger can lead to actual murder. It happens today and it happened at the time Jesus is teaching. In fact, He, Himself, becomes a victim of such anger from those who put Him on the cross.

Unhealthy anger is a pervasive emotion in American culture. It may even be public enemy number one. It is both the effect of sin and the instigator of more sin. It has led to actual murder. Jesus says in 5:21 that violation of the sixth commandment, "you shall not murder," will bring serious accountability (Exod. 20:13). True enough. Then Jesus raises the bar from the codebook to the heart, and says, "But I tell you that the anger that motivates such action is just as accountable and just as culpable and dangerous as the action itself" (paraphrase mine).

The reply may be thought or said, "Well, I only said, 'Raca,' I didn't actually hurt or touch anyone physically. It's only a contemptible word. Don't be so touchy" (5:22a).[8] "On second thought, I may have said, 'you fool,' but what's so bad about that (5:22b)? I really didn't mean to assail anyone's heart or character or morality." "Anger and insult are ugly symptoms of a desire to get rid of somebody who stands in our way" (Stott 85). Jesus teaches that such bad anger puts a person dangerously close to, or on the path of, the divine judgment of hell itself.[9]

In the 1990s "hate crime" legislation began to surface in some state legislatures in the United States, and was passed in some jurisdictions. Its purpose is to punish crimes against people more severely if it is determined that hate motivated a crime against a person. It seeks to differentiate actions prompted by hate and those actions that are not premeditated by hate. Jesus' teaching goes one step further: The anger of the heart is just as dangerous and culpable as the act of anger perpetrated against another. Such anger places both the giver and the receiver in danger.

Jesus reveals three levels of unhealthy anger that indicate negative progression, which says, "anger that goes unmanaged grows unhealthier and becomes more dangerous." Level one is anger in the heart with someone (brother?), but no words are spoken. This anger can endanger, or even kill, one's heart. Level two is anger in the heart that begins to treat someone with disrespect. This anger hurts or endangers the relationship. Words are spoken. Level three is anger in the heart that characterizes another person's heart and condemns it. This anger can kill the relationship with another and endanger the angry person's destiny. On all levels, accountability for the bad anger is certain.

Jesus gives two examples and then teaches that unhealthy anger requires immediate attention. First (5:23-24) is in worship and inside the family of God. Worship is a heart issue that involves expressing one's love to God. Giving to God is a heart issue, because Jesus goes on to say that treasure and heart are inseparable (6:21). Eugene Peterson paraphrases it this way:

> "If you enter your place of worship and, about to make an
> offering, you suddenly remember a grudge a friend has against

you, abandon your offering, leave immediately, go to this friend and make things right. Then and only then, come back and work things out with God" (*The Message*).

What is the point? Do not let anger fester with a fellow Christian. Take care of it quickly, Jesus teaches. Unhealthy anger requires immediate attention. Bad anger destroys relationships and even communities of faith. The old adage that "a grudge is like swallowing poison and hoping the other person dies" is a clear description of how bad anger works. Even if the other person wants nothing to do with resolution and forgiveness, one's heart is clear when the effort is authentically made.

Second (5:25-26) is in court and inside the family of man. It is about the integrity of the heart. Winning a case in court is not most important. There is a danger in being right. It is the danger of no grace. Courts do not resolve anger; people do. One can actually win a case in court and be the loser because of the bad anger of an opponent. Anger can take the heart prisoner and is far worse than actual confinement. The Christian does not want to be in either prison. Settling the case Jesus' way restores the heart, and potentially, the relationship. Jesus' way takes charge of the situation, saves the believer from further difficulty, heads off any prison time (literally or spiritually), and brings reconciliation and maybe a friendship. Peterson paraphrases Jesus' teaching in this way:

"Say you're out on the street and an old enemy accosts you. Don't lose a minute. Make the first move; make things right with him. After all, if you leave the first move to him, knowing his track record, you're likely to end up in court, maybe even in jail. If that happens, you won't get out without a stiff fine" (Matt. 5:25-26 *The Message*).

Jesus knows there is good anger and bad anger. The kind of bad anger Jesus refers to is *orgē,* a brooding, inward anger, as differentiated from *thymos*, an anger that flares up.[10] In this teaching passage, He shows the importance and the means of managing bad, brooding anger.

Anger is a secondary emotion—secondary to fear and anxiety (Bilodeau 30). Anger is not a primary emotion that occurs before one knows what is happening. Thus anger can be managed if an awakened mind is applied to it (Carter 6). Jesus awakens our mind, teaches us how to manage it, and motivates us to choose to handle anger God's way. Returning to 5:21 and the connection of murder to bad anger, Stott concludes: "If we want to avoid committing murder in God's sight, we must take every possible positive step to live in peace and love with all men" (86).

NOTES

[1]Brackets mine. Jesus concludes the body of the Sermon with a second reference to the Law and Prophets: "So in everything, do to others what you would have them do to you, for this sums up the law and prophets" (Matt. 7:12).

[2]The six antitheses are designed to show that Jesus demands more than outward conformity. Inward conformity must be present if one desires to obey the commandment. It is here

that our need for grace becomes acute. We need God's gracious provision in order to keep the commandments from the heart.

[3]This idea is taken from his general writings and sermons.

[4]This author prefers "managing anger" instead of the more popular "anger management" because the emphasis is on the managing, not the anger.

[5]Positive examples include Eph. 4:26, "In your anger do not sin . . ." as well as the parable of the wedding banquet (Matt. 22:1-14; cf. Luke 14:16-24).

[6]This idea is taken from his general writings and sermons.

[7]The word for anger, *orgizomai*, is found eight times in the New Testament (Matt. 5:22; 18:34; 22:7; Luke 14:21; 15:28; Eph. 4:31; Rev. 11:18; 12:17). Anger depicts an "inner mental attitude of indignation, wrath, hatred, and fury usually targeted at a specific person, thing, or event" (Harris vol. 4 379; cf. Num. 22:22; Prov. 16:30).

[8]Both anger and contempt is forbidden. The term "Raca" is an Aramaic term of abuse (contempt). According to Carson, the term means "empty" and "could perhaps be translated 'you blockhead'" (*The Sermon on the Mount* 41).

[9]A distinction must be made between the anger or wrath of God and the anger or wrath of humans. The human anger that Jesus warns against is an "irrational and uncontrollable emotion, containing much vanity, animosity, malice and the desire for revenge . . . God's anger is absolutely free from all such poisonous ingredients" (Stott, *Romans* 71). Moo agrees: "God's reaction to sin is not the 'anger' of an emotional person, it is the necessary reaction of a holy God to sin" (60; cf. Rom. 1:18).

[10]The difference may be noted by studying *thymos* in Luke 4:28 and Acts 19:28. Both words, *orgē* and *thymos,* are condemned as vices (e.g., Eph. 4:31; Col. 3:8; Verbrugge 926).

5 ■ Adultery

Matthew 5:27-30

Fred Johnson

²⁷You have heard that it was said, "Do not commit adultery."
²⁸But I tell you that anyone who looks at a woman lustfully has already
committed adultery with her in his heart. ²⁹If your right eye causes
you to sin, gouge it out and throw it away. It is better for you to lose
one part of your body than for your whole body to be thrown into hell.
³⁰And if your right hand causes you to sin, cut it off and throw it away.
It is better for you to lose one part of your body than
for your whole body to go into hell.

Jesus now turns His attention from the sixth commandment (5:21-26) to the seventh, "You shall not commit adultery" (Exod. 20:14; Deut. 5:18). Jesus' purpose is to offer a second example that illustrates a "righteousness that surpasses that of the Pharisees and the teachers of the law" (5:20). The Pharisees and scribes (teachers of the Law) had reduced their understanding and application of the seventh commandment to an external obedience only. Those who desired to keep the seventh commandment could do so by abstaining from physical adultery. Jesus points to the true intention and application of the seventh commandment. According to Jesus, sexual purity begins with the heart (5:28). Jesus thus "penetrates to the deeper spirit of the law," insisting that internal obedience and external conformity are required to obey the commandment (Hagner 112).[1] Purity of heart is the righteousness demanded by Jesus in contrast to an artificial righteousness that results from external obedience alone.

In examining the righteousness demanded by the seventh commandment, Jesus focuses on sexual perversion (adultery, 27), sexual passion (lust, 28), and sexual purity (deliverance, 29-30). By limiting the seventh commandment to an external obedience alone, Stott asserts that the Pharisees and scribes were guilty of teaching "a conveniently narrow definition of sexual sin and a conveniently broad definition of sexual purity" (87). Stott's assessment is painfully modern, as contemporary secular culture hungers for unlimited sexual freedom. MacArthur aptly summarizes the spirit of our day:

> Ours is a day of unbridled indulgence in sexual passion. People propagate, promote, and exploit it through the most powerful and pervasive media ever known to man. It seems to be the almost uninterrupted theme of our society's entertainment. . . . Mass media uses sex to sell its products and to glamorize its programs. Sex crimes are at all-time highs, while infidelity, divorce, and perversion are justified. Marriage, sexual fidelity, and moral purity are scorned, ridiculed, and laughed at. We are preoccupied with sex to a degree perhaps never before seen in a civilized culture (300).

Jesus' teaching on sexual purity could not be timelier for the twenty-first century Christian living in a culture bent on rampant sexual hedonism. Sexual identity and expression are no longer viewed as moral issues. The only questions asked concerning the acceptability of premarital and extramarital sexual activity are "Is it socially acceptable?" "Is it personally rewarding?" "Does it enrich human life?" or "Does it harm anyone?" (Lawson 74). Disregard for this teaching of Jesus has brought nothing but broken marriages, broken homes, and broken lives.[2]

SEXUAL PERVERSION (V. 27)

Jesus stood firm on the Mosaic commandment forbidding adultery (Exod. 20:14; Deut. 5:18). Adultery is sexual perversion, according to Jesus, for it "violates the sanctity of the marriage bond" (Lawson 75). Jesus taught that marriage was instituted by God and was to be understood as a permanent covenant between one man and one woman for life (Gen. 2:18; Matt. 19:6; Mark 10:9). The relationship is exclusive in that a man "will leave his father and mother and be united to his wife, and they will become one flesh" (Gen. 2:24).

The biblical idea of marriage, however, goes beyond mere companionship. This union involves romantic passion. God-ordained romantic longing is beautifully expressed in the Song of Solomon "where marriage is pictured as the satisfaction of this longing" ("Marriage" 538). The marriage relationship, furthermore, is the most intimate of all relationships in that the "natural consummation of romantic love is sexual union" ("Marriage" 538). Marital love and sexual union are characterized as the strongest, most powerful force that a man and woman may experience within the bonds of marriage: "Under the apple tree I roused you . . . for love is as strong as death, its jealousy unyielding as the grave. It burns like blazing fire, like a mighty flame" (Song of S. 8:5-6). The proverb writer, using the imagery of a fountain, speaks of joy and sexual satisfaction in the context of covenant love and faithfulness to your wife: "May your fountain be blessed, and may you rejoice in the wife of your youth. A loving doe, a graceful deer—may her breasts satisfy you always, may you ever be captivated by her love" (Prov. 5:18-19).[3]

The Bible is not prudish or pornographic when it speaks of God's design for sexual expression and enjoyment within marriage. It is a divine gift. With the invitation to embrace what God has designed, however, comes a strict prohibition. Sexual expression and activity are restricted to one's spouse, period. Violators of sexual fidelity within marriage are guilty of adultery.[4]

Adultery in the Greco-Roman world was understood as "sexual intercourse of a married woman with a man other than her husband" (Hawthorne 594). The Old Testament, however, broadens this view to include any man who has sexual relations with another man's wife. For example, the Proverbs writer warns, "Can a man walk on hot coals without his feet being scorched? So is he who sleeps with another man's wife" (Prov. 6:28-29). The New Testament likewise forbids adultery: "Marriage should be honored by all, and the marriage bed kept pure, for God will judge the adulterer and all the sexually immoral" (Heb. 13:4). Although Paul clearly bans adultery (1 Cor. 6:9), his teaching is couched within the larger context of instruction on sexual ethics. According to Paul, Christian sanctification requires abstinence from *porneia,* that is "sexual immorality" (1 Thess. 4:3; Gal. 5:19; Col. 3:5; cf. 1 Cor. 10:8). This Greek word is used to "denote any kind of illegitimate—extramarital and unnatural—sexual intercourse or relationship" (Wright 871).[5] The implications of the Bible's holistic teaching on sexual ethics become clear: "the satisfying of sexual desires is not wrong, and marriage is its appointed setting" (Wright 873).

Jesus intends His teaching on the seventh commandment to extend beyond husbands, wives, and the sexual perversion of adultery. "Anyone" (28) is general and cannot be restricted to a married man. Likewise, "woman" (28) can refer to a married or unmarried woman. A single man's lustful look (at a single or married woman) is just as wicked as the lustful look of a married man upon a single woman or another man's wife. The reverse is also true. What is said of a man is equally accurate in regard to a woman (Lenski 226; MacArthur agrees 302; cf. Rom. 1:26). Jesus quotes the seventh commandment in order to teach and demonstrate the deeper intent of the Law as applied to all sexual conduct. He does so simply by "labeling *lust* adultery" (Carson, *The Sermon on the Mount* 43, italics mine). Sexual purity is a matter of external and internal conformity to God's standard of sexual behavior. Accordingly, all Christians, both men and women, are called to know and obey God's standards of sexual passion, practice, and fulfillment.

SEXUAL PASSION (V. 28)

God designed both sexual purity and sexual passion. Sexual passion within marriage is joyful intimacy. Sexual passion outside of marriage, according to Jesus, is breaking the commandment of God. Jesus now stresses the purity to which the Law points. According to Jesus, the person who lusts, but does not commit the physical act of adultery, is just as guilty as the one who indulges in the physical act. Jesus simply makes no distinction between internal impulses and outward activities. Both can be pure or perverted.

Several years ago our Sunday school class decided to have a class outing. We decided a movie night would be fun and went to see *Schindler's List*. The movie depicts the horrors of life in the Krakovw-Plaszovw concentration camp, led by Untersturmführer Amon Göth. In one scene, a Jewish girl is raped. Nudity filled the screen. I admit that I was embarrassed as I watched. On one side of me sat my wife, on the other side sat the preacher's wife. Though embarrassed, I did not lust. The truth is my sense of shame blocked the awakening of any desire to lust.

In dealing with sexual passion, Jesus is not prohibiting the sexual instinct; it is God-ordained. Nor is Jesus, I believe, dealing with the "momentary arousal of sexual desire" (Fisher 75; Hunter agrees 52). Sexual desire can be awakened in an instant. Jesus asserts that we are guilty of adultery when the look turns to lust, that is, when the look accompanies the desire to engage in sexual activity (real or imagined). Jesus is addressing the "deep-seated lust which consumes and devours, which in imagination attacks and rapes, which mentally contemplates" illicit sexual encounters (Carson, *The Sermon on the Mount* 44; Hagner agrees, 121).[6] This is the look that wants the freedom of sex without the responsibility or accountability that God demands (Fisher 75).

Dr. Marion Henderson, the esteemed preacher and professor we desire to honor with these essays, points out that Jesus is speaking of "the look that persists and continues" (52; Lenski translates, "But I say to you that every man looking at a woman . . . " 225). Jesus is speaking about the one who keeps on looking "in order to lust after her" (Hunter 52; Hagner agrees 120). The continual looking is purposeful. It is a calculated look in order to awaken sexual impulses.[7] This is the man who deliberately fosters lust by looking at a woman as a sex object, who fantasizes perverted sexual conduct through erotic materials, whether books or magazines. This is the woman who fosters lust through videos, explicit sexual lyrics in songs or the Internet. Stott is correct, "Deeds of shame are preceded by fantasies of shame" (88). This intentional desire to awaken lust, according to Jesus, is equally sinful in God's sight as the physical act of adultery (Mounce 43).

An alternative view understands the relationship between looking and lusting as one of result instead of purpose (McNeile 64). The NIV translation lends itself to this interpretation: "But I tell you that anyone who looks at a woman lustfully," that is, anyone who continues to look with the result that you lust. This understanding is desirable for two reasons. First, it leaves room for the kind of looking that is God-honoring. Physical attraction is not evil in itself (ask Adam). But physical attraction must be monitored in order to stay God-honoring. When my wife and I were dating, I was very much physically attracted to her (as well as spiritually, intellectually, and emotionally). But if I let my guard down, accompanied by certain sexually stimulating circumstances, and if I refused to deal with it when I knew I had crossed the line to lust, the result of this combination was sin. Second, as we shall see, Jesus instructs us on how to maintain sexual purity (vv. 29-30). What kinds of circumstances turn looking into lusting? How should we respond?

Was David at fault for seeing Bathsheba naked (2 Sam. 11:1-4)? I don't think so. It was not the casual glance due to an "unavoidable exposure to sexual temptation" that led to David's sin (MacArthur 303). David's adultery was the continual looking (due to circumstances) and in the conscious yielding to sexual stimulus. Sin would not have happened if David had looked in a different direction and refused to submit to the sexual allurement. David, however, yielded to the temptation, invited Bathsheba into his bedroom, and physically committed adultery.

Jesus is clear on the subject. The looking, which results in lust or purposes to lust, does so because sin is already in the heart. The lustful looking is but the "expression of a heart that is already immoral and adulterous" (MacArthur 303). Jesus taught that the seat of sin is the heart (see Luke 6:43ff.; cf. Matt. 7:17-20). If the heart was pure, the lustful look would not take place (Lenski 226). It needs to be noted that the idea of sinning in the heart is already contained in the Ten Commandments where one is "forbidden to covet, among other things, the wife of a neighbor" (Exod. 20:17; Hagner 44; cf. Stott 87; Carson, *The Sermon on the Mount* 44). This is precisely Paul's point in a moving confession, "For I would not have known what coveting really was if the law had not said, 'Do not covet'" (Rom. 7:7b). In other words, the Law had always stressed the importance of the heart.[8] Paul now agonizes with the reality of obeying this command, "but sin, seizing the opportunity afforded by the commandment, produced in me every kind of covetous desire" (Rom. 7:8a; Jones 232).

Jesus sees the thoughts in our hearts that are "on the ready for murder and adultery. . . . He sees the impure glances and the furious eagerness of our imagination" (Thielicke 43). Here is our sovereign Lord who stretches His scepter even over the innermost recesses of our hearts. King Jesus not only demands holy actions, but commands holy desires. When faced with the righteousness that God requires, Paul concluded: "What a wretched man I am!" (Rom. 7:24a). The diagnosis is bleak. That conclusion, however, led to a doxology, "Who will rescue me from this body of death? Thanks be to God—through Jesus Christ our Lord" (Rom. 7:24b-25)! Paul confessed his struggle with sin and in the same breath acknowledged his salvation through Christ. The Psalmist puts forth the same cry and the identical solution: "Wash away all my iniquity and cleanse me from my sin. For I know my transgressions, and my sin is always before me. . . . Create in me a pure heart, O God, and renew a steadfast spirit within me" (51:2,3,10). Once our hearts are cleansed unto salvation by the grace of our Father's love, Christians are called to the task of continual heart cleansing in order to obey our Father's commandments and enjoy His divine blessing.

SEXUAL PURITY (VV. 29-30)

Jesus proceeds to point the way to sexual purity.[9] Some scholars suggest that Jesus either anticipates or immediately responds to an objection raised by one of His hearers. Jesus meets the protest that asserts the problem is really with the eye and not the heart. The objector claims "that he cannot help it that his eye inflames him to lust" (Lenski 227). Consequently, Jesus draws from the "fallacious excuse the equally fallacious conclusion as to the remedy" (Lenski 227). The cure for the protester's claim is the removal of his own depraved eye. Furthermore, Jesus ridicules their position by mentioning the right eye only. Removing the right eye still leaves the left eye and lust is inevitable (same logic for right hand). Even if one removes both eyes, lust still emerges in the "mind's eye" (Jones 243). Jesus disallows the rationalization of the one who would "shield his heart by a reference to the eye" (Lenski 227). The seat of sin remains in the heart, which in turn controls the eye.

Although we would not deny the line of reasoning above, a better interpretation sees Jesus using hyperbole to stress the importance of dealing drastically with temptation that leads to sexual perversion. Breaking the Law is sin. The consequence of sin is eternal punishment in hell.[10] Therefore, radical action must be taken to shun the cause of illicit sexual temptation. Better the plucking out of an eye or removal of an appendage than the whole body cast into hell. Jesus is certainly not advocating any form of self-mutilation in an effort toward spirituality. The image "emphasizes the crucial importance of taking whatever measures are necessary to control natural passions that tend to flare out of control" (Mounce 43).[11] MacArthur aptly summarizes the call to sexual purity: "Just as the outward act of adultery reflects a heart that is already adulterous, the outward act of forsaking whatever is harmful reflects a heart that hungers and thirsts for righteousness" (305).

Biblically, to be at the right side of someone or something was identified as being in the special seat of honor or place of importance (cf. 1 Kgs. 2:19; Ps. 45:9; Acts 2:33-34; Heb. 1:3; Matt. 25:31-46). Most likely Jesus mentions the right eye and hand in order to emphasize what is the most important or prominent. The right eye was considered to have the best vision; likewise, the right hand, the best skills (Carson, *Matthew* 151). The reference to the right hand may not refer to activities. Several other options have been proposed. The right hand is mentioned because intellectual adultery (lust) is a kind of theft (you are stealing another man's wife; Carson, *The Sermon on the Mount* 44). Spurgeon holds that Jesus refers to one's profession (28). Some suggest that the right hand is used euphemistically to refer to the male genitals or to the "offence of the hand" referring to masturbation (Deming 134).[12] In this context, it seems best to understand Jesus' reference to the right as meaning that which is most important. Consequently, the point Jesus graphically makes is that even the most important, precious, or cherished looking or activities must be jettisoned if they cause one to sin (Mounce 43; MacArthur 304; Jones 243).

The above interpretation is further preferred when we consider the verb Jesus uses: "If your right eye or hand causes you to sin. . . ." The verb is used of a bait stick in a trap. Hunters would fix the trap with a bait stick to lure the animal. When the animal went for the bait, the stick would spring the trap (Barclay 148; Fisher 75). Because of the importance of obeying God's standard of sexual purity, whatever triggers or causes impure thoughts or actions (real or imagined) must be expunged quickly and decisively.[13] To deliberately "foster lust by erotic books, plays, films and magazines is to fly in the face of this commandment" (Green 75).

The contemporary significance of applying Jesus' words cannot be overstated. Christians are bombarded with advertisements and enticements that invite sinful thoughts and activities. Applications must be authentic and forthright. If my eyes or hands cause me to sin sexually, I must in the future deliberately decline those things that corrupt. I must not read certain literature, watch certain movies, or align myself with activities that have a strong possibility of causing sexual sin.

Stott wants to be careful about laying down any law (legalistic requirements) related to what books, magazines, movies, or activities Christians may indulge in. Certain people "can see explicitly sexual pictures (on paper or film) and remain entirely unscathed, while others would find them terribly corrupting" (90). We understand Stott's appeal to guard against unbridled legalism. However, the grammar of these verses indicates that Jesus is not just speaking hypothetically. In other words, Jesus is speaking about an eye or hand that does cause a person to sin sexually.[14] Christians who know God's standards of sexual purity, who sin sexually (by eye or hand) are the first to know this side of heaven. When sin happens, we must pinpoint the cause and eradicate it.

A student once confessed to me that he would never buy pornographic literature; however, he renewed his subscription every year to *Sports Illustrated* to satisfy his craving for sexual stimulation. He admitted that he sinned sexually every February (swimsuit issue). Of course I am not advocating that every Christian needs to cancel their subscription. I would advocate it for this particular student (or at least have in place an accountability strategy when the swimsuit issue arrives).

Because of the subtlety of sexual allurement resulting in sexual sin in our culture, we propose a further delineation that will help us maintain sexual purity. Indeed, we are to rejoice when the momentary arousal of sexual passion is squelched before it leads to sin. However, living in a sexually perverted secular environment, the Christian needs to ask, "Why did I look in the first place? Why did I go to this place? Do I look at sexually stimulating material that I would never have looked at a few years ago? Has my spiritual sensitivity toward perverted sexual stimulation decreased?" Honest answers to these questions will serve as a personal early warning detection alarm of potential pollutants. Once the alarm sounds, there must be no compromise, no accommodation, no concession or negotiation, only confrontation of contaminants which lead to sexually immoral thoughts or deeds. To God be the glory.

NOTES

[1]Jesus uses the identical reasoning in Matthew 5:21-26 where internal anger equals external murder.

[2]James Dobson asserts that sexual immorality is the primary issue eroding contemporary society (see the *Focus on the Family* Web site for a full discussion, www.family.org).

[3]In 1 Corinthians 7:1-7, Paul emphasizes the importance of sexual union within the marriage relationship.

[4]The consistent witness of the Old Testament sees adultery as an act of sexual immorality so dreadfully wicked that it is punishable by death (Lev. 20:10; Deut. 22:22). The New Testament likewise sees adultery as appalling, punishable by God Himself: "Blessed are those who wash their robes, that they may have the right to the tree of life and may go through the gates into the city. Outside are the dogs, those who practice magic arts, the sexually immoral, the murderers, the idolaters and everyone who lives and practices falsehood" (Rev. 22:14-15; cf. 1 Cor. 6:9).

[5]Forbidden activities include any sexual activities outside monogamous heterosexual marriage. Paul admonished the Ephesian Christians: ". . . among you there must not be even a hint of sexual immorality . . . because these are improper for God's holy people" (Eph. 5:3).

[6]The Greek word translated "lusting" denotes a strong desire of any kind. It is used in a positive way only three times in the New Testament (Luke 22:15; Phil. 1:23, 1 Thess. 2:17). The rest of the occurrences are used in a negative sense (e.g., Rom. 13:14; Gal. 5:16, 24; Eph. 2:3; 2 Pet. 2:18; 1 John 2:16). We live in a culture that continues to diminish God's view of adultery—how much more is this the case in regards to sexual lusts (Carson, *The Sermon on the Mount* 44)?

[7]The New American Standard Bible brings out this idea more clearly than the NIV, "But I say to you, that everyone who looks on a woman to lust for her...."

[8]Cf. 1 Sam. 16:7; 1 Kgs. 8:39; 1 Chr. 28:9; Luke 16:15; John 2:25; Acts 1:24.

[9]Verses 29-30 appear elsewhere in the Gospels (see Matt. 18:8-9; Mark 9:43-48). Most likely, this teaching of Jesus was used on more than one occasion in different contexts (Hagner 119; Stott 89).

[10]The Aramaic word "Gehenna" is often translated "hell," the opposite of paradise (Keener 58). The name refers to the valley of Hinnom (cf. Josh. 15:8; 18:16) where human sacrifices were offered to Molech, a pagan deity (cf. 2 Kgs. 23:10; Jer. 7:31). This location later served as the place where garbage was burned. The "constant burning there made the valley a particularly suitable metaphor for eternal punishment" (Hagner 117).

[11]As a young man, Origin (early church leader; c.185-c.254) took Matthew 19:12 literally and castrated himself (Schnucker 734).

[12]Deming bases his conclusion on readings from the Babylonian Talmud. For example, Rabbi Tarfon said, "A hand touching his genitals is to be cut off. . . ." (*b.Nidda.* 13a-b; in Deming 133).

[13]Job was aware of the connection between a sinful heart and lustful eyes. Consequently, he determined to post a sentinel over his eyes to guard against sexual impurity, "I have made a covenant with my eyes; how then could I gaze at a virgin . . . if my step has turned. . . ." (Job 31:1,7-8).

[14]The grammar assumes the reality of the "if" clause for the sake of the argument/discussion. Thus, "since your eye and hand cause you to sin."

6 ■ Divorce & Remarriage

Matthew 5:31-32

Don Green

³¹It has been said, "Anyone who divorces his wife must give her a certificate of divorce." ³²But I tell you that anyone who divorces his wife, except for marital unfaithfulness, causes her to commit adultery, and anyone who marries a woman so divorced commits adultery.

The third application of Jesus' principle—that the disciple's righteousness should surpass that of the Pharisees and teachers of the Law—is in the realm of divorce and remarriage. In contrast to each of the other applications in Matthew 5:21, 5:27, 5:33, 5:38, and 5:43, Jesus does not begin by saying, "You have heard that it was said." Rather, He introduces this topic by simply saying, "It has been said." With this shift in how this teaching is introduced, Jesus is connecting this saying with what precedes, thus this teaching further defines the distinctive regarding His view of adultery. As John R.W. Stott observes, "The third antithesis (about divorce) follows the second (about adultery) as a natural sequence. For in certain circumstances, Jesus now says, remarriage by or to a divorced person is tantamount to adultery" (92). Or as Carson says:

> The OT not only points toward insisting that lust is the moral equivalent of adultery (vv. 7-30) but that divorce is as well. This arises out of the fact that the divorced woman will in most circumstances remarry (especially in first-century Palestine, where this would probably be her means of support). That new marriage, whether from the perspective of the divorcee or the one marrying her, is adulterous (*Matthew* 152).

Jesus' teaching on the subject of divorce and remarriage is found in four texts—Matthew 5:31-32; Matthew 19:3-12; Mark 10:2-12; and Luke 16:18. (Paul's teaching in 1 Cor. 7 is the only other New Testament reference.) What Jesus says in the Sermon on the Mount should be understood in light of three important contextual factors:

1) the practice of divorce in the 1st century Roman world;
2) the interpretation of Deuteronomy 24:1-4 in Jesus' day;
3) the teaching of Jesus on this subject in Matthew 19:3-12.

THE PRACTICE OF DIVORCE IN THE
FIRST CENTURY ROMAN WORLD

When Jesus spoke these words in the 1st century Roman world, divorce and remarriage were commonly accepted. According to Staton, "The historian Seneca records that people got married in order to get divorced and got divorced in order to marry again" ("Divorce the Divider: Part Three—Jesus and Divorce" 7). He also notes that even in 1st-century Palestine "many of the people in Jesus' crowds had been divorced and remarried" (7).

Michael Green observes that, although the practice of divorce was common in both the Greco-Roman world and the Jewish community, there were differences in perspective. He writes:

Divorce was rife throughout ancient society in the first century. It required no formality in Graeco-Roman circles: a written or oral notification sufficed. . . . But Jewish teaching on the strength of the marriage bond was exceedingly high, not only in the Old Testament but in rabbinic Judaism. Divorce could only take place when a man finds some indecency in his wife and puts her away with a writ of divorce (Deuteronomy 24:1). The precise meaning of "indecency" split the conservative school of Shammai from the liberal school of Hillel. The former restricted it to unchastity. The latter allowed it for burning the toast at breakfast! Accordingly, there soon developed a great disparity between the ideals and the practice in Judaism concerning divorce. Given the fallenness of human nature it is easy to see how the interpretation of Hillel won the day with the men (76).

THE INTERPRETATION OF
DEUTERONOMY 24:1-4 IN JESUS' DAY

Throughout this discourse to His disciples, Jesus is revealing God's intention for human relationships over and against the Mosaic provision, not as it was given, but as it was interpreted and practiced by the Jews. Thus, Jesus' teaching about divorce is offered in light of the Mosaic provision in Deuteronomy 24:1-4. He reveals the true intention and implications of that provision, thus revealing what God originally intended for His people.

He is contrasting the true import and intent of the Law as it is authoritatively interpreted by Himself with the perversions and distortions of the Law as it was interpreted by pharisaical externalism. Jesus' teaching on this subject runs counter to the prevailing Jewish perspective on divorce and stands in contrast with the current Jewish practice of divorce in His day in several ways:

1) Jesus relaxes the dissolution of marriage in the case of adultery by

the death penalty as required in Deuteronomy 22:22. Since Jesus permits divorce in the case of adultery, He does not invoke the death penalty for that sin. John 4:18 and John 8:4 are examples of this perspective.

2) Jesus restricts the common practice of dissolution of marriage for any and every reason as some had interpreted Deuteronomy 24:1. At the same time, He notes that the only indecency which could be grounds for divorce is marital unfaithfulness and that the consequence of divorce for any other reason is more stringent. The second marriage is not only a defilement (Deut. 24:4), but adultery.

3) Jesus requires that responsibility be shared by the man as well as the woman. In Greco-Roman culture, a woman was under the authority of a man—either her father or her husband; consequently divorce was a husband's prerogative.

4) Jesus reinforces God's original intention for marriage as stated in Genesis 2:24.

5) Jesus restates Moses' provision for divorce not as a command but as a concession.

6) Jesus regards divorce seriously in a culture that treated it lightly.

Jesus' allusion to Deuteronomy 24:1 is neither a quotation from the Hebrew nor the Septuagint, as He seems to paraphrase the provision with His short statement, "whoever divorces his wife, let him give her a certificate of divorce." It should not be misconstrued from this statement that men had either the right or obligation to put away their wives with God's approval. Matthew 5:31 merely states that if a man did put his wife away, he was required by the law to give her this legal document, the bill of divorce.

The revolutionary teaching of this passage is Jesus' statement in verse 32, "anyone who divorces his wife, except for marital unfaithfulness, causes her to become an adulteress." He is saying that the only reason that would even satisfy the Mosaic provision for divorce is *porneia*. This is the meaning of that "indecency," which causes a wife to find no favor in her husband's eyes (Deut. 24:1). The word *porneia* may refer to prostitution, unchastity, fornication, sexual immorality, or sexual sin of a general kind that includes many different behaviors. This word is used in such texts as Matthew 15:19; Mark 7:21; John 8:41; Acts 15:20; 1 Corinthians 6:18; 7:2; 2 Corinthians 12:21; Galatians 5:19; Ephesians 5:3; 1 Thessalonians 4:3 (Swanson).

Staton concludes, regarding the meaning of this word, "Probably the best translation of this word would be simply 'sexual immorality'" ("Divorce the Divider: Part Three—Jesus and Divorce" 10). In this context and in Matthew 19:9, the word refers to every kind of sexual immorality that in practice has the same effect as adultery—the breaking of the one-flesh bond of marriage (see how Paul addresses this kind of behavior in 1 Cor. 6:16-20). The result of this putting away without proper cause (the exceptive clause is omitted by Mark and Luke) is that the husband makes his wife an adulteress, and whoever would remarry her also commits adultery.

Two reasons could be cited to explain why Jesus does not state the exceptive clause in Mark and Luke:

1) In the 1st century, no Jew, Roman, or Greek would have questioned that adultery constituted grounds for divorce.

2) Matthew's Gospel was written primarily for a Jewish audience. So in Matthew 5:31-32, Jesus is contrasting the prevailing Jewish attitude toward divorce with God's intention. Likewise, in Matthew 19:3-12 Jesus is responding to a qualified question from the Pharisees, "Is it lawful for a man to divorce his wife for any and every reason?" that used the language of the Shammai-Hillel debate.

Regarding the absence of the exceptive clause in Mark, Instone-Brewer observes,

"First-century Jewish readers would have mentally inserted the phrase 'for any matter' into the question the Pharisees asked Jesus. . . . They would have done this not only because they were familiar with the debate, but also because the question made no sense without it. The question, 'Is it lawful to divorce a wife?' could only be answered by 'Yes, it says so in the law'" (135).

Jesus' teaching in Matthew 5:31-32 can be summarized as follows:

1) the one acceptable reason for divorce is *porneia* ("sexual immorality");

2) the effect of divorce is viewed from the woman's point of view as she is made to be an adulteress if she is divorced by her husband for any other reason and remarries;

3) the remarriage of the divorced woman is also viewed as adultery for the man who marries her.

THE TEACHING OF JESUS ON THIS SUBJECT IN MATTHEW 19:3-12

The more complete treatment of this subject in Matthew 19 is viewed as the pivotal passage that provides perhaps the best commentary on Matthew 5:31-32. It presents not only the exceptive clause in a context but also the first statement about the second marriage of the husband who divorces his wife. The former issue was noted in Matthew 5:32 and the latter is mentioned in Mark 10:11 and Luke 16:18, but both elements are included in Jesus' teaching in Matthew 19:3-12.

What Jesus says about divorce in Matthew 19:3-12 must again be interpreted in light of the Mosaic provision for divorce, as He is answering the Pharisees' question about the legality of divorce for any reason. Since this was the debated issue of His day between those of the Shammai school (who advocated divorce for only one reason) and the Hillel school (who advocated divorce for any and every reason), He is being put to the test to see which view He would take. Origen explains the test in this way:

"If He said, 'It is lawful' He would be accused of permitting divorce for trifle reasons. If He said, 'It is not lawful,' He would be accused of permitting a man to dwell with a woman even with her sins" (505).

Consider these contrasts in this exchange between Jesus and the Pharisees that shed some light on how a disciple's attitude toward marriage, divorce, and remarriage will differ from that of the Pharisees.

Pharisees' Question	Jesus' Answer
based on what the Law says about divorce (Matt. 19:3)	based on what the Creator says about marriage (Matt. 19:4-6)
from Hillel's perspective of divorce "for any and every reason" (Matt. 19:3)	from Shammai's perspective of divorce for "one reason"— "marital unfaithfulness" (Matt. 19:9)
focused on what Moses commanded (Matt. 19:7)	focused on what Moses permitted (Matt. 19:8)
assumed divorce and remarriage would be common	assumed divorce and remarriage would be rare (Matt. 19:10-12)

Jesus does not immediately and directly answer their question, "Is it lawful for a man to divorce his wife for any and every reason?" However, He begins with the first principles of marriage as they are recorded in the opening chapters of Genesis to show that in God's eyes it is not lawful for a man to divorce his wife for any and every reason. Since God joins people together, man does not have the right to separate them. The reason that this is true is because in the covenant of marriage God takes two people and makes them one flesh in the marriage relationship. On the basis of these ideal principles of marriage, Jesus affirms that man should not divorce his wife for any reason.

The misunderstanding of the Jews regarding God's will for marriage and Moses' provision for divorce is even more evident in the second question that the Pharisees asked Jesus in verse 7, "Why then did Moses command that a man give a certificate of divorce and send her away?" It seems most reasonable to interpret this question to imply that Moses required a man to put away his wife in certain circumstances and to give her the bill of divorce. The Pharisees were thus saying, "If marriage is indissoluble according to the original institution and man is not to dissolve the union, how is it that Moses commands divorce?" Jesus answers this question in such a way that one must conclude that in the beginning God intended that there should be no divorce but that "because of the hardness of heart," He permitted it. He answers in verse 8, "Moses permitted you to divorce your wives because your hearts were hard." Deuteronomy 24:1-4 was not given to condone the practice of divorce, but to concede to human weakness. From the beginning, it was not God's intention that marriage should be dissolved except by the separating power of death (cf. Rom. 7:2-3). The only reason God ever permitted it was hardness of heart. This is the starting point of marital failure whether it is on an individual level or a larger national level.

Jesus then proceeds to discuss the issue of remarriage, as He says in verse 9, "anyone who divorces his wife, except for marital unfaithfulness, and marries another woman commits adultery." According to Guy Duty, divorce was not only a common occurrence in the Old Testament, but also was remarriage. "In the Bible, the right to divorce carries with it the right to remarry. Jesus approved the Jewish divorce law that allowed remarriage, but he restricted this Jewish divorce law to the cause of fornication" (18). Further indication that divorce implied remarriage is the meaning of the word for divorce. Staton notes that the Greek word means "a release (freedom) . . . a total dissolving . . . the opposite of being bound"; thus "A divorce allowed those involved to remarry without sin" (7).

The disciples react to Jesus' revolutionary teaching by saying in verse 10, "If this is the situation between a husband and wife, it is better not to marry." They clearly understood the full implications of Jesus' teaching about the ideal of marriage and the indissolubility of it. To them and the audience in Jesus' day the attractiveness and advisability of marriage seemed to be contingent upon the possibility of an easy divorce and the prospect of a better second marriage. Since it had such restrictions, it was to the disciples somewhat unwelcome, but surely not as unwelcome as a life of abstinence and celibacy.

A SUMMARY OF JESUS' TEACHING
ON DIVORCE AND REMARRIAGE

When one brings together all that Jesus says on the subject of divorce and remarriage, the following conclusions may be drawn:

1) God's intention is that marriage should be permanent (Matt. 19:4-6; Mark 10:6-9).
2) God permits divorce only because of the hardness of man's heart (Matt. 19:8; Mark 10:5).
3) The only acceptable reason for divorce is "marital unfaithfulness" (Matt. 5:32; Matt. 19:9).
4) If a woman is divorced for any other reason and remarries, she commits adultery (Matt. 5:32; Mark 10:12).
5) If a man divorces his wife for any other reason and remarries, he commits adultery (Matt. 19:9; Mark 10:11; and Luke 16:18).
6) If a man divorces his wife for any other reason and she remarries, he causes her to become an adulteress (Matt. 5:32).
7) If a man marries a woman who was divorced for any other reason, he commits adultery with her (Matt. 5:32; Luke 16:18).

Instone-Brewer offers what he considers to be six specific guidelines that Jesus taught which are often overlooked and were contrary to what

other 1ˢᵗ century Jews taught:
1) Monogamy—an individual can be married to only one person at a time.
2) Marriage should be lifelong—and it is against God's will to break up a marriage.
3) Divorce is not compulsory—even in cases of adultery.
4) Divorce is allowable—if there is a stubborn refusal to stop committing adultery.
5) Marriage is not compulsory—so infertility is not a ground for divorce.
6) Divorce for any matter is invalid—and so remarriage after this divorce is adulterous (178).

Obviously there are many other issues that are not addressed by Jesus. For instance, He says nothing about what a couple should do if they have remarried after an invalid divorce and are in an adulterous relationship. Yet His teaching brings much-needed perspective on the various views regarding divorce and remarriage. Historically there have been at least four different views on this topic of divorce and remarriage (House):
1) No divorce and no remarriage
   This has been the position of the Roman Catholic Church since they maintain that "adultery gives the right of separation from bed and board but does not sever the bond of marriage nor does it give the right to dissolve that bond" (Murray 35).
2) Divorce but no remarriage
   "This was the view of the majority of the early church fathers" (Stein 193).
3) Divorce and remarriage for adultery and desertion
   "This interpretation is associated with Erasmus and is the view of the Protestant Reformers. Many evangelicals hold this view today" (Stein 193). In 1 Corinthians 7, Paul makes provision in the case of an unbeliever who deserts or divorces a believing spouse (see Staton, "Divorce the Divider: Part Four—Paul and Divorce").
4) Divorce and remarriage under a variety of circumstances
   This was a popularly held view in Jesus' day and is still a popularly held view both in the church and outside the church.

What one must not forget is that, in spite of differences of interpretation, there are some commonly held perspectives. "All exegetes agree that Jesus saw divorce as a tragedy . . . any divorce denotes a failure of the divine purpose . . . there is no so-called good divorce" (Stein 192). Jesus was clear and concise in His teaching on this topic. He treated the subject seriously in a culture that treated it lightly. May we model His approach in applying His principles to our lives.

In his treatment of the Sermon on the Mount, Dallas Willard poses the bottom-line question and offers a sound perspective:

> Is, then, divorce ever justifiable for Jesus? I think it clearly is. His principle of the hardness of hearts allows it, though its application would require great care. Perhaps divorce must be viewed somewhat as the practice of triage in medical care. Decisions must be made as to who cannot, under the circumstances, be helped. . . . Divorce, if it were rightly done, would be done as an act of love. It would be dictated by love and done for the honest good of the people involved. Such divorce, though rare, remains nonetheless possible and may be necessary. If it were truly done on this basis, it would be rightly done, in spite of the heartbreak and loss it is sure to involve (*The Divine Conspiracy* 172).

May we in our ministries model Jesus' approach in applying biblical principles to our lives. May we in our marriage commitments model the sixty-year marriage of Marion and Vera Henderson. And may we in our attitude toward divorce and remarriage model Dr. Marion Henderson's sensitivity to real life situations and his refusal to let Jesus' teaching be applied in a legalistic, unloving way.

7 ▪ Truth

Matthew 5:33-37

Lynn R. Laughlin

*[33]Again, you have heard that it was said to the people long ago,
"Do not break your oath, but keep the oaths you have made to the Lord."
[34]But I tell you, Do not swear at all: either by heaven, for it is God's throne;
[35]or by the earth, for it is his footstool; or by Jerusalem, for it is the city of the
Great King. [36]And do not swear by your head, for you cannot make
even one hair white or black. [37]Simply let your "Yes" be "Yes," and your
"No," "No"; anything beyond this comes from the evil one.*

"Then you will know the truth, and the truth will set you free" (John 8:32). Have you ever heard that statement? Do you believe it? The problem seems to be, "What is truth?" One man asked another man this question almost 2,000 years ago. The question arose out of a trial and the dialogue between the judge and the accused. The accused had indicated that anyone who listened to him was on the side of truth. When the judge heard this statement, he immediately asked the question, "What is truth?" The judge's name was Pilate and the accused, Jesus.

Jesus' entire ministry was about truth. He wanted His followers to be people of integrity. From the outset of His ministry, Jesus wanted His disciples to hear the truth. Though, just as important, He wanted them to speak the truth and to be people who could live the truth.

THE PROBLEM WITH OATHS

Part of the problem stemmed from the fact that even within the religious world of Judaism one could work or word his way around the truth by offering an oath. If the oath contained certain key words, then the speaker was not obligated to hold up or carry through that which he had just affirmed by oath. How hypocritical! And yet, even today within the religious world, there may not be statements bearing oaths; but there is a certain amount of untruth. We must be careful not to point our finger at people in the time of Christ and indicate that they had a serious problem, while neglecting the "plank in [their] own eye" (Matt. 7:3).

The problem of truth telling has existed since the Fall. That seems to be how many things have happened: God has a great idea (truth), and then man tries to put his stamp of ownership upon what God has ordained. The ownership here deals with specific commands that God has given and the erroneous interpretation man has put upon God's Word. Jewish tradition was raised as the true standard, as compared to the Old Testament and the Mosaic Law.

Jesus faced a serious problem because of the traditions that had grown up around Scripture. These traditions had indeed become the Law, as they had to do with the external or that which could be seen by man. These practices were superficial in nature and in no way represented the heart of the Practitioner. Their hearts were not right with God, as they had created their own righteousness. God looks upon the heart and judges man by that standard. David, in his last words to Solomon, said:

> "And you, my son Solomon, acknowledge the God of your father, and serve him with wholehearted devotion and with a willing mind, for the Lord searches every heart and understands every motive behind the thoughts" (1 Chr. 28:9).

When Samuel stood before Jesse's sons in Bethlehem to anoint the new King, God reminded him that "Man looks at the outward appearance, but the Lord looks at the heart" (1 Sam. 16:7).

John MacArthur points to five principles that help with the study at hand. The first principle is that the spirit of the Law is more important than the letter. The second principle is that the Law is positive as well as negative. Its purpose is not only to prevent both inward and outward sin, but to promote both inward and outward righteousness. The third principle is that the Law is not an end in itself. Fourth, God alone is qualified to judge, because He alone can judge men's hearts. Fifth is that every human being is commanded to live up to the perfect, divine standard to which the Law points. Because that command is impossible for man to fulfill, God Himself has provided fulfillment through His Son, Jesus Christ (MacArthur 287).

In this text, Jesus is in the midst of six illustrations as to how God's Word had been perverted by Jewish traditions. In the fourth illustration, He deals with the concept of truth and how the kingdom person conveys truth through the simplest of words. Words that are spoken do not need the addition of oaths to strengthen them, as they should stand alone. In each of the six illustrations, Jesus demonstrates a radical departure from the teaching of the rabbis by showing how they had distorted the Law in highlighting the outward righteousness and making that aspect alone preeminent. Inward righteousness is what Jesus wants to hold up as the key to obeying Scripture.

The unfolding of the fourth illustration can be seen in three distinct areas. First, there is the Mosaic Law as stated in Scripture; second, the perversion of the Law by Jewish tradition; and third, the simplification of the Law by Jesus.

"Again, you have heard that it was said to the people long ago, 'Do not break your oath, but keep the oaths you have made to the Lord'" (Matt. 5:33). This is not a direct quotation from the Old Testament. Rather, it is a composite of several Scriptures on oaths in which one is to call upon God to witness his vow. It also implies that God is to punish this one if he does not keep the oath.

These are the Scriptures from the Old Testament:

1) "You shall not misuse the name of the LORD your God, for the LORD will not hold anyone guiltless who misuses his name" (Exod. 20:7).

2) "Do not swear falsely by my name and so profane the name of your God. I am the LORD" (Lev. 19:12).

3) "When a man makes a vow to the LORD or takes an oath to obligate himself by a pledge, he must not break his word but must do everything he said" (Num. 30:2).

4) "If you make a vow to the LORD your God, do not be slow to pay it, for the LORD your God will certainly demand it of you and you will be guilty of sin" (Deut. 23:21).

The two words for oaths that Jesus uses are two different Greek words, but they are similar in meaning. The verb *epiorkeō* means "to swear falsely or to perjure oneself." The other word is *horkos,* which means "to enclose as with a fence or to bind together" (MacArthur 321). So, an oath is an affirmation of the truth of a statement, while asking God to be the Judge if indeed the statement is false or not carried out. (This swearing has nothing to do with the use of bad words or cursing, as is the meaning of that word today.)

There is provision throughout Scripture as to the acceptance of oaths. What is of interest is that this is both prior to and after the Law. Abraham made several oaths in affirming statements that he made (Gen. 14:22-24; 21:23-24; 24:1-4). David swore an oath with Jonathan (1 Sam. 20:16-17). There are many passages in the Old Testament that verify the acceptance of oaths (Josh. 9:15; Judg. 21:5; Ruth 1:16-18; 2 Sam. 15:21; 2 Chr. 15:14-15).

We find instances of God using oaths in both the Old and New Testaments. The most famous is His oath to Abraham after he was willing to offer Isaac (Gen. 22:16-17). The author of Hebrews also makes mention of God's oath to Abraham (6:13-17) and indicates the reason for God making that oath. It is not that God cannot be trusted outside of oaths, but that the significance of this statement is clearly eminent. (Other such references are found in Ps. 89:3,49; 110:4; Jer. 11:5; and Luke 1:73.)

Even Christ Himself uses words that have the tone of an oath. For instance, "Truly I say to you" or "I tell you the truth," found just a few verses prior in the Sermon on the Mount (Matt. 5:18,26) and as He continues in the Sermon (6:2,5,16). In John, this oath is stated more strongly, "Truly, truly . . . " (John 1:51; 3:3; 5:19); but (as can be noted) this is done to call special attention to what is being stated. There are some (Quakers, Jehovah's Witnesses) who have taken this prohibition of oaths to apply to court and entering public office. However, even Jesus accepted the oath concept in court, as He responded to Caiaphas that He was the Christ, the Son of God (Matt. 26:63-64).

The New Testament also contains the use of oaths, as Paul calls God as his witness (Rom. 1:9; 2 Cor. 1:23; 1 Thess. 2:5,10). It would appear that if Paul understood the words of Jesus to do away with oaths, he indeed would have obeyed. The only other reference to oaths is what James said, and that was a simple repeating of the words of Jesus. We will discuss later the importance of this prohibition.

Now we will turn our attention to what Jesus indicated was the real source of the problem—the perversion of the Law by Jewish tradition. He was seeking honesty and truthfulness, and so He said:

> "But I tell you, Do not swear at all: either by heaven, for it is God's
> throne; or by the earth, for it is his footstool; or by Jerusalem, for it
> is the city of the Great King. And do not swear by your head, for
> you cannot make even one hair white or black" (Matt. 5:34-36).

Jesus had not come to destroy the Law, but to make it complete. What Jewish tradition had done to the Law was to pervert it and pull the attention of the true believer away from the heart of the Law and to be filled with form and formula.

As John Stott points out, they argued that what the Law was really prohibiting was not taking the name of the Lord in vain. False swearing, they concluded, meant profanity (a profane use of the divine name), not perjury (a dishonest pledging of one's words) (Stott 100).

In one whole tractate (short treatise) of the Mishnah, consideration is given to oaths that are binding and to those that are not. The reason for the oaths that are non-binding was because of phraseology; i.e., by Jerusalem, not binding; toward Jerusalem, binding (Carson, *The Sermon on the Mount* 47). Consequently, if you were familiar with the proper terminology, you could appear to be very forthright and truthful, when in reality you were practicing deception. This is totally unbefitting to the kingdom person.

Jesus points out how misguided this had become. If you think that swearing by heaven negates your vow, you have missed the point. Even though you did not use God's name, you used heaven, which is God's throne. If you think that swearing by earth created a loophole, then you are wrong again, because the earth is the footstool of God. If you thought you could use Jerusalem and slide by, not so, because that city belongs to Him. And if you thought you could swear by the color of your hair, you thought wrong, because that is beyond your control. Jesus comes at this problem again in Matthew when He states:

> "Woe to you, blind guides! You say, 'If anyone swears by the tem-
> ple, it means nothing; but if anyone swears by the gold of the tem-
> ple, he is bound by his oath.' You blind fools! Which is greater; the

gold, or the temple that makes the gold sacred? You also say, 'If anyone swears by the altar, it means nothing; but if anyone swears by the gift on it, he is bound by his oath.' You blind men! Which is greater: the gift, or the altar that makes the gift sacred? Therefore, he who swears by the altar swears by it and by everything on it. And he who swears by the temple swears by it and by the one who dwells in it. And he who swears by heaven swears by God's throne and by the one who sits on it" (Matt. 23:16-22).

Through rabbinic tradition, truthfulness had become an art. Actually, the ability to recite an oath had become a game of deceit. So, the righteousness of the scribes and Pharisees, that Jesus called us to surpass by having a higher standard, had much of its content founded in these kinds of traits.

THE SIMPLICITY OF TRUTH

"Simply let your 'Yes' be 'Yes,' and your 'No,' 'No.' Anything beyond this comes from the evil one" (Matt. 5:37). Jesus' attempt here is to simplify this whole matter. The Law had been distorted by man, so now Jesus was going back to the Law and helping to fulfill it. The mature Christian seeks to have his words accepted as valid truth without any additions. William Hendrickson states it this way:

> What we have here in Matthew 5:33-37 (cf. Jas. 5:12) is the condemnation of the flippant, profane, uncalled for, and often hypocritical oath, used in order to make an impression or to spice daily conversation. Over against that evil Jesus commends simple truthfulness in thought and deed (Hendrickson qtd. in MacArthur 324).

Even the way that Jesus expressed the simplification caused some rabbinic traditions to say that this expression "yes, yes," (doubling) is an oath. This phrase of "yes, yes" and "no, no" can be translated to say "your 'yes' is to be 'yes' and your 'no' is to be 'no.'" James repeats this by stating, "Let your 'Yes' be yes, and your 'No,' no" (Jas. 5:12). The subject under consideration in Matthew is not so much the taking of a vow as it is the necessity of speaking the truth at all times. Jesus inevitably penetrates behind all legislation to the essential principles it intends to express. To legalize His teaching is to destroy it. His rules reach far beyond any ability of external regulation to satisfy. They call for nothing short of complete inward surrender to God's purpose and nature (Mounce 45). The heart of the matter is truthfulness, since Christ stated that He was "the way and the truth and the life (John 14:6). We must make every effort to be people of the truth. Our entire persona must be that of truthfulness. We must make every effort to be filled with the truth and then allow that truth to flow forth in every word we speak and action that we perform. It is not enough that we claim to have the truth. It is only when we speak the truth and live the truth that we have become obedient believers. Jesus was tired of the games that the religious leaders were playing. He wanted His followers to be above the pettiness of oaths and to let their every day speech pronounce them truthful.

Maybe a stronger case for simplification in our day is that with the idea of one bringing in an oath, it usually causes the other party to think this is not the truth. It creates suspicion when this kind of affirmation is brought into the picture.

If you need more than a simple yes or no, Jesus states that it comes from the evil one or from evil. In either case, the final resting-place of all evil is Satan. Jesus called him a "liar and the father of lies" (John 8:44). The evil within our hearts pulls us in the direction of Satan, as we are tempted to speak words that are not true. We sometimes shy away from saying that this statement is a lie and a lie is sin. We need to be aware that that is how Satan deceives.

One of the implications of this passage is the recognition of that sin within our lives. We are so good at drawing lines and removing concepts; but, lest we get too far from the truth, let us consider "truth has no degrees or shades." A half-truth is a whole lie, and a white lie is really black. God has never had any standard lower than absolute truthfulness. Of every person He desires "truth in the inner most being" (Ps. 51:6). Among the things He especially hates is "a lying tongue," and "lying lips" (Prov. 6:16-17; 12:22). The destiny of liars is the lake of fire (Rev. 21:8). God's absolute, unchanging standard is truth and sincerity in everything (MacArthur 325-26).

The other implication is that of all forms of exaggeration, hyperbole, and the use of superlatives may cause us to cross over the line of truth. We are prone to bolster our position or make our case stronger with exaggeration. We add to the story to make it more exciting or intense. We claim to have done something, when in reality we have never been there or done that. We often tell a brother or sister that we will pray for them, and by omission we have failed to keep our word. Knowing that, instead of indicating that you will pray for someone or something, try praying immediately; and that will take care of the omission. D.A. Carson adds:

> . . . you who with me are teachers and preachers—how often do
> we fudge the evidence to make a point, or dogmatize in areas
> where we know nothing, in the hope that dogma will mask our
> ignorance? I am not speaking of the honest mistake, but of deceit
> (*The Sermon on the Mount* 48).

God calls for us to be holy, as He is holy. That means being truthful, as He is truthful. Our endeavor is to live out the truth and to be people of integrity, so that others will know when we say "yes," we mean "yes" and they will know our "no" means "no." God help us to do nothing short of this.

8 ■ Give to the Evil Person

Matthew 5:38-42

Neal Windham

³⁸You have heard that it was said, "Eye for eye, and tooth for tooth."
³⁹But I tell you, Do not resist an evil person. If someone strikes you
on the right cheek, turn to him the other also. ⁴⁰And if someone wants
to sue you and take your tunic, let him have your cloak as well.
⁴¹If someone forces you to go one mile, go with him two miles.
⁴²Give to the one who asks you, and do not turn away
from the one who wants to borrow from you.

> **"Personal success or personal satisfaction is not
> worth another thought."** —Teilhard de Cardin

While on the surface it might seem that modern Israelis and Palestinians have understood Moses' words "Eye for eye and tooth for tooth" all too well, it is clear that many have not even begun to glimpse what Jesus had in mind when He quoted this familiar maxim in the Sermon on the Mount (Exod. 21:24; Matt. 5:38). Unlike some of His Jewish contemporaries, our Lord did not stop with "Eye for eye and tooth for tooth." His daring "But I say . . ." eventually jettisoned the freshly chosen disciples out of their secure worlds of tightly woven, self-serving Midrash into an outrageous and extravagant new way of seeing people, a realm of extraordinary giving to the other, including even the evil other. Perhaps there is yet hope for the Middle East, hope for the world.

Among contemporary readings of this text, neither Walter Wink's "nonviolent resistance" (Wink 199); nor Glen Stassen's "transformative peacemaking ethic" (Stassen 257); nor Richard Horsley's "local interaction with personal enemies" (Horsley 17); nor John Dominic Crossan's "(being) stripped of . . . layers of protection and entitlement" (Crossan 138) is singularly capable of giving adequate contemporary expression to Jesus' full, intended meaning. Instead, at its very core, this passage is telling us that the kingdom of heaven has absolutely nothing whatsoever to do with following self-preservation instincts, but rather offers the disciple a new pattern of unprecedented giving, especially toward those who are evil. As such, Matthew 5:38-42 is much broader in scope than merely shaming an enemy or naming a victim (as some have suggested), much fuller in its implications than quietly offering peaceful resistance or even boldly trumpeting noble-minded pacifism in times of war (as others have exclaimed). In this text, Jesus is systematically dismantling the profound and universal human tendency to take care of self at the expense of all others. Matthew 5:38-42 is therefore a text that speaks with remarkable precision and directness to the self-absorbed, postmodern West.

SETTING THE CONTEXT

R.E.O. White has called attention to Matthew's focus upon ethics for a community confused about discipleship: "Christians seemed to have forgotten that the highest end of all their faith, experience, and profession is right living. . . . They needed nothing more desperately than a strong reminder of the moral teaching of Jesus" (62). So Jesus' words about turning the other cheek and going a second mile are deliberately intended to extend the notion of right living beyond the misleading casuistry of the scribes and Pharisees, whose righteousness the disciples must exceed in order to enter into the kingdom of heaven (Matt. 5:20).

Actually, the entire Sermon on the Mount is a microcosm of Matthew's steady attention to right living. Of its six "You have heard . . . but I say" sections begun in Matthew 5:21, four are carefully paired: adultery (5:27-30) with divorce (5:31-32); and eye for eye (5:38-42) with love of enemy (5:43-48)—each clearly geared toward ethics. While the thematic pairing of the first two is quite obvious (adultery and divorce go hand-in-hand for Jesus' audience, the latter automatically following upon the former), the pairing of the last two may not be quite so obvious. But when we consider such statements as "turn the other cheek" and "let him have your cloak as well" (both in the fifth section) alongside "love your enemies" and "pray for those who persecute you" (both in the sixth section), the thematic connection becomes much clearer. The manner in which a disciple treats an evil person (v. 38) is closely related to the manner in which that same disciple treats an enemy (v. 44). And all of this leads to godly perfection (v. 48), to right living—in a word, to love.

What is so significant here is that our section is the penultimate example of what it really means to fulfill the Old Testament (Matt. 5:17). That the final section on loving enemies is without a doubt the most comprehensive of the six so-called antitheses[1] is hard to argue. Its closing words, "Be perfect, therefore, as your heavenly Father is perfect," seem to seal the argument. But we must remember that these words on loving enemies appear as the second of a pair of concerns begun in our text, Matthew 5:38. Together, sections five and six then bring the argument for love as the highest fulfillment of Torah to a stunning climax.

Further, all of this has to do with right relationships. Actually, the entire Sermon is about right relationships: to people in general (5:7-12); to an estranged brother (5:21-26; 7:1-5); to members of the opposite sex (5:27-30); to spouses (5:31-32); to the needy (6:1-4); to those who observe how disciples fast (5:16-17); to those outside the community of faith (5:13-16,43-48;7:6); and, of course, ultimately to God Himself (5:3-6; 6:5-15,25-34; 7:7-27).

Right relationships in a book about right living, especially as that right living reflects on the community of faith in the world—this is the Sermon on the Mount. This is Matthew 5:38-42.

A FAMILIAR AND ABUSED TEACHING (V. 38)

Jesus' citation in verse 38 of what has become known through the Romans as *lex talionis* (the principle of exact retribution, not more or less) has its roots in the Old Testament (Exod. 21:24; Lev. 24:19-20; Deut. 19:21). It was also found in the Code of Hammurabi (eighteenth century BC Babylon).[2] The principle was undoubtedly designed both to entrust appropriate punishment to civil authorities (Deut. 19:17-18) and to prevent personal revenge (Carson, *Matthew* 155), which might extend as far as the destruction of an entire family (Hill 127). By New Testament times, monetary compensation was offered in restitution as an alternative to maiming the offender.[3] That the principle was not to be practiced at the personal level is well illustrated by the fact that David twice had the opportunity to destroy Saul, who was trying to kill him, and twice refused to harm "Yahweh's anointed" (1 Sam. 24:6; 26:9-11).

DON'T "RESIST" THE EVIL ONE? (V. 39A)

But *lex talionis* was and is about more than providing exact and equal retribution. Matthew makes this quite clear by using the much-debated *mē antisthnas* ("Do not resist")[4] the "evil person." Whether we translate *antisthnai* as to oppose, resist, fight, or stand against is no easy call; but in any case it would appear that disciples do not engage in verbal attacks on their opponents. Of the dozen verses in which some form of *anthistēmi* appears in the New Testament, at least six clearly refer to verbal opposition (Luke 21:15; Acts 6:10; 13:8; Gal. 2:11; 2 Tim. 3:8; 4:15). Two (Rom. 9:19 and 13:2) imply standing up against higher authorities of various kinds (a chief means of which would presumably be verbal), while another two (Jas. 4:7 and 1 Pet. 5:9) call specific attention to resisting the devil. Interestingly, these last two references, both from the General Epistles, couple such resistance with a quotation of Proverbs 3:34, which in the Hebrew means, "God mocks the mockers, but gives grace to the humble." Once more, there is evidence of verbal resistance.

But this is not just any verbal resistance. Guelich (219ff.) has effectively argued that Jesus is teaching His disciples not to take the offender into a court of law. Specifically, He draws upon four key parallels between

Deuteronomy 19:16-21 and Matthew 5:38-42 in order to demonstrate that Jesus' words should be understood in this way.[5] Thus understood, Jesus is teaching His disciples not to fight with words in a court, but to speak with radical generosity when struck on the face, sued, drafted to carry a load, asked to provide a loan, or act in any similar circumstance. Again, Matthew 5:38-42 teaches us that the kingdom of heaven has absolutely nothing whatsoever to do with following self-preservation instincts, but rather offers the disciple an outrageous new way of demonstrating love for all people, but especially opponents: give them not only what they demand, but more than they demand.

Is this hyperbole? Perhaps. Jesus uses hyperbole at other points in the Sermon (e.g., Matt. 5:29-30).[6] Frankly, however, hyperbole can become an easy excuse for easing the demands of our Lord. Further, it becomes very difficult to determine just what is and is not hyperbole. Once we identify "going the second mile" as hyperbole in section five, do we at the same time conclude that "except for marital unfaithfulness" is also a figure of speech in section two? Perhaps it is. There are endless forms of debilitating abuse in countless marriages, and some of these situations are clearly intolerable. But, while recognizing the importance of identifying figures of speech correctly, should we not operate under the assumption that unless the words of Jesus cannot be construed literally, we should at least attempt to understand them at face value? In our case, not taking someone to court, going the second mile, and giving to the one who asks could undoubtedly have been understood quite literally in Jesus' day. And, if we are willing to allow it, so could turning the other cheek.

Of course, we must be very careful not to limit Jesus' teaching only to these four examples. To do so would be to practice a form of legalism similar to that of the scribes and Pharisees, who seemed to know the letter, but not the spirit, of the Law. There is a much deeper, underlying current in the flow of this text, and this we will seek to understand as we examine the details of the four illustrations provided by our Lord.

The illustrations are broadly based and have various points of reference in their several applications. Jesus is showing us that we should practice the principle of selflessly giving more than is demanded when we are treated: (1) as Victims of Shameful Acts (v. 39b); (2) as People under God's Law (v. 40); (3) as People under Human Authority (v. 41); and (4) as Compassionate Caregivers (v. 42). The respective reference points for these four applications are: (1) the Mishnah (*Baba Kamma* 8:6), (2) the Torah (Exod. 22:25-27; Deut. 24:12-13), (3) Rome (Matt. 27:32), and (4) again the Torah (Exod. 22:25).

WHEN TREATED AS VICTIMS OF SHAMEFUL ACTS (V. 39B)

The Mishnah's[7] *Baba Kamma* ("The First Gate") 8:6 reads:
If a man cuffed his fellow he must pay him a *sela* (four *zuz*).
Rabbi Judah says . . . one hundred *zuz*. If he slapped him he must

pay him 200 *zuz. If (he struck him) with the back of his hand he must pay him 400 zuz.* . . . . This is the general rule: *all is in accordance with a person's honor* (Danby 343, emphasis mine).

It is very likely that Jesus had this or some similar rabbinic tradition in mind when He told His disciples to turn the other cheek.[8] If a direct slap on the face was costly, a backhanded blow was doubly so; and this is precisely what Jesus describes in verse 39b, assuming the attacker is right-handed. Having struck the disciple's left cheek with the palm of his right hand, he would naturally use the back of the same hand to then strike the turned right cheek. It was a shameful deed, as *Baba Kamma* requires a large restitution (400 *zuz*) "in accordance with the person's honor." What *Baba Kamma* does not envision is the willful act of submission in offering the right cheek as well. This was Jesus' own radical spin on the apparently familiar tradition. Its significance lay in the fact that the disciple was indeed offering the attacker more than he was expecting. Not eye for eye and tooth for tooth, but two cheeks for none. The disciple will not attack at all!

That the emphasis is not upon pacifism or nonviolent retaliation as tactics of war is clear from the fact that this text envisions only two people, as Horsley would say, involved in a local dispute. Turning the other cheek is not about Rome or Zealots or anything of the sort. It is about how people treat each other in the daily grind of life, where disputes are bound to erupt, as tempers naturally flare. It is much easier to talk about pacifism and nonviolent retaliation as theories of war than to discuss how we should treat parents, siblings, friends, and (especially in this passage) personal enemies in everyday life. Such safe distancing must, however, be avoided at all costs. This illustration invades our private worlds of retaliation, retribution, revenge, and resentment right where we live. Moreover, in the very spirit of Jesus Himself, the disciple should offer the other cheek both physically and mentally, both publicly and privately, both volitionally and emotionally. It is an unselfish act of giving without thought of personal consequence.

Of course, this does not mean that disciples should tolerate ongoing abuses, physical or otherwise, which allow evil to go unchecked and oppressors to go unpunished, through neglect. Civil abuses should be handled in the appropriate setting, a court of law (cf. Rom. 13:1ff.). What is extremely unfortunate here is that when these matters are not handled among believers at the personal level or in the church as they should be (Matt.18:15-18), they sometimes do get to the public courts, as will no doubt be the case in the pedophilia crisis in the Roman Catholic Church. Such cases do enormous and, in some cases, irreparable damage to the church throughout the world. Jesus' teaching on transforming relationships at the personal level through selfless giving offers the disciple a much-needed alternative to courtroom hecklers and their ridicule of the church.

WHEN TREATED AS PEOPLE UNDER GOD'S LAW (V. 40)

Where Jesus is likely responding to a known Jewish tradition in the first illustration, the roots of the second come directly from the Old Testament itself (Exod. 2:25-27; Deut. 4:12-13). In both texts, the cloak (or outer garment) is taken in pledge for a loan transacted, but only until sunset, at which time the cloak was returned to its owner, "because his cloak is the only covering he has for his body. What else will he sleep in?" (Exod. 2:27a). The basis for the teaching is compassion, as Exodus further points out, "When he cries out to me, I will hear, for I am *compassionate*" (Exod. 2:27b, emphasis mine).

In Jesus' example, the disciple has been taken to court and sued[9] for his undergarment. Amazingly, our Lord is saying that the disciple should give up not only that for which he is sued, but also this important Old Testament entitlement (the cloak), in order to more than satisfy the demands of both lender and Law. Such an action would presumably flabbergast his opponent (not to mention the court), leaving the borrower destitute and literally naked.[10] In effect, Jesus turned the Old Testament precept upside-down and inside-out, making the one called upon to show compassion rather the object of an unprecedented act of kindness. On a larger scale, it would be analogous to giving up not only the required restitution (say, $1,000,000) in an automobile accident leaving a plaintiff physically impaired, but throwing in a house, leaving the defendant utterly destitute.

WHEN TREATED AS PEOPLE UNDER HUMAN AUTHORITY (V. 41)

The third illustration calls attention to the Roman practice of pressing a civilian into service[11] for a prescribed distance, one Roman mile (*milion*; Latin *mille*). Obviously, among Jews the order would have been tolerated at best and hated at worst. To go two miles would, it seems, have been inconceivable. The procedure (or something like it) is mentioned once in Matthew's Gospel (27:32), where Simon of Cyrene was forced (*angareusan*) to carry the cross of our Lord on His way to Golgotha. Interestingly, this is the only other instance of *angareuō* ("to press into service") anywhere in Matthew's Gospel.[12]

Thus, in addition to personal and Jewish legal applications of the principle of giving more than is required or anticipated, our Lord has the audacity to involve Rome! Green observes, "The first mile renders to Caesar the things that are Caesar's; the second mile, by meeting oppression with kindness, renders to God the things that are God's" (Manson 160 qtd. in Green 86). Today, when on occasion we hear of people intentionally paying more than their fair share of taxes in order to alleviate national debt or failing social security reserves, we generally think them crazy. What might our Lord say about such an attitude?

WHEN TREATED AS COMPASSIONATE CAREGIVERS (V. 42)

"Give *to the one who repeatedly asks*," says Jesus in verse 42a (emphasis and translation mine),[13] calling attention to the well-known Jewish practice of almsgiving (cf. 6:1-4). Verse 42b ("Do not turn away from the one who wants to borrow from you") likely takes us again to Exodus 22, but rather than calling attention to the disciple as one who borrows (as in the second illustration above), the disciple is here the one who lends to the needy (Exod. 2:25). In no way is he to turn away the one who is asking.[14] This is fully in keeping with Old Testament casuistic law, which demanded generous lending "if there is a poor man among your brothers. . . ." (Deut. 15:7-8). Moreover, "The law required that the gleanings of the field, the olive tree, and the vineyard should be left for the poor, the sojourner, the fatherless, and the widow (Lev. 19:9, 10; 23:22; Deut. 24:19-22)" (Tenney 1 110). Thus Jesus is reinforcing standard Old Testament teaching as well as current Jewish piety.[15]

It is intriguing that in verse 42 no sum is specified. Jesus does not clearly require more than is asked, but rather, only what is asked. This is not characteristic of Matthew 5:38-41, with its repeated attention to giving more than is required or expected.[16] Nor is the one asking in verse 42 clearly an adversary, as in the other three illustrations.

Still, the disciple is required to offer something, in keeping with the six giving imperatives scattered throughout verses 39-42[17]; and in light of Jesus' focused attention to giving more than is required or expected in verses 39-41, does it not seem reasonable to suggest that He is again telling His disciples to offer the beggar or borrower more than either Old Testament Law or Jewish piety demanded or expected? To self-absorbed, consumer-driven middle and upper class Americans, the message of Jesus in Matthew 5:42 is painfully clear: "You must change your entire orientation toward money. Rather than borrowing and owing for all you can get, give generously—beyond your sense of duty—to all who are in real need."

CONCLUSION

There is a subtle, forward-looking undercurrent winding its way through this troubling text, one which to this point has gone unnoticed. With its attention to allowing an adversary to twice strike a hard blow to the willingly offered face of the disciple, to taking not some but all of his clothing, to seeing the Lord's follower go twice the required distance, and to the disciple's giving freely to anyone who asks; one cannot help but recall our Lord's passion, for in it Jesus fulfilled every single aspect of this veiled prophecy in the heart of the Sermon on the Mount. Viewed in this way, Matthew 5:38-42 constitutes passive, cruciform ministry, anticipating our identity with Christ's own passion (Gal. 2:20).

When he was very young, perhaps only three, my son Luke (now twenty-one) came to the car one Sunday morning after church crying, "They nailed him in! They nailed him in! Why did they nail him in?" My intense desire to track down and strangle his Sunday school teacher was eclipsed only by the more profound reality which just then began to sink in; namely, that as the only son of God's man, the preacher of that church,

Luke might be wondering, much like Isaac bound and waiting, if his own father would permit him to endure a fate similar to Christ's. No one has ever lived the words of Matthew 5:38-42 quite like the submissive, passive Jesus. We cower at the thought of enduring the cross with Him. When viewed as entirely selfless, sacrificial giving, with no thought of personal outcome, Matthew 5:38-42 is not less but more radical than we at first surmised. Hyperbole? I seriously doubt it. No, this is calculated passion.

In truth, the gospel is always about giving more than we had expected, about abandoning every last instinct of self-preservation in favor of the greater good, the fuller blessing of consideration for others—the very passion of my dear mentor and friend, Dr. Marion Henderson, who has always given not only more, but all he has for the cause of Christ.

NOTES

[1]Are the six sections begun in Matt. 5:21 antitheses or fulfillments? In favor of antitheses, we may call attention to the implicit and explicit contrasts which Jesus makes between what has "been heard" and what "I say." In favor of fulfillments are Matt. 5:17 ("I came . . . to fulfill" the Law and Prophets) and the weaker translation of *dev* as "and," not "but" (though this is problematic, especially in 5:44). Given the strong purpose statement about fulfillment at the head of the entire section, these six sections are, I think, geared more to fulfillment of Old Testament Torah than to contrast with contemporary interpretations of Torah, though both elements are clearly present in the text.

[2]"If a seignior has destroyed the eye of a member of the aristocracy, they shall destroy his eye. If he has broken a(nother) seignior's bone, they shall break his bone. . . . If a seignior has knocked out a tooth of a seignior of his own rank, they shall knock out his tooth" (Code of Hammurabi 196-7, 200; in Pritchard 175). Davies and Allison cite additional texts outside the Old Testament, including Jubilees 4.31-32 and the Apocalypse of Peter, 7-17.

[3]Josephus *Antiquities* 4.280 cited in Keener, *Matthew* 196.

[4]Wallace acknowledges the imperatival use of the infinitive, though he does not cite this text (608).

[5]"First, the setting of Deuteronomy 19:16 involved the hypothetical trial of a false witness. . . . Second, the false witness had accused (*anteste*) his brother in court (19:18). Third, the penalty was based on the *lex talionis* principle by assigning to the false accuser the same penalty that would have been incurred by the accused. And fourth, the reason given for such action was to remove the *evil one* (*ton poneron*) from the community. All four elements found in Deuteronomy 19:16-21 constitute the premise and antithesis of 5:38, 39a" (Guelich 220).

[6]Or is it metonymy? Where hyperbole focuses upon exaggeration for emphasis, metonymy works by association, i.e., saying one thing ("the White House") while referring to another (the President). Could it be that Jesus' words about severing an eye or hand from the body actually *referred* to severing oneself from a specific environment in which adultery was likely to take place?

[7]A collection of rabbinic teachings brought together around AD 200.

[8]Though Isaiah 50:6 clearly *agrees* with the fundamental teaching of Jesus here.

[9]This meaning of *krino* is well attested in the ancient literature (BAGD 452-3).

[10]Keener observes that "the poorest people of the Empire (. . .) had only an inner and outer garment (*IVP Bible Background Commentary* 60).

[11]The verb *angareusei*, a Persian loanword, means "press into service" or "requisition" (Davies and Allison 546). Cf. Epictetus, *Diss.* 4.1.79: "If there is a requisition and a soldier seizes it (your donkey), let it go. Do not resist or complain, otherwise you will be first

beaten, and lose your donkey after all" (cited in Davies and Allison 547).

[12]There is only one additional instance in the entire New Testament, the parallel text in Mark 15:21. The paucity of uses of *angareuō*, coupled with the actual mention of this practice in 27:32, lends credence to the notion that the Roman custom of drafting available civilian help is precisely what Matthew has in mind.

[13]The present tense participle is emphatically placed prior to the imperative *dos*.

[14]*Mē apostraphēs* is a negative prohibition, meaning something like, "Don't turn him away" (Wallace 469).

[15]On the point of Jewish piety, see R. Bultmann (Bromiley 223-224) and Staudinger (Balz 429).

[16]Still, Guelich observes a general lessening of requirements as in verse 41 there is a "legal obligation," while in verse 42a there is a "less binding, religious obligation," and in verse 42b there is "the least binding obligation of a personal loan" (252).

[17]"Turn" (v. 39), "Give" (v. 40, *aphes*), "Go" (v. 41), "Give" (v. 42a, *dos*), and "Do not refuse" (v. 42b).

9 ■ Love

Matthew 5:43-48

Danny D. Clymer

⁴³You have heard that it was said, "Love your neighbor and hate your enemy."
⁴⁴But I tell you: Love your enemies and pray for those who persecute you,
⁴⁵that you may be sons of your Father in heaven. He causes his sun to rise on
the evil and the good, and sends rain on the righteous and the unrighteous.
⁴⁶If you love those who love you, what reward will you get? Are not even
the tax collectors doing that? ⁴⁷And if you greet only your brothers,
what are you doing more than others? Do not even pagans do that?
⁴⁸Be perfect, therefore, as your heavenly Father is perfect.

INTERPRETATIONS

Jesus states, "You have heard that it was said, 'Love your neighbor and hate your enemy.' But I say to you, Love your enemies and pray for those who persecute you" (Matt. 5:43-44). The precept of the Law which Jesus quotes—"Love your neighbor"—is found in Leviticus 19:18. The context of Leviticus shows that your neighbor is by implication confined to a compatriot, for the whole verse reads: "Do not seek vengeance or bear a grudge against one of your own people, but love your neighbor as yourself[1]: I am the Lord." But the supplementary clause added by Jesus—"and hate your enemy"—is not based upon any implication in this text, nor is the command "hate your enemies" found anywhere else in the Old Testament.[2]

This fact is supported by Jesus' claim: "Do not think that I have come to abolish the Law and the Prophets; I have not come to abolish them but to fulfill them" (Matt. 5:17). Before Jesus interprets the Law, He makes it clear that what He is going to teach is in absolute harmony with the Law and Prophets. Thus, when He says, "love your enemies," He is not teaching anything new, but only interpreting accurately what the Law really means.

Matthew 5:20 also argues against the idea that Christ was correcting the Law. By substituting Pharisees and the teachers of the Law (5:20) for the Law and the Prophets (5:17), Jesus shows that He was speaking of the official Jewish interpretation of the Old Covenant and not of its literal meanings. He proposes that His teaching is in contradiction to the teaching of the Pharisees and the teachers of the Law. They were considered holy people; yet Jesus is here teaching that because of their misunderstanding and misinterpretation of the Law, they were sorely lacking in true righteousness. This observation lends strong support to the fact that Pharisaical and scribal additions to the Law existed, which He is about to reject. The righteousness which must exceed that possessed by the Pharisees and the teachers of the Law He then defines.

It may be further argued that the formula[3] Jesus uses to introduce the laws makes it clear that He is not referring merely to the Law of Moses. The phrase *tois archaiois* ("to the people long ago," 5:21) may be variously translated, and only the context can decide its meaning. "*tois archaiois* might mean: in ancient times, to the ancients, or by the ancients. The second is in accord with N. T. usage. . . ."[4] Jesus does not say, "You have read in the Law," or "It is written in the Law." He says, "You have heard," thus showing the true teaching of the Law, as opposed to what was taught in the synagogues, as an explanation of it.

ENEMIES

However, when Jesus says, "Love[5] your enemies, and pray for those who persecute you . . ." (5:44), He is demanding something that has never before been said so succinctly, positively, and forcefully. This is not to say that the basic idea is new with Jesus, for there are other parallels in Judaism:

1) Proverbs 25:21: "If your enemy is hungry, give him food to eat; if he is thirsty, give him water to drink";
2) Job 31:29-30: "If I have rejoiced at my enemy's misfortune or gloated over the trouble that came to him—I have not allowed my mouth to sin by invoking a curse against his life—";
3) Testament of Joseph 18:2: "If any one seeks to do evil unto you, do well unto him, and pray for him, and you shall be redeemed of the Lord from all evil";
4) Testament of Simeon 3:5-6: "For if a man flees to the Lord, the evil spirit runs away from him, and his mind is lightened. And henceforward he sympathizes with him whom he envied and forgives those who are hostile to him, and so ceases from envy";
5) Aristeas, paragraph 227: "The king expressed his approval and asked the next, 'To whom ought a man show liberality?' And he replied, 'All men acknowledge that we ought to show liberality to those who are well disposed towards us, but I think that we ought to show the same keen spirit of generosity to those who are opposed to us that by this means we may win them over to the right and to what is advantageous to ourselves. But we must pray to God that this may be accomplished, for He rules the minds of all men.'"[6]

Who Jesus has in mind when He speaks of enemies (*echdrous*) is not easy to determine. On the whole, the Jews were living in a state of political and social feuds. They scorned the Greeks and despised the Romans. Even within the borders of their own land, the Shammaites were considered outcasts. The Galileans were frequently ridiculed by the orthodox southerners, and Samaritans were avoided like a plague. There was a mutual strain between the scrupulous Pharisees and the *Am ha-arets* (common people) whom the former viewed as illiterate and disreputable.

Contextually, the enemies may have been Roman soldiers (5:41), money-lenders and legal suitors (5:40), personal enemies or religious opponents (5:39). In the rest of Matthew, the enemy may be someone in your household (10:36), the devil (13:25,28), or your personal enemies whom God judges (22:44). The reference to those who persecute you (5:44) in no way serves to indicate which enemies are primarily in mind in the original use of the saying, for although to persecute with a personal object is used in the New Testament primarily of religious persecution, it is not impossible that the obligations imposed by the Roman occupational forces are regarded subjectively as a form of religious persecution.

The fact, however, that Jesus does not specifically identify the enemy is further reinforced when He says that God ". . . causes his sun to rise on the evil and the good, and sends rain on the righteous and the unrighteous" (5:45b). Jesus' emphasis is upon the identification with God. It is God who makes or causes His sun to rise, and He sends the rain. But what is even more significant here is that He does this without discrimination. In order to make the marvelous nature of the Father's love stand out all the more conspicuously, the two pairs of recipients are arranged chiastically, the emphasis falling neither on the evil (A) nor the good (B), nor upon the righteous (B) or unrighteous (A). Sun and rain descend on all alike and, in so doing, reveal the Father's love which is given to all indiscriminately.

Verses 46 and 47 qualify this love to a somewhat greater extent. Those who refuse to include their enemies and their persecutors in their love are putting themselves on a moral and spiritual level with the very people whom they despise, namely, in Jesus' day the tax collectors and pagans. Matthew, the man who records this, having himself been a tax collector (Matt. 9:9), was no stranger to the intense hatred with which especially the teachers of the Law and Pharisees regarded the people who belonged to this class. The low esteem in which tax collectors were held appears from such passages as Matthew 9:10,11; 11:19; 21:31,32; Mark 2:15,16; Luke 5:30; 7:34; 15:1; 19:7.

As tax collectors were despised, so also were the pagans. They were considered to be idolaters and oppressors (both politically and religiously). By pious Jews, the pagans were regarded as unclean (John 18:28), in fact as dogs (Matt. 15:26,27). For a Jew to have dinner with an uncircumcised pagan was unthinkable (Acts 11:2). They, therefore, like the tax collectors, were treated with extreme scorn.

It is understandable that this hatred was mutual. As the Jews treated the pagans with scorn, so they themselves received similar treatment (John 18:35; Acts 16:20; 18:2). It was not, therefore, surprising that the pagans were found saluting[7] only those whom they loved. But Jesus says, "And if you greet only your brothers, what are you doing more than others?" (5:47). Jesus again requires something more, reflecting back on the overall principle from 5:20. He shows that the standard for the Pharisees and the teachers of the Law in this last respect is actually no better than that of the despised tax collectors and pagans.

INDISCRIMINATE LOVE

One can now understand the background of Jesus' command: "Be perfect, therefore, as your heavenly Father is perfect" (5:48). Altogether the word *teleios*, here rendered "perfect," is used three times in Matthew: twice in 5:48 and once in 19:21. It comes from a word meaning end or goal (*telos*) and is commonly translated perfect or complete (Moulton 629). When one examines the actual content of the word, however, he notices that this alters the context and circumstances of the moment. He demands them to be that which the Pharisees, the teachers of the Law, the tax collectors and pagans are not: indiscriminate in love. One must be complete and rounded in love, not one-sided or partial. He must be impartial and all-loving as the Father in heaven, Who ". . . causes His sun to rise on the evil and the good, and sends rain on the righteous and the unrighteous (5:45b)." One must be perfect because his Father is perfect. And he must be perfect in the same sense and in the same way that his Father is perfect. The Father's perfection here consists in His love for everyone.[8]

The parallel passage in Luke helps to further enlighten the meaning when the writer says, "Be merciful, just as your Father is merciful" (6:36). Be perfect, as your Father in heaven is perfect, by being merciful, even as your Father in heaven is merciful. The Greek word used in Luke for merciful (*oiktirō*) is not the usual New Testament word for mercy, but is a word meaning to have compassion on someone.[9] In the plural form, it is sometimes translated tender mercies. The Father is compassionate toward all men, and so must His children be. Jesus says, "Love your enemies and pray for those who persecute you, that you may be sons of your Father in heaven" (5:44-45). In other words, one is to love both neighbor and enemy as God loves them, and to do this he must actually be a son of God. Only those who have God for their Father share His love and compassion and are able to do what He does—include all men in His love.

It is fairly obvious that the meaning Jesus gives to the command, "Be perfect," is derived from the context. The usage of *teleios* in Matthew 19:21 only lends support to this thesis. Jesus says, "If you want to be perfect, go, sell your possessions and give to the poor, and you will have treasure in heaven." The phrase if you want to be perfect corresponds to you lack in Mark 10:21 and Luke 18:22. The word perfect in this case indicates the opposite of lacking, namely, giving up one's material possessions. In other cases (contexts) a different course of action may be needed for a man to be perfect as the Father is perfect.

APPLICATION

It is easy to read and write about this perfect love. It is so hard to apply it in everyday life. I guess that is why God allowed me to witness this kind of love in the lives of Doc and Vera Henderson. I saw it in the classroom in his teaching and her hospitality (great pies!!). I experienced it on the staff of the South Fork Church of Christ where I served with them for three years. I can testify to it from the twenty years we labored together on the campus of Lincoln Christian College where many discussions took place and decisions were made, and this indiscriminate love prevailed when all was said and done. I watched Doc and Vera apply this God-like love to their family in both the easy and difficult times.

It may be the true story surrounding Tom Dace's death that will help you understand Matthew 5:43-48. Tom returned from a prayer breakfast with some of the men of the South Side Christian Church in Springfield, Illinois, to an apartment house he was remodeling on Scarritt Street. When he started up his circular saw that morning, the noise awakened Frank Sherry who was sleeping off a hangover from drugs and alcohol. In a stupor, Frank came down the stairway, picked up a claw hammer, and proceeded to hit Tom numerous times. Tom never regained consciousness and died the next day.

Several days later, Tom's wife Florence went to the county jail where Frank was being held and requested to see him. When the police realized there was no animosity in the tone of her voice, and after a thorough search, she was allowed to see Frank.

She stood looking into the cell while holding Tom's Bible in her hand. She said to Frank, "You have done a terrible thing. You have taken away my husband, my livelihood, and my Christian partner. I am not here to condemn you, but to love you." She went on to say, "You owe it to me to read this book. On the inside cover Tom has written what one must do to become a Christian. I want you to read that." Frank said nothing. He took the Bible, and Florence left.

Months later Florence went to see Frank at a maximum security prison. Sitting with him in the cafeteria, Florence heard the good news. Frank was now a Christian. He led in a devotion from a large Bible that had every page marked with passages he wanted to remember. Frank proceeded to confess his sins and ask Florence and God for forgiveness.

Florence stood and threw her arms around Frank and said, "God forgives you and so do I." Years later Florence was the main reason Frank was released from prison. She wrote letter after letter to the parole board explaining how Frank was not only harmless, but now helpful to society.

Frank is currently involved in a prison ministry that spans several southern states. The story of his conversion and the God-like love he received from Florence later inspired a woman to write a song she called, "The Woman Who Had Love in Her Eyes." Florence Dace showed a watching world what Jesus taught about perfect love.

NOTES

[1] It is important to observe that the words *as yourself* are lacking from Jesus' quote. This may have been done to allow the two expressions *love your neighbor* and *hate your enemy* to reveal their antithetical natures more distinctly. Cf., Olof Linton, "St. Matthew 5,43," *Studia Theologica,* 18(1964) 74-5.

[2] Nowhere in Jewish literature is there known to be a command to hate one's enemies.

[3] For a discussion of the structure see W.D. Davies, *The Setting of the Sermon on the Mount,* 5-13.

[4] A.B. Bruce, *The Synoptic Gospels,* The Expositor's Greek Testament, Vol. I. Ed. by W. Robertson Nicoll (Grand Rapids: Eerdmans, 1961) 106.

[5] C. Spicq says it well when he defines love here. He states, "Some kind of warm feeling for a sinner or for an unpleasant person is not demanded, at least not expressly. Primarily, *agapan* means to show respect or kindness. Even to enemies we owe esteem, fair treatment, and help in time of need" (Spicq, Vol. I 11). See also Horst Balz and Gerhard Schneider, eds., *Exegetical Dictionary of the New Testament* (Grand Rapids: Eerdmans, 1990) 10.

[6] The translations of Testament of Joseph, Testament of Simeon, and Aristeas may be found in the edited work by James H. Charlesworth, *The Old Testament Pseudepigrapha: Apocalyptic Literature & Testaments,* Vol. 1. The *Mishnah* offers some parallels to the above as well: Aboth 1:12; 2:16; and 4:24.

[7] The word salute (*aspazomai*) obviously denotes here and elsewhere more than to welcome or greet. It is a demonstrative expression of friendliness, which implies hearty wishes for the other person's welfare and happiness (see also 3 John 15).

[8] It must be noted that this text is not a treatise for Universalism. This love which Jesus establishes cannot be understood as condoning the sins or imperfections in the character of others, nor does it imply that God will save everybody regardless of their relationship with Him.

[9] W. Bauer, *A Greek-English Lexicon of the New Testament and Other Early Christian Literature,* Third edition. Trans. by W.F. Arndt and F.W. Gingrich, Revised and edited by F.W. Danker (Chicago: Univ. of Chicago Press, 1952) 700.

10 ▪ Giving to the Needy

Matthew 6:1-4

Harold Merritt

*¹Be careful not to do your "acts of righteousness" before men,
to be seen by them. If you do, you will have no reward from your
Father in heaven. ²So when you give to the needy, do not announce it
with trumpets, as the hypocrites do in the synagogues and on the streets,
to be honored by men. I tell you the truth, they have received their
reward in full. ³But when you give to the needy, do not let your left hand
know what your right hand is doing, ⁴so that your giving may be in secret.
Then your Father, who sees what is done in secret, will reward you.*

For the followers of Jesus Christ, an upright life is not optional. It is essential. Righteousness is a significant theme in Matthew's Gospel and particularly in the Sermon on the Mount, which highlights the need for Christians to display godly character as well as conduct. The word righteous is used no less than seventeen times in Matthew, from the description of Joseph (a "righteous man," 1:19), to the glorious destiny of God's faithful ("the righteous to eternal life," 25:46), to the righteousness of Jesus Himself ("that innocent man," 27:19). The noun righteousness is found seven times with five of these references concentrated in the Sermon on the Mount.¹ The last of these five leaves no doubt regarding what righteousness Jesus has in mind as He focuses attention on God's kingdom and His righteousness (6:33). It is a life lived in the intentional pursuit of God's will in response to His gracious forgiveness and acceptance.

The emphasis on the disciples' righteousness found in 6:1-18 is a part of the larger treatment of the subject which begins in 5:6, where Jesus pronounces a blessing on those who hunger and thirst for righteousness. In 5:10, a further blessing is extended to those who are persecuted because of righteousness. This is followed in 5:20 by a solemn warning to the disciples, "unless your righteousness surpasses that of the Pharisees and the teachers of the Law, you will certainly not enter the kingdom of heaven." In the rest of chapter five, Jesus spells out what that means by stressing the necessity of being godly in attitude as well as in action. The Pharisees and teachers of the Law treated God's commands legalistically, leading to external compliance without internal commitment. They kept the letter of the Law, but disregarded its spirit. Jesus, however, teaches that the commands must be obeyed from the heart. Using six illustrations, He insists that the Law be internalized, calling for the inner qualities of gentleness, purity, faithfulness, honesty, and love in order to mirror the very character of God Himself (5:21-48).

In 6:1-18 the theme of righteousness continues, but with a shift in emphasis. From the inner moral significance of the Law, Jesus now turns to the exercise of the three prominent acts of Jewish piety: charitable giving (6:2-4), prayer (6:5-15), and fasting (5:16-18). Again His focus is on the attitude of the heart. These expressions of religious devotion are not to be marked by self-promotion, but by pure motives that flow from genuine faith in the Father. Not only the central point, but also the structure of the three paragraphs is the same. Each begins with a prohibition of exploiting the religious practice to draw human applause, as the hypocrites do. This is followed in each case by the pointed observation that they will receive what they desire, but nothing more. Contrasted with the prohibition is a prescription describing how the religious observance should be carried out. Finally, there is the promise of the Father's recognition and reward.

THE PRINCIPLE STATED (V. 1)

In 6:1, Jesus states the fundamental principle which applies to all three of the religious practices, not just the first: "Be careful not to do your 'acts of righteousness' before men, to be seen by them. If you do, you will have no reward from your Father in heaven." Just as 5:17-20 stands as a general introduction followed by six examples, so 6:1 stands as a general introduction followed by three examples. The phrase "your righteousness" which occurs in 5:20 is repeated in 6:1 but is somewhat obscured by the NIV's translation, "your acts of righteousness." Jesus assumes that His disciples would engage in these activities. He does not say if you give or pray or fast, but when you do these things, then this is the manner in which you should do them. All three are significant spiritual disciplines that relate to our love for God. Giving to the poor glorifies Him as well as provides needed assistance to others. Praying recognizes God's fatherly care as well as our creaturely dependence on Him. Fasting promotes greater self-denial and devotion to the One who took up His cross and died for us. Clearly Jesus expected that His followers would pursue these spiritual disciplines. His concern was to instruct them regarding the spirit in which these practices should be carried out in order to please and honor God.

Motive is the central issue. Jesus warns His hearers not to parade their acts of piety for the purpose of gaining the attention and admiration of others. To do so is to forfeit the blessing of their Father in heaven. Obviously God is not pleased when we do the right things for the wrong reasons. The danger is evident in the opening words of 6:1: "Be careful." The verb employed here occurs five more times in Matthew as Jesus warns against false prophets (7:15), aggressive adversaries who will persecute believers (10:17), and the faith-destroying influence of the Pharisees and Sadducees (16:6,11-12).

At first glance, it appears that the opening words of chapter 6 contradict the teaching of 5:16. There Jesus commands, "let your light shine before men, that they may see your good deeds and praise your Father in heaven." In 6:1, He seems to say the opposite: "Be careful not to do your 'acts of righteousness' before men, to be seen by them." The discrepancy, however, is only apparent, not real. France goes to the heart of the matter by addressing the key issues:

> The disciple's life is inevitably, and rightly, public, but that does not entitle him to show off his religious devotion; there is a world of difference between living a conspicuously good and godly life (5:13-16) and striving to gain a reputation for piety. The difference lies not only in the motive, but in the result: the former brings glory to God, the latter only to the performer (131).

The New Testament elsewhere confirms the public visibility of believers' faith and values. Paul observes in 1 Timothy 5:24-25, "The sins of some men are obvious, reaching the place of judgment ahead of them; the sins of others trail behind them. In the same way, good deeds are obvious, and even those that are not cannot be hidden." As to motives, those whose highest aim is to be seen by men are not among the pure in heart who are promised that they will see God (Matt. 5:8).

The promise of a reward from our heavenly Father stated in 6:1 is mentioned repeatedly in 6:1-18. The teaching on reward in Matthew is more extensive than in any other Gospel (Hagner 140). The idea of a reward for God-centered living and service is an important part of Jesus' teaching. In the previous chapter, Jesus promises a great reward for those who are persecuted for His sake (Matt. 5:12) and the loss of reward for people who love only those who love them in return (Matt. 5:46). In 6:1-18, Jesus stresses that a proud display in giving, praying, and fasting that aims at human reward necessarily precludes divine reward. The two are incompatible. To seek the praise of men is to forfeit the blessing of God.

Jesus' words, of course, were not spoken in a vacuum. The concept of a reward is firmly rooted in the Old Testament. It is found in the Torah (Gen. 15:1), the books of history (Ruth 2:12), the wisdom literature (Prov. 25:22), and the prophets (Jer. 17:10). It also played an important, if somewhat more subtle, part in first-century Judaism. It was, as we might expect, related to the keeping of the Law, with a final accounting on the day of judgment (Guelich 276).

For Jesus, divine reward seems to have both present and future dimensions, although the primary emphasis is on the latter.[2] Both are promised in Matthew 19:28-31; those who have left all for the sake of Christ may anticipate the Father's blessing in this age and in the age to come (cf. also

Mark 10:29-31; Luke 18:28-30). Jesus clearly states in Matthew 16:27, "For the Son of Man is going to come in his Father's glory with his angels, and then he will reward each person according to what he has done." God's gracious and undeserved compensation on judgment day is the central point of the Parable of the Workers in the Vineyard (Matt. 20:1-16). The prospect of a reward at the final judgment is also seen in Jesus' Parable of the Talents (Matt. 25:14-30). When the master returns after a long absence, he settles accounts with his servants and praises those who have fulfilled his instructions: "Well done, good and faithful servant! You have been faithful with a few things; I will put you in charge of many things. Come and share your master's happiness" (Matt. 25:21,23).

The early church, following their Master's lead, also taught that believers could expect a reward. John seeks to motivate his readers by speaking of being "rewarded fully" (2 John 8), of "rewarding your servants the prophets" (Rev. 11:18), and of Christ bringing His reward with Him at His return (Rev. 22:12). With a backward glance, the writer of Hebrews portrays Moses as anticipating his reward (Heb. 11:26).

Paul informs the Corinthians that on judgment day Christian leaders in particular will be rewarded according to the quality of their work (1 Cor. 3:8,14). He also reminds them that all believers will be compensated in accordance with their deeds (2 Cor. 5:9-10).

At first sight, divine rewards may appear objectionable. If it is sinful to perform a religious act to gain a human reward, is it not also sinful to do so to gain a reward from God? This would, of course, be true if we assume selfish motivation apart from a genuine relationship with God. But here we must distinguish between rewards that flow naturally from a relationship with God and rewards that are alien to this relationship. Stott (131-32) draws attention to the helpful comments of C.S. Lewis:

> We must not be troubled by unbelievers when they say that this promise of reward makes the Christian life a mercenary affair. There are different kinds of rewards. There is the reward which has no natural connexion (*sic*) with the things you do to earn it, and is quite foreign to the desires that ought to accompany those things. Money is not the natural reward of love; that is why we call a man mercenary if he marries a woman for the sake of her money. But marriage is the proper reward for a real lover, and he is not mercenary for desiring it. . . . The proper rewards are not simply tacked on to the activity for which they are given, but are the activity itself in consummation (2).

Jesus Himself serves as our model: "Let us fix our eyes on Jesus, the author and perfecter of our faith, who for the joy set before him endured the cross, scorning its shame, and sat down at the right hand of the throne of God" (Heb. 12:2). Likewise, Jesus' disciples are motivated by their devotion to Him not simply by the thought of reward. The reward is an intrinsic part of their loyalty to their Lord.

It is also worth noting that there is no question of a believer deserving a reward. When Jesus' disciples have done all they can, they can only say, "We are unworthy servants; we have only done our duty" (Luke 17:10). God, then, rewards faithful believers because of His grace, not because He is indebted to them. His gracious reward is infinitely greater than any human effort could possibly deserve.

Such generosity expresses the loving nature of God, whom Jesus describes as our Father in heaven. Although other words are used of God in the Sermon on the Mount (God, Lord, and the great King), Jesus' favorite designation is Father, which He uses seventeen times in these three chapters. Even in the beatitudes, where the term is not used, His fatherhood is clearly implied: "Blessed are the peacemakers, for they will be called sons of God (5:9)." Our status as God's children reflects His Father/child relationship with believers. It is not surprising, then, to find God's paternal care associated closely with richly rewarding His children for their obedience in attitude as well as action.

THE PRINCIPLE APPLIED TO
GIVING TO THE POOR (VV. 2-4)

In 6:2-4, Jesus applies the warning of 6:1 to the practice of giving to the poor. The Old Testament has much to say about caring for the poor.[3] A key passage is Deuteronomy 15:7-11, which commands the Israelites not only to give to the poor among them, but also to do so with a compassionate heart. The words open-handed, freely, and generously are set over against hardhearted, tightfisted, and grudging heart. Jesus, of course, shared this deep concern for the poor (Matt. 11:5; 19:21; 25:35-36). His care for them, as well as His view of money, is encapsulated in His well-known proverb, "It is more blessed to give than to receive" (Acts 20:35).

First-century Judaism made such charitable giving a religious priority,[4] but often the spirit of that giving was far from right. The opportunity to express care for others was contaminated by self-promotion. According to Carson, "Rabbinic writers also warn against ostentation in almsgiving . . . the frequency of the warnings attests to the commonness of the practice" (*Matthew* 163).

In Matthew 6:2, Jesus warns against such abuse of charitable giving: "So when you give to the needy, do not announce it with trumpets, as the hypocrites do in the synagogues and on the streets, to be honored by men. I tell you the truth, they have received their reward in full." Both the motive and the corresponding manner of giving are faulty. To contribute in a deliberately conspicuous way betrays a heart focused on self, not on God. Accordingly, Jesus warns His disciples not to make their giving a spectacle, as the hypocrites do.

Although the hypocrites are not specifically identified, there can be no doubt that Jesus is referring to the Pharisees and teachers of the Law, whose superficial righteousness He roundly condemns in 5:20ff.[5] The word is unambiguously applied to the Pharisees and teachers of the Law in Matthew 15:7, where Jesus denounces their evasion of responsibility to care for their parents in their old age. This Jesus sees as a matter of motive, a matter of the heart, as is apparent from His quotation of Isaiah 29:13: "These people honor me with their lips, but their hearts are far from me. They worship me in vain; their teachings are but rules taught by men" (15:8-9). Likewise in Matthew 23, Jesus repeatedly calls the Pharisees and teachers of the Law hypocrites, as He seven times pronounces woe upon them due to their inconsistency. He prefaces the woes with two significant observations, which have a bearing on our text in chapter six. The first is that the Pharisees and teachers of the Law "do not practice what they preach" (23:3), and "Everything they do is done for men to see" (23:5). It is probably no coincidence that the word translated "to see" is precisely the same word as in 6:1, although translated differently ("to be seen").[6]

As those contexts suggest, the word "hypocrite" conveys the idea of an actor, one who plays a part[7]. Its religious application is to those who pretend to be pious, when in fact they are not (Danker 1038). It is this pretense which is exposed in Matthew 6:2. The Pharisees and teachers of the Law appear to be models of spirituality, but the manner of their giving reveals that they are devoid of devotion to God.

In their desire for attention, Jesus says they announce their giving with trumpets in the synagogues and in the streets. In an attempt to understand this in a literal sense, several suggestions have been put forward. One is that trumpets were actually blown to indicate large donations in order to encourage others to be generous. There is, however, no evidence of this practice. A more likely suggestion is that it refers to the blowing of trumpets to signal fast days at which gifts were given to meet some urgent need. Another possibility is that Jesus is alluding to the deliberate clanging of coins dropped into collection boxes found in the temple and in synagogues. Those in the temple were horn-shaped to discourage theft. Most likely, however, the blowing of trumpets is figurative like our own expression "to blow your own horn."[8] The metaphorical understanding also seems to fit well with Jesus' description of the high profile public performance the Pharisees and teachers of the Law loved to make (Matt. 23:5-7): "Everything they do is done for men to see," including how they dress, where they sit, and the title with which they are greeted.

Donations to the poor were not exempt from their staged efforts to be honored by men. The verb "to be honored" implies a tragic truth. It is used elsewhere in Matthew only of glorifying God (5:16; 9:8; 15:31). In their pride, the hypocrites placed themselves on the throne of God, accepting the praise which is rightfully His alone (Davies and Allison 581-82). It is impossible to honor God and to honor self at the same time. The two are mutually exclusive.

In addition, these theatrical benefactors disqualified themselves from receiving any spiritual benefit from God. Jesus states the sad reality this way, "I tell you the truth, they have received their reward in full." The verb translated "they have received" was a commercial term in the first century that conveyed the idea of receiving full payment and giving a receipt for it (Danker 102). The actors have the reward they want, the admiration and applause of others; but that is all they will receive. Since they have been paid in full, they will receive no blessing from God.

In 6:3-4a, Jesus explains the right way to give: "But when you give to the needy, do not let your left hand know what your right hand is doing so that your giving may be in secret." This may be taken literally, instructing disciples to give discreetly using only one hand to avoid catching the eye of others (Gundry 102). But more likely it is to be understood figuratively. "The expression may simply mean that we are to avoid all scheming and planning for our own advantage in human attention" (Augsburger 85). As Jeremiah 17:9 testifies, there is nothing as deceitful as the human heart. Just when we think we have disciplined our desires, it is then that mixed motives may contaminate our loyalty to God. Constant vigilance is required to ensure that He is the motivational center of our heart and life. Our giving should be so unself-conscious that we are hardly aware of it ourselves. This very spirit is highlighted in Matthew 25:37-40. There the righteous are described as blissfully unaware of their service to others and therefore to Christ. Their service is so natural and selfless that there is neither concern for self-congratulation, nor appetite for attention.

This is not to suggest that we be inattentive or careless in our financial stewardship. There is ample teaching in the New Testament to the contrary.[9] We are held accountable for all that God has placed within our care. Rather, Jesus' point is that we must give no opportunity for secret pride to develop within our hearts. A model of such self-forgetful giving is to be found in the Macedonian Christians. Paul says of them, "they gave themselves first to the Lord and then to us in keeping with God's will" (2 Cor. 8:5). With little thought for their own limited resources, they gave beyond their ability to the even more impoverished Jewish Christians of Jerusalem. In such sensitive and compassionate hearts, there is no room for spiritual conceit or for the desire to advertise one's generosity, only sincere concern for others in need and eagerness to do the Father's will. In this sense, the giving is in secret. Although it may be noticed by others, it is not done to be seen by others.

Such secret giving comes with a promise: "Then your Father, who sees what is done in secret, will reward you." This promise, which was first stated negatively in 6:1, is repeated in relation to prayer (6:6) and fasting (6:18). It has three key elements. First, the basis of the promise is the personal relationship that exists between God and the believer. This is conveyed by the words *your Father*. The pronoun *your* is singular, as it is also in 6:6 and 6:18. This phrasing, found only here in the first three Gospels, points to the individual nature of this relationship. It is a remarkable reality of the gospel that God desires to have this intimate association with every believer.

The second element is the Father's flawless insight into our motives. He sees what is done in secret. In 6:6 and 6:18 He is described literally as "the one who is in secret" (NIV, "who is unseen"). Our hidden considerations and humble contributions correspond to our Father's nature. This crucial fact was impressed upon Samuel in the course of locating and anointing David as king of Israel: "Man looks at the outward appearance, but the Lord looks at the heart" (1 Sam. 16:7). Jeremiah also stresses God's penetrating vision: "I the Lord search the heart and examine the mind to reward a man according to his conduct, according to what his deeds deserve" (Jer. 17:10). As this text reveals, no matter how others see us, God's perfect perception links deeds with motives.

Third, there is the promise of the reward itself. The greatness of this promise is seen by contrasting it with the reward the hypocrites pursued. Over against the fleeting admiration of men stands the eternal blessing of the Father Himself. Although the nature of the reward is not described here, it certainly does not involve the promise of material prosperity. The so-called health and wealth gospel finds no basis here. Nor does the reward involve public recognition in this life. Although the King James Version states that the disciples will be rewarded openly, this reading is absent from some of the most important early manuscripts.[10] The reward would seem to include, however, the present joy of knowing we are doing God's will in caring for others in need and the prospect of His praise and presence in His eternal kingdom (Matt. 25:34-36; 1 Cor. 4:5-6). In that kingdom, there will be no needy. Meanwhile we are to commit ourselves to giving to the poor, expressing the Father's compassion for the Father's glory.

NOTES

[1]The related verb appears twice in Matthew (11:19; 12:37) and the word unrighteous appears once only and that in the Sermon on the Mount (5:45). These and other statistics cited later in the chapter are taken from Clapp, Friberg, and Friberg, *Analytical Greek Concordance of the Greek New Testament.*

[2]While Stott (132) understands the reward as probably relating to this life, Guelich (280) associates it with the final judgment. Carson (*Matthew* 164) thinks it includes both.

[3]Some significant passages include Lev. 19:9-10; Deut. 24:19-22; Ps. 112:9; Prov. 22:9; 31:20; Isa.10:1-4; Jer. 22:15-16; Zech. 7:8-10.

[4]For a detailed description of the nature and organization of Jewish relief for the poor, especially in Jerusalem, see Jeremias (126-34).

[5]The word hypocrite occurs only seventeen times in the New Testament and always on the lips of Jesus. Significantly, it is found thirteen times in Matthew but only three times in Luke and once in Mark.

[6]Compare *tōn anthrōpōn pros* to *theathēnai autois* (6:1) with *pros to theathēnai tois anthrōpois* (23:5) (Aland, et al., *Greek New Testament*).

[7]For an exploration of the question of whether Jesus' use of the word *actor/hypocrite* was influenced by the presence of the Hellenistic theater at Sepphoris near Nazareth, see the intriguing article by Batey.

[8]A fuller discussion of these possibilities is given in Carson (*Matthew* 163-4), Davies and Allison (579–80) and Hagner (139).

[9]Some key passages are Acts 2:44-45; 1 Cor. 16:1-4; 2 Cor. 8-9; 1 Tim. 6:17-19.

[10]After assessing the manuscript evidence, Metzger (*A Textual Commentary on the Greek New Testament,* 12) observes, "The point in the whole section, however, is not so much the openness of the Father's reward as its superiority to mere human approval (compare verses 6 and 18)."

11 ▪ Pure Prayer

Matthew 6:5-8

Greg Lee

*⁵But when you pray, do not be like the hypocrites, for they love to pray
standing in the synagogues and on the street corners to be seen by men.
I tell you the truth, they have received their reward in full. ⁶When you pray,
go into your room, close the door and pray to your Father, who is unseen.
Then your Father, who sees what is done in secret, will reward you.
⁷And when you pray, do not keep on babbling like pagans, for they think
they will be heard because of their many words. ⁸Do not be like them,
for your Father knows what you need before you ask him.*

HYPOCRISY (V. 5)

Rarely does Jesus stray from teaching about our human tendency to
emphasize outward actions while disregarding the inward motivations we
ought to examine and nurture. Here He continues this theme of His mountainside message, while adding specific instruction on the practice of
prayer. The guiding principle of His teaching is simple: when you pray,
you will be rewarded based on your motivations. A sincere prayer to God
is sincerely answered by God; but if the true purpose of your prayer is not
God-directed, then it will not be God-answered. Earlier in the message,
Jesus addressed the importance of our attitudes, using a litany of unques-
tionably evil examples (murder, adultery, divorce, etc.). The force of His
words begins to penetrate the listener's heart when He uses the subsequent
righteous examples (almsgiving, prayer, and fasting) to demonstrate the
spiritual poison of unrighteous motives.

Examples highlighted in Matthew's Gospel lend credibility to Jesus'
teaching on prayer. Whereas Luke frequently records cases of Jesus seeking
a lonely place to pray (Luke 5:16; 6:12; 9:18; 11:1; 22:41), Matthew makes
record of two powerful prayers that serve as bookends to Jesus' public ministry. Jesus begins that ministry alone with God in the desert (4:2) for forty
days of spiritual preparation for immediate temptation by Satan and long-
term ministry with the masses. His ministry climaxes as He pleads with His

Father alone in Gethsemane (26:36) committed to God's way, but clearly desiring another. No one would mistake these two instances of prayer as anything but sincere, seeking the attention of God alone.

Commentators routinely use the opening phrase of this passage to emphasize the assumption that people are praying. D.A. Carson says that Christ "presupposes that his followers *will* pray" (*The Sermon on the Mount* 58). Although it is reasonable to believe that Jesus expects His listeners to pray, He intends a different application for this phrase. As He prepares to address the manner in which people pray, He uses the phrase "When you pray . . ." as a device to bring about a mental image in the minds of His listeners. If I were to say, "When you eat, do not use a fork," you would immediately think of the three meals you eat each day and how difficult it would be to eat them without a key utensil; you would not stop to consider how I assume that you routinely eat. Similarly, for the devout Jew who would stop to pray three times each day, a variety of prayer-time images would have immediately come to mind. When Jesus opens with the phrase "When you pray," He is setting the scene for His teaching to come.

Most people today can quickly think of others who seek attention by changing their persona when they begin to pray in public; perhaps the pitch of their voice drops an octave or the flowery language of past centuries takes over. Jesus condemns such prayerful "stage acting" (MacArthur 364). The word hypocrite takes its meaning from the theatrical world where men would hide their faces with a mask to portray another character. Using religious actions to draw the accolades of others had become an art form, but Jesus asserts that prayer ought to be authentic. There is nothing more futile or ridiculous than acting as someone you are not when addressing God, since the all-knowing Creator Himself made you and sustains you.

It is worth noting that Jesus does not condemn the customary practice of praying three times each day. In fact, His lack of negative comments regarding this routine could be regarded as a quiet affirmation. Such a habit can be helpful if it does not become so legalistic that the ritual replaces the relationship (Dan. 6:10).

Jesus delineates His understanding of the aforementioned hypocrites here. In their culture, all devout Jews were expected to stop and pray at 9:00 A.M., 12:00 noon, and 3:00 P.M. each day. Such a system undoubtedly interrupted any number of daily activities. You can imagine the scene when carpenters ceased their hammering, authors paused their writing, and rabbis suspended their teaching in order to observe the sacred rite of prayer. However, some would actually calculate their schedules to position themselves in busy intersections and public forums like the synagogue when the bell tolled for prayer times, so that they could draw the attention of many around them. You can easily picture these men as stage actors when they appear surprised that they ended up in front of a crowd at prayer time—again!

Jesus condemns such actions passionately. His frustration is not directed at those who stood to pray in public,[1] but is focused on those who did so for the purpose of attracting the attention of others. These hypocrites squandered their opportunity to address God Himself for the cheap reward of impressing those nearby. They might as well have taken their tithe and, instead of giving it to God, used the money to buy lavish clothing and gaudy jewelry to draw attention to themselves. By taking something that was intended for God and perverting it for self-promotion, these men demonstrated that they did not love to pray, but rather loved to be seen by men.

Our tendency to value outward reputation over inner relationship is a systemic problem that was apparent long before Jesus' teaching. When choosing a king for Israel, Samuel discovered that "The LORD does not look at the things man looks at. Man looks at the outward appearance, but the LORD looks at the heart" (1 Sam. 16:7). This continues to be a primary challenge for the Christian in today's image-obsessed world. The devoted believer is faced with a difficult question: Am I more concerned about my character and my personal relationship with God or about my reputation and the perception of those around me? Ironically, Jesus reminds us that while prayer grants us God Himself as our audience, these pretenders had only gained the attention of other people.

Since the synagogue is mentioned in this verse, it is sometimes applied to prayer in a corporate worship setting, although Jesus is specifically referring to personal prayer. We need to be mindful of Christ's teaching regardless of the setting, however, because even public prayer ought to be personal. Christians easily can be tempted to offer prayers directed toward the human audience rather than toward God. To resist that tendency, believers should evaluate their motivations by monitoring aspects such as tone and phrasing when offering prayers in the presence of others. On the other hand, it would be shameful to swing to the legalistic extreme and eliminate the practice of public prayer in an effort to avoid being seen by men. Such a rigid view is not supported in the New Testament,[2] as evidenced by Jesus teaching the model prayer a few verses later and addressing God with the plural pronoun "Our Father . . ." (Matt. 6:9). Christ-followers should not eliminate this spiritually healthy practice simply to avoid the possibility of having impure motives; instead, they must continually assess their purposes as they practice prayer in the presence of others.

The ludicrous nature of praying to an audience other than God is exposed here. While God gives us access to His throne and "is able to do immeasurably more than all we ask or imagine" (Eph. 3:20), the hypocrite denies himself these rewards in return for the recognition of others when he is done acting his part. God behaves like the perfect gentleman in that He listens attentively when you speak to Him, but does not eavesdrop while you are actually speaking to someone else. In the end, God honors your motivation. If you petition Him sincerely, then you should anticipate His rewards. However, if your primary motivation is to be seen by others, that notoriety will be granted—nothing more, nothing less.

It is not unusual for Jesus to teach that a change in action may produce a change in attitude. He understands the reciprocal relationship that attitude and action have. Conventional wisdom may advise us to get our heart right first and then let righteous action flow from it, but Jesus teaches the opposite later in the chapter when He addresses our treasures (Matt. 6:21). He claims that how we use our money may greatly affect the passions of our heart. Similarly, praying in a private place not only signifies that we do not need to be noticed, but also assists in keeping our motivations pure.

PRIVACY (V. 6)

The NIV phrasing your room leaves an inaccurate impression for those who have a room at home to call their own. Most Palestinian homes had only one room with a door you could close that served as a closet or storeroom (Keener, *Matthew* 138). The lowliness and loneliness of the prayer closet Jesus refers to stands in stark contrast to the prominence of the open street corners and synagogues He addressed before.

The reference to a prayer closet suggests that you come to God alone, knowing that what you say there will be held in secret. Have you noticed that the potential for intimacy in conversation directly correlates to the number of people involved? It is much more difficult to be open with a large group of people than with a small group because intimacy depends on trust and transparency. When speaking with only one person, I am more likely to reveal the private portions of my dreams, struggles, and passions than I am when addressing a larger crowd. Frequently, I pray aloud prior to the service of the Lord's Supper at the church where I serve. Only moments later as I receive the bread and cup, I pray silently to God. In which prayer do you suspect that I am more revealing about the sin in my life and more in awe of the sacrifice God made for me? It is in my silent prayer where, in a one-on-one situation, I can open my heart without reservation to the Father.

Praying in secret to God is the only way you can ensure that your most personal thoughts will not be compromised. Confiding in a close friend can be encouraging, but there always remains the possibility that your thoughts will become known to others. Writing in a journal or diary can also be beneficial, but such a practice allows for no response outside of your own reflection. Furthermore, private prayer leads to a reinforced faith. If no one but God is privy to the petitions you bring, then when God rewards your prayer, there will be no doubt as to the source of the reward.

HUMILITY (VV. 7-8)

It is important to understand that while other passages in both the Old and New Testaments endorse shorter prayers (Eccl. 5:2; Mark 12:40), length itself is not the primary issue Jesus wishes to address at this time, nor is repetition. In fact, Jesus Himself spends an entire night in prayer (Luke 6:12). He also endorses repeatedly and persistently praying on the same topic when He tells His followers they should "always pray and do not give up" and then asks rhetorically, "Will not God bring about justice for his chosen ones who cry out to him day and night?" (Luke 18:1,7).

After unsettling His listeners with the previous indictment of showmanship, Jesus draws them back once again to the visual image of their prayer time by reiterating the simple phrase, "When you pray. . . ." He then takes this opportunity to rebuke them for another ugly tendency common to the Jewish prayer life—mindless, lengthy, excessively flattering prayers.

During their daily prayer times, the Jews had a ritual of offering repeated prayers. First they would recite the *Shema*, followed by a series of eighteen additional prayers called *Shemoneh 'esreh* (Barclay 192). While these prayers are beautifully written and have spiritual value, they were often recited with empty repetition. What must have begun as a well-intentioned religious habit, now played out as a mechanical, rather than spiritual, exercise. This thoughtless echoing had numbed them to the point that they no longer understood how prayer works.

John MacArthur explains their custom of long, laudatory prayers by stating, "Verbosity was confused with meaning and length was confused with sincerity" (363). The ability to use many words had long been mis-understood by the ancients, who believed it would aid in gaining access to and preference from deities. Michael Green comments about their practice: "Pagans tended to think that God could be bludgeoned into acquiescence if you prayed long enough" (80). The Jews seemed to have adopted this philosophy. Additionally, many had fallen into the pagan practice of adding flattering titles and reminders of the good deeds they had done when they offered their daily prayers. Pagans believed that such wordy diatribes would aid in gaining preferential treatment from the deity[3] Heavily Jewish, both Christ's listeners and Matthew's written audience would have been ashamed and shocked by these comparisons to the Gentiles.

If Jesus teaches against trying to sway God with compliments and praises, should we then cease offering praises to Him? No; once again, the issue is motive. Parents are regular recipients of this selfish flattery tactic. When a child begins with cajoling compliments, a discerning parent is astute enough to know that he is being primed for an ensuing request. God is equally unimpressed by empty praises selfishly offered to Him with only the reward in mind. Yet, properly motivated adoration is necessary because it acknowledges the attributes of God. Jesus models these two verses later when He gives instruction on how to pray by extolling, "Our Father in heaven, hallowed be your name" (Matt. 6:9). The purpose of beginning a prayer with sincere admiration is not to adjust God's view of me and what I deserve, but to adjust my view of God and what He deserves. Babbling attempts to coax God into answering my request, but humble praise prepares me to make the proper request.

The pagans viewed divine beings through the lens of their own humanity, presuming that these deities doled out their provisions in the same impersonal manner as the vendors with whom they bartered at the market. With rewards on the line, they felt the need to wheel and deal in their prayers. Bribing the gods with opulent sacrifices, appeasing them with unending flattery, and even swindling them with empty promises were all within the realm of acceptability.

When Christ sternly warns, "Do not be like them," He is condemning the pagans' cold, selfish, merchant-oriented approach to their gods. He builds a contrasting picture of God as a Being Who is interested in a personal relationship with us by using the more intimate word Father. He refers to Him by this name three times in these four verses and no less than ten times in the broader context of almsgiving, prayer, and fasting. Our God is rightly pictured as One who knows your needs (and desires for them to be filled) even before you ask Him. He simply awaits your humble, sincere request. The hypocrite's spiritual posture is arrogant and does not fully acknowledge the distinct differences between God and man. The correct attitude to have before God is one of humility and teachability because, "By praying, we are instructing ourselves more than we are Him" (Martin Luther qtd. in MacArthur 369).

A growing awareness of God's omniscience is key to a proper relationship with Him. Our Father both "sees what is done in secret" (5:6) and "knows what you need before you ask" (5:8). Yet, from the beginning of time, mankind has hopelessly tried to hide his worst (even from the God who sees everything), hindering intimacy with the Father. Our efforts to conceal sin are no more successful than Adam and Eve's attempt to take cover among the trees. Conversely, we are tempted to conspicuously call attention to our prayers and good deeds, afraid they will go overlooked. The irony is that the rightful recipient of your prayers and service not only notices, but also foreknows both your actions and the motivations that produce them.

In the end, we would do well to take note of an observation by D.A. Carson. He clarifies why this passage, as well as other teachings of Christ, challenge us to do study before making knee-jerk application. "Jesus has a way of preaching in absolute categories even when he is primarily addressing himself to fairly specific conditions" (*The Sermon on the Mount* 60). Short-sighted analysis could lead some to conclude that Jesus is against lengthy and public prayers, until you harmonize this teaching with His words and examples in other settings. It then becomes clear that Jesus is not primarily concerned with the questions of what and how. He presents motive as the defining factor, forcing us to ask why. Praying on the street corner might well be fine for the purpose of setting a godly example or for the purpose of encouraging some lonely fellow there. Christ's condemnation here is focused on those who are praying in public for the purpose of man's applause.

While I was in the midst of studying this passage, its application was made real to me at the conclusion of a Bible study one evening. We gathered to pray and sat silently waiting for someone to agree to voice the prayer. A man whose faith is young, but blazing surprised me by volunteering. He listed our requests on a piece of paper and then said, "Okay." Before we could even bow our heads, he began with "God, please answer our prayers" and then went on to list the first four requests using simple words and phrases. When he came to the fifth one, he could not recall from his scratched notes what he was to pray for, so he stopped and asked, "What was this one about?" After I explained it, he said, "Oh yeah" and then continued with the last few petitions. Never have I heard a more straightforward and unpretentious prayer. The only eloquence was in his sincerity. His pause to direct a question to me was a subtle illustration that the words of the prayer were not intended for me, but for God. The tone was unassuming; the prayer was raw; the relationship was real. Above all, his motivation was pure, and therefore his prayer was heard—by God.

NOTES

[1] In our passage, Jesus is not specifically calling attention to people who stood when they prayed. Standing was a common position for prayer in that day (Mark 11:25; Luke 18:11,13) as were kneeling, sitting, and prostrate positions.

[2] Actually the opposite is true. Later in Matthew, Jesus gives preference to praying with a plurality of people (18:19-20) and Paul instructs Timothy to encourage public prayer, even to "lift up holy hands in prayer" (1 Tim. 2:8).

[3] Jesus was concerned with this babbling content. The word used to give this description is *battalogeō*, the most unique word of the passage in that it occurs no other place in the New Testament or in secular literature. Built from an existing word, the translation of babbling likely gives us an excellent picture of Matthew's intention (Carson, *Matthew* 166).

12 ▪ The Model Prayer

Matthew 6:9-15

Keith H. Ray

⁹This is how you should pray: "Our Father in heaven, hallowed be your name,
¹⁰your kingdom come, your will be done on earth as it is in heaven.
¹¹Give us today our daily bread. ¹²Forgive us our debts, as we also have forgiven
our debtors. ¹³And lead us not into temptation, but deliver us from the evil one."
¹⁴For if you forgive men when they sin against you, your heavenly Father
will also forgive you. ¹⁵But if you do not forgive men their sins,
your Father will not forgive your sins.

THE CONTEXT

Traditionally, this passage is referred to as the Lord's Prayer. While it certainly describes Jesus' teaching to the disciples, it was intended to be their model prayer. John MacArthur has rightly named it "the Disciples' Prayer." It is a skeletal prayer for believers to flesh out with their own words of praise, adoration and petition (MacArthur 374). This model or paradigm of prayer, in fifty-seven Greek words, outlines for the believer the appropriate content in conversing with God. Its comprehensiveness and brevity are marks of its genius. Martin Luther captured this brilliance when he wrote: "The right method is to use few words . . . the fewer the words the better the prayer. . . . Few words and much meaning is Christian. Many words and little meaning is pagan" (Ebeling 15).

The context of this passage clarifies the need for the model prayer. Both the surrounding pagan culture and Jewish culture had their own practice of prayer. This confusion led the disciples to Jesus, seeking instruction for appropriate prayer. It is important to recognize that the context is already addressing the giving of alms and fasting. Now their attention is turned to how they should pray and not what they should pray (Matt. 6:9a).

Prayer for the disciple is crucial as it relates to fasting and giving. We cannot give a fast properly unless we are in constant communion with God. Fasting is meaningless apart from prayer, because apart from prayer it is apart from God (MacArthur 372). Any religious ritual unaccompanied by prayer easily becomes routine. This routine was the target for Jesus' teaching. Routine praying was prevalent with both Jewish and pagan culture. The Jews had relied upon formulas like *Shemone Esreh* (*Eighteen Benedictions*, qtd. in Scott 43), and the pagans offered ritualistic formulas believing that the use of a lot of words secured their prayers (Ebeling 11). Both Jews and pagans thought God could be bludgeoned into acquiescence if you prayed long enough (Green 81). The model prayer was intended to end once and for all the confusion regarding appropriate prayer.

It is, however, ironic that the very context of this passage forbids meaningless repetition in prayer and that the very prayer suggested to counter that, is so abused. "For no prayer has been repeated more than this one, often without understanding. . . ." (Carson, *The Sermon on the Mount* 61). Contemporary Christians need to hear again the power of prayer and be wary and warned about naïve repetition.

THE STRUCTURE

Having recognized the intent of Jesus' teaching on prayer and the context in which it was presented, we now turn to its structure and design. In its simplest form the prayer consists of four main parts: (1) the address, (2) thou petitions, (3) we petitions and (4) doxology (Harner 10). Within the frame of the structure lie seven petitions, all of which focus on essential human needs.[1]

The prayer itself has two levels of focus. The first and primary focus is God's glory and the second is our human needs. Equally important is the order of the prayer. God's glory precedes human need. Obviously, Jesus is trying to show that a proper disposition toward the Father is a priority, if not an appropriate attitude.[2] Thus, the power of prayer does not depend so much on words, as upon the spirit in which we offer it (Hare 120). Further analysis of the text reveals that divine glory and human need run parallel to the true emphases of this prayer: The kingdom of God (glory) and forgiveness (human need) (Matt. 8:13; John 4:24). We will give further attention to these two elements later in this chapter. Glorifying God includes petitions on behalf of God's name, His kingdom, and His will. Man's needs, on the other hand include petitions for one's bread, one's forgiveness, and one's protection from temptation. Providing the basic premises from which we pray, it is amazingly freeing in other ways. "It makes no mention of where to pray, a time to pray, or the attire and position for prayer . . . it is appropriate to pray in any attire, at any time, in any place and under any circumstance" (MacArthur 373).

The model prayer brings with it a refreshing simplicity and brevity, freedom in the act of praying itself, and an unparalleled comprehensiveness. In fact, the prayer has a way of turning the frequent ambition of prayer to align God's will with our agenda, to do just the opposite. True prayer for the Christian centers on God's glory. Jesus' model prayer focuses on the sovereignty of God, not the pursuit of His gifts and promises. It turns the believer in the direction of seeking God's glory and obedience to

His will. God's agenda then becomes the agenda for the one praying. It affirms God's sovereignty, righteousness, and majesty and seeks to conform our desires and our purposes to His will and glory (MacArthur 375).

THE ADDRESS

The tone of prayer is set by the opening words of adoration. It puts the believer in the appropriate mental position for the rest of the prayer. This prayer is less concerned with proper protocol in approaching deity, than with truth, thus enabling us to come to Him in the right frame of mind (Stott 146). He is a holy, heavenly daddy that makes His awesome nature, sovereign character, and His intimate spirit available to meet with us in prayer.

This use of *abba* in addressing God was a new concept for Jews, accustomed to His sovereign nature. It introduced a new understanding and relationship with God. Jesus had the audacity to speak of God and to God in such a way to be perceived as offensive, disrespectful, and worldly (Ebeling 17). After all, *abba* described the intimacy of a child addressing his father. Jesus repeatedly used this intimate title in all of His praying except His prayer on the cross: "My God, my God, why have you forsaken me?" (Matt. 27:46). The fatherhood of God conjured images of the Old Testament where God works in history as helper, redeemer, ruler, protector, and disciplinarian with whom He has a Covenant.

The entirety of the prayer hinges on this single reality. If we have an intimate Father, He will hear and care for our requests for His coming kingdom, forgiveness of sin, and protection from temptation (Harner 56).

Additionally, this intimacy is balanced with and supplemented by the reverent desire that His name be treated as Holy. What appears to be a paradox in having an intimate Father who is in heaven, is really a statement of His sovereignty (McNeile 78). The heavenly description expresses His absolute superiority to all reality (Eph. 3:15; 4:6) (Lochman 23). This intimate Father is able to address any and all of our needs. Since He is beyond our comprehension and above all, we cannot doubt that whatever we ask of Him, He is able to do. He is sovereign (Scott 84-85).

Jesus brings the disciples into a new awareness of this fatherly relationship and a sense of confidence that comes from a sovereign Father. This intimate vocabulary was to the Jews a reassurance of God's reality and continuing care for them (Deut. 32:6,9-10,12,15b). It reminded them that God was in heaven and still concerned about the suffering and persecution they were experiencing on earth (Harner 27). Again, this not only was a convincing reminder of God's care, but a point of amazement that they were eligible for this level of intimacy with their already awesome God (Carson, *The Sermon on the Mount* 64). The paradox of sovereignty and intimacy make this model prayer a complete paradigm shift from any Jewish or pagan concept of prayer. Ebeling summarizes the impact of their new relationship: "We are sons, not slaves, not prisoners, not condemned criminals in the death-cell of the world, but free men who are summoned to life" (19).

THE PETITIONS

The model prayer has an appropriate opening in its address to the heavenly Father. That fatherly tone beckons the one praying to bring his petitions. Jesus directs those petitions into two categories: The thou petitions are directed to the nature and work of God; and the "we" petitions address the side of human need (Harner 58-9).

While it is uncommon to describe God as a being that has need, Ebeling suggests that "the most important petition is concerned with the greatest need. Our greatest need is to attend to His and to take up His cause" (Ebeling 24). This prayer makes it immediately clear that we attend to the needs of God by expressing our concern for His glory in relationship to His name, rule, and will (Stott 146).

The petitions clearly indicate the two emphases within the prayer. One is the overt attention to the kingdom of God,[3] and the second is the role that forgiveness plays in that kingdom. Seeking the heavenly and holy Father calls the one in prayer to His agenda. Praying "your will be done" unifies the prayer. This unifying factor is the result of our recognition that God will assert His sovereign will; and, on the other hand, we through obedience to that will, do our little part in moving it forward (Scott 95). We do not change His will; He changes ours. We must first look upward and declare our faith in the God who reigns in heaven. This majestic and eternal purpose reminds us that the world belongs to God. Truly, our loftiest faith in God must have its outcome in ordinary living (Stott 96).

The central thrust of the kingdom gives focus to the petition: inherent to Jewish tradition is this kingdom perspective. Ancient rabbis contended that "a prayer in which the kingdom of God is never mentioned is not true prayer" (Scott 92). The Talmud clearly stated that "a prayer that does not have the kingdom of God is not a prayer" (MacArthur 379). Not only was Jesus modeling the appropriate reference to the kingdom, but also He reminds us that whatever you ask for, should be commensurate to the purpose and will of God (John 12:28; 2 Cor. 6:2). Thus, the prayer for His kingdom to come, occurs whenever His will is done. Mounce suggests that perfect obedience to His will awaits the final arrival of the King. In the meantime, we can experience His sovereign rule by living lives of obedience (53-4).

On a more practical level, MacArthur raises a very important issue. When praying for His will to be done (or a way of inaugurating His kingdom), it implies our awareness of His will through His Word and, second, a desire to do His will (67). Obviously the desire to be in His Word and discern His will is a significant challenge to the contemporary church. This, however, has been the blessing of serving with Dr. Henderson. His commitment to Christ, and his practice of reading and studying God's Word have been an example to me of how I may begin to discern the will of God.

These petitions urgently seek the fulfillment of a holy God's desire to accomplish His purpose as set out in the initial humanity of His Son Jesus Christ.[4] The kingdom motif draws the believer to the sovereign and eschatological intention of God. Harner further states that God's salvation, too, is extended throughout all of His creation: "on earth as it is in heaven" (80).

The comprehensiveness of this is beautifully stated by James Orr:

The kingdom of God is "a natural and universal kingdom and dominion of God embracing all objects, persons, and events, all doings of individuals and nations, all operations and changes of nature and history, absolutely without exception . . ." (qtd. in McClain 22).

To pray for anything less is to miss the comprehensiveness of this prayer and its implication for the disciple of Christ.

The prayer shifts in 6:11 from God's glory to man's needs, or as mentioned earlier, from the thou to the we petitions. These petitions appeal to the whole person. Daily bread provides the physical needs; forgiveness, the emotional and mental needs; and escape from temptation provides the spiritual dimension (MacArthur 388). Additionally, the emphasis on the kingdom of God demands a new ethical standard flowing out of the reign of God. Scott contends that the whole prayer is contained in this one petition for the kingdom: "We ask for daily bread that we might work for the kingdom; for God's forgiveness that we may be worthy to enter it, for power to resist temptation that we may never wander from the road that leads to it" (Scott 92).

This new standard arises when sin is recognized, dealt with; and forgiveness is identified as a kingdom ethic. Forgiveness is the foundation from which God's reign and provision are derived in the work of progress. Forgiveness is a central theme of this passage. MacArthur captures the essence of this element when he says, ". . . everything leads to, or issues from, forgiveness" (392).

FORGIVENESS

The model prayer introduces to us and reminds us that nothing is more important in the Christian life than forgiveness of others. A holy God, who has intentions of bringing His kingdom to earth will manifest it with the most heavenly ethic—the ethic of forgiveness. Five times within the prayer and the following verses this vital subject is mentioned. Within the judgmental and divisive culture of Judaism, Jesus reintroduces forgiveness as the most necessary ingredient for kingdom living.

The relationship of being forgiven and forgiving others is a key to this kingdom ethic. To pray "forgive us our debts (sins) as we forgive others" sets up a curious sense of formula. John Stott says it rather succinctly, "God forgives only the penitent, and one of the chief evidences of penitence is a forgiving spirit" (149). Even more simplistically, MacArthur puts it this way: "God deals with us, as we deal with others" (394). Again, the model prayer elicits from the believer an unprecedented ethic of forgiveness.[5] The Apostle Paul urges a divisive church to "forgive each other just as God in Christ, also has forgiven you" (Eph. 4:32). Michael Green has captured the complexity and seeming conditionality of divine and human forgiveness: "It's not as if God won't forgive you unless you forgive those who have wronged you . . . He can't. How can we receive His gracious pardon with open hands, if our hands are clinched tightly against those who had wronged us?" (82).

The prayer is simple and profound; let forgiveness flow from the grace of God into the human experience to achieve this new kingdom. This may very well be the most needed, most profound gift from God as the primary offering of the gospel of Christ.

This prayer ends with a petition that implicitly recognizes our own helplessness before the devil. The one praying hopes to bring vindication through Jesus, who alone can vanquish him. (Carson, *Matthew* 174). It serves as a reminder that we have not arrived spiritually. This shortfall calls for an appeal to the Father to deliver us from ourselves, our sin, and our inconsistency in the face of temptation. This is a safeguard against presumption, a false sense of security, and self-sufficiency (MacArthur 396). The wording is awkward when it says "lead us not into temptation." While numerous debates exist over its meaning, Carson suggests that a litotes figure of speech is a way of expressing something by negating the contrary (*The Sermon on the Mount* 70). His example would be the phrase not a few, meaning "many." In the case of the prayer, we are requesting that the Father lead us away from temptation. He goes on to suggest that we "consciously depend upon God for physical sustenance, and sense our dependence upon Him for our moral triumph and spiritual victory" (Carson, *The Sermon on the Mount* 71).

The significance of this prayer for deliverance is emphasized when you recognize that the verb form is a command. It is the picture of a servant-child of God who lives in the kingdom of forgiveness, seeking desperately a deliverance from the evil one by the willing and able hand of the Father.

The prayer sums up the teaching of Jesus in a most succinct way. It expresses the longing the disciples should feel for the action of God. This would occur by setting up His kingdom through their daily dependence upon Him, their relationship of reconciliation with Him and their fellow man, and their need of His power to preserve them from yielding to temptation (Morris 455). To that we say, "Amen." This prayer is a very succinct guideline for appropriate prayer. Approaching the heavenly Father in prayer requires adequate recognition of His nature and His kingdom. It teaches us the right approach to a sovereign holy God. It elicits from us the call to conform to His will and His kingdom. It implies that His kingdom takes preeminence in our lives. We are urged to live out that kingdom priority through a life of forgiveness.

For the praying Christian there is confidence that God will provide for all of our needs. Our greatest needs are forgiveness from Him and for others. In our utter dependence upon Him, we find deliverance from evil and the strength to face challenges of earthly living. In the end we receive the blessing of a kingdom that far exceeds our greatest expectation.

NOTES

[1]Scott and others have identified the basic prayer as 1) Let your name be hallowed, 2) Your kingdom come, 3) Your will be done, 4) Our needs be met, 5) Our sins forgiven, 6) Lives led away from temptation, 7) Our deliverance from evil (Scott, 79ff.).

[2]M.L. Jones states it quite profoundly, "man is at his greatest and highest when upon his knees he comes face to face to God" (245).

[3]Kingdom of God was a central theme of Christ's ministry and the teaching of the Old Testament (Exod. 15:18; Ps. 145:13; Mark 10:15; Luke 12:32).

[4]Petitioning God to make His name Holy is actually asking that He manifest the holiness of His name by intervening in history and bringing a new time of salvation to men (see Harmer, 65) (Ezek. 36:23; Isa. 29:23).

[5]We are reminded of the role of our confession in forgiveness (1 John 1:9).

13 ■ Fasting

Matthew 6:16-18

David Butts

[16]When you fast, do not look somber as the hypocrites do, for they disfigure their faces to show men they are fasting. I tell you the truth, they have received their reward in full. [17]But when you fast, put oil on your head and wash your face, [18]so that it will not be obvious to men that you are fasting, but only to your Father, who is unseen; and your Father, who sees what is done in secret, will reward you.

Fasting is not a popular subject in the church. While I was growing up, I do not recall ever hearing a sermon or lesson on fasting. It was certainly there in the pages of Scripture, but we viewed it somewhat like sacrifices in the Old Testament—interesting, but irrelevant as far as practicing it today is concerned. Richard Foster, noted Christian author, writes:

> In a culture where the landscape is dotted with shrines to the Golden Arches and an assortment of Pizza Temples, fasting seems out of place, out of step with the times. In fact, fasting has been in general disrepute both in and outside the Church for many years. For example, in my research I could not find a single book published on the subject of Christian fasting from 1861 to 1954, a period of nearly one hundred years. More recently a renewed interest in fasting has developed, but we have far to go to recover a biblical balance (*Celebration of Discipline* 47).

Is fasting so easily dismissed from a biblical viewpoint? It is an important question to deal with, considering the rise of interest in fasting among Christians within the past decade. In the mid-1990s I received an invitation from Bill Bright, founder of Campus Crusade, to participate in a gathering in Orlando, Florida, with a group of Christian leaders. Christian leaders gathering is not unusual; however, the purpose for our gathering was most unusual. We were invited to come for three days of fasting and prayer. What occurred during those three days was so powerful that there continues to be a national emphasis on fasting, not only in that one yearly gathering, but within churches and Christian organizations around the United States and many other countries.

The question, then, is critical for us to address today. Is fasting an Old Testament practice intended to phase out with the advent of the church, or is it a biblical practice that God intended to be used by His people for all time? Jesus' teaching on the topic in Matthew 6:16-18 in the Sermon on the Mount assumes even greater relevance for us today with the increased emphasis on fasting.

WHAT IS FASTING?

First of all, what is fasting?[1] To fast is to go without food for a spiritual purpose. In Scripture, it is nearly always linked with prayer. John R.W. Stott explains:

> Strictly speaking, it (fasting) is a total abstention from food. It can be legitimately extended, however, to mean going without food partially or totally, for shorter or longer periods. Hence of course the naming of each day's first meal as "breakfast," since at it we "break our fast," the night period during which we ate nothing (*Christian Counter-Culture* 136).

To properly grasp the intent of Jesus' teaching on fasting, it is vital to see it in the larger context of His immediately previous teaching on prayer and giving. In all three areas of service to God (prayer, giving, and fasting) the Lord is giving a corrective teaching to the abuses of the Pharisees. Taken out of this context, Christians today will have an unbalanced view of any of these three spiritual disciplines.

For instance, in the Lord's teaching on prayer, He instructs us to pray in our closets. Is Jesus teaching against public prayer, or praying in groups? There are some believers today who mistakenly believe so. This is taking the teaching out of context. Jesus was dealing with the tendency of some Jewish religious leaders to pray loudly and eloquently in very public places so that others would be impressed by their spirituality. To correct this ostentatious display of public piety, He instructs us to pray for the right reason: to be heard by our Father in heaven.

The same corrective teaching is given about giving, and in our text, concerning fasting. The tendency among many of the leaders of the Jews, especially among the Pharisees, was to fast on a regular basis. Among the most religious, fast days would occur twice a week, typically on Monday and Thursday.[2] On those days they would demonstrate to the public that they were fasting by their outward appearance. They would wear old clothes, or clothes that were ripped, to show their grief. Their hair would not be combed and some would smear ashes on their faces. All of these things were carefully calculated to demonstrate their piety and to let everyone know they were fasting.

Fasting in this way was not an act of worship or piety, but a self-serving demonstration of worldly religion. Jesus saw through this façade and clearly pointed out that these religious hypocrites received just what they wanted, not the approval of God but of men. He said in verse 16, "they have received their reward in full." This reward was not from God, but from gullible men who were impressed by this outward show of piety. Martin Luther wrote, "It was not Christ's intention to reject or despise fasting. It was His intention to restore proper fasting" (qtd. in Smith 6).

FASTING SHOULD HAVE WHAT ATTITUDE?

To those given to such outward displays of religious ostentation, Jesus basically told them to come back to reality. "Quit acting like something you're not," would be a good paraphrase of Jesus' instructions. His command to put "oil on your head and wash your face" is simply good hygiene. D.A. Carson suggests, "Oil does not here symbolize extravagant joy but normal body care (cf. Ruth 3:3; 2 Samuel 12:20; Psalm 23:5; 104:15; 133:2; Ecclesiastes 9:8; Luke 7:46)" (*Matthew* 176).

Just as we might expect, Jesus does not jump into the details of fasting—how to, why, for how long, etc. His concern is about the intent of the heart while we are fasting. Is it an act done for God, or just to impress others with our spirituality? He does not even address the question with which we began: Should Christians fast today? Or does He?

Notice the structure of the teaching method used by Jesus as He deals with giving, prayer, and fasting. In Matthew 6:2, He says, "So when you give. . . ." Then in 6:5, He continues in the same vein, "And when you pray. . . ." It really should not surprise us then to read in 6:16, "When you fast. . . ." No serious scholar, or for that matter, Christian would suggest that giving or prayer is not for believers today. The same serious attention needs to be given to fasting.

Jesus expected that His followers would fast. He wanted to make sure they did it in a proper attitude. In a clear teaching on the matter of fasting in Matthew 9:14-15, we read:

> Then John's disciples came and asked him, "How is it that we and the Pharisees fast, but your disciples do not fast?" Jesus answered, "How can the guests of the bridegroom mourn while he is with them? The time will come when the bridegroom will be taken from them; then they will fast."

Jesus clearly stated that there will come a time when His followers would fast. After the Lord was no longer present with them in the body, the practice of fasting would assume greater significance, and would become a normal practice for Christians.

As a matter of fact, fasting is seen as a normal part of the Christian experience from the crucifixion until today. The book of Acts records several instances that seem to be normative for the church: "While they were worshiping the Lord and fasting. . . ." (Acts 13:2). "Paul and Barnabas appointed elders for them in each church and, with prayer and fasting committed them to the Lord, in whom they had put their trust" (Acts

14:23). Bill Bright, founder of Campus Crusade, writes, "While fasting and prayer are mentioned only twice in the book of Acts, the discipline apparently was common practice in the Early Church" (12).

Certainly the evidence is in Scripture that permits fasting, but does this text or others require Christians to fast? The best overview of this question is presented by Bill Bright in his powerful book, *The Coming Revival* (12):"Is fasting a commandment? Where does God make it clear that He requires us to fast today?" (12).

After examining the laws of the Old Covenant and the teachings of the New Covenant, David R. Smith concludes: "The Jews were commanded to fast in Old Testament times, in a prescribed manner, (but) there is no similar command to Christians." But he adds:

> Early law was but a type of that which was to be written on the hearts of believers, after they had experienced the New Birth . . . although fasting is not commanded in the New Testament, it is a duty which Christians do perform. . . .
>
> Other authoritative sources agree with this position. Not one argues against spiritual fasting for today. Rather, all encourage it as a grace God has provided for the revival of the individual and the Church (qtd. in Bright 13).

WHY SHOULD WE FAST?

We must eventually come to the question: Why fast? What is its purpose? I see at least three purposes in Scripture for fasting:

1) It humbles us before God.
2) It helps us focus on God.
3) It empowers us through God for service.

God's Word tells us that God opposes the proud, but lifts up the humble. How can we walk in humility before our God? Fasting is the biblical way by which we humble ourselves before Him. Ezra said this in Ezra 8:21: "There, by the Ahava Canal, I proclaimed a fast, so that we might humble ourselves before our God and ask him for a safe journey for us and our children, with all our possessions." And God blessed that humility by providing a safe journey for Ezra and his people as a result of their fasting and prayer.

Humility is a place of receptivity before the Lord. We place ourselves beneath God with open hands to receive from Him. We recognize that we are not God. We do not have all the answers. We desperately need to hear and receive from God. That was the situation in Judah during Jehoshaphat's day. An army from several nations was on the march against them. Outnumbered and in despair, they turned to God and fasted and prayed. Their fasting put them in a place of humility where they could pray the right prayer. Jehoshaphat's prayer, after they had fasted, was not a prayer asking God to bless their efforts or to do what they wanted Him to do. Rather, it was an astonishing prayer of humility in which they said,

O Lord, "we do not know what to do, but our eyes are upon you" (2 Chr. 20:12). Fasting brings us to a proper place of humility before God where we are able to pray such a prayer of faith and dependence.

Daniel is a good example of a man who fasted in such a way as to humble himself before God. In Daniel 9:3 we read, "So I turned to the LORD God and pleaded with him in prayer and petition, in fasting, and in sackcloth and ashes." From this place of humility came a powerful answer from God that resulted in the release of a nation from captivity.

Fasting also helps us to focus ourselves upon God. Doing without food for a period of prayer helps us to put away distractions and turn to Jesus. We are living in a day in which Jesus is calling His church back into an intimate relationship with Him, not just reading books about Him, or listening to others speak of Him, but coming directly to Him and getting to know Him deeply. Fasting is of great assistance as we desire to move closer to Him, because we turn our attention to His agenda rather than our own.

A friend of mine, Christian author Steve Hawthorne, told me recently of a seven-day fast he experienced as he was seeking direction for ministry. At the end of the fast, another friend asked him if he received the guidance he was seeking. Steve replied, "Probably not, but I do know the Guide better now." What a wonderful picture of how the Lord fulfills His promise that if we will come near to Him, He will come near to us (Jas. 4:8).

In the New Testament, the story of the prophetess Anna is a great example of one who lived a life of prayer and fasting, so as to focus on the Lord.

> There was also a prophetess, Anna, the daughter of Phanuel, of the tribe of Asher. She was very old; she had lived with her husband seven years after her marriage, and then was a widow until she was eighty-four. She never left the temple but worshiped night and day, fasting and praying (Luke 2:36-37).

She was truly a woman focused upon the purposes and plans of God. Her years of worship, prayer, and fasting paid off, as she received the great privilege of seeing the Christ child and proclaiming His coming to those around her.

Fasting also is a way for us to be empowered by God for service. There seems to be a release of spiritual power when fasting and prayer are combined. The great men and women of God down through the ages have come to God in prayer and fasting to receive power for greater ministry. Jesus Himself launched His ministry after a forty-day fast. Esther went to the king for mercy and salvation for Israel. It was her day of greatness and ministry to God's people. But it happened after observing a three-day fast with the people of Israel.

In Acts 13 and 14, we have two different accounts of leaders being set apart for service through fasting. Paul and Barnabas were sent off on their first preaching trip by a group of fasting leaders in Antioch. Then, with prayer and fasting, the two set apart elders in the churches for continued leadership and ministry. Something significant can happen when

Christians fast in preparation for service.

I believe the reason for empowerment goes back to the first two points. We humble ourselves and draw near to the Lord through fasting and prayer. Then we are ready to receive power to be used in God's service in an even greater way than before. Having learned humility and intimacy, we are able to be entrusted with greater power as we realize that it is not because of our ability, but rather God working in us. Stott sums it up this way, "Whatever our reasons, Jesus took it for granted that fasting would have a place in our Christian life" (*Christian Counter-Culture* 139).

God is raising up a people who will surrender their lives to be used by Him in these critical days. In fasting there is a surrender of our lives and habits to Him. And He always takes us up on our offers of surrender and subsequent service.

NOTES

[1]While fasting in the ancient world was common among many religions (especially out of fear of demons, in preparation to meet the gods, and in connection with magic), it was especially well established among the Jews. In the Bible, fasting was closely tied to mourning (1 Sam. 31:13), receiving revelation from God (Exod 34:28; Deut. 9:9; Dan. 9:3ff.; 10:2f.), times of emergency (Judg. 20:26; 1 Sam. 7:6), prayer (Jer. 14:12; Neh. 1:4), confession (Neh. 9:1ff.), and perhaps the Day of Atonement (Lev. 16:29ff.), the only prescribed fast in the Law. In the New Testament era, fasting was a sign of inner conversion (Matt. 6:16ff.) and a requisite to missionary service (Acts 13:1ff.). The epistles do not however mention fasting. See *nēstis, nēsteuō, nēsteia*," (Behm, Bromiley 632-33; and Brown 1, 611-13).

[2]An early Christian document, *Didache*, has Christians fasting on Wednesdays and Fridays, so as not to be confused with the Jews (*Didache* 8). Interestingly, this brief book appears as early as AD 90 and probably no later than AD 120. Apparently, the church(es) associated with *Didache* had not caught the essence of Jesus' teaching about the nature of and motives for fasting.

14 ■ Treasure

Matthew 6:19-24

Gene Appel

[19]Do not store up for yourselves treasures on earth, where moth and rust destroy, and where thieves break in and steal. [20]But store up for yourselves treasures in heaven, where moth and rust do not destroy, and where thieves do not break in and steal. [21]For where your treasure is, there your heart will be also. [22]The eye is the lamp of the body. If your eyes are good, your whole body will be full of light. [23]But if your eyes are bad, your whole body will be full of darkness. If then the light within you is darkness, how great is that darkness. [24]No one can serve two masters. Either he will hate the one and love the other, or he will be devoted to the one and despise the other. You cannot serve both God and Money.

I have something at my house that would not mean much to you, but it means a great deal to me. It is a snow ski-rack that can hold several pairs of snow skis and poles. It is made of a beautiful piece of cherry wood, and in the corners there are some snow-scapes painted in oil. If you are a skier, that rack might be useful to you; but it would not be a treasure to you. However, it is a treasure[1] to me.

The wood used to be a piece of cherry paneling in my late father's office—in the office where he studied, prayed, read the Bible, and put messages together. Also it is a treasure because my mother had it made into a ski-rack, and then she hand painted the winter scenes in the corner with her own hands. I know it would not mean much to you—but it is a treasure to me.

Treasures are things we try to keep because of the value we place on them. We go to great lengths to hold on to them, to protect them, because we treasure them.

Both of our daughters have a favorite blanket. One of them has been particularly obsessive about hers, which she has slept with every night of her life. At one time it was a beautiful handmade quilt. Eight years later it is an emaciated, thread-bare, lining-exposed, transparent rag that you might use to check the oil in your car, or scrub the floor, but you would not treasure it. Many times we have suggested retiring this blanky. We have attempted to replace this blanky. But it is very clear that to one little girl in our home it is a treasure.

Everybody has treasures. Even homeless folks will go to great lengths and even risk their lives to hold on to a few items that might seem ridiculous to other people. But to them, the items in their shopping cart are treasures. Maybe there is a photograph, a letter, or an ornament (Willard, *The Divine Conspiracy* 204). We reveal what our treasures are by what we try to protect, secure, hold onto, no matter what.

In Matthew 6:19-24, Jesus forces us to do some uncomfortable wrestling with the issue of our financial treasures. To Jesus, this is not a matter of just money. It is a matter of the heart. It is not a matter of physical possessions, but of our spiritual priorities. It is not just a matter of this life, but eternal life.

Jesus compels us to wrestle with three questions that really reveal where our treasure is. He forces us to take off our mask and be honest with ourselves in an area where we easily deceive ourselves.

WHAT HAS YOUR HEART? (VV. 19-21)

Jesus indicates that our heart tends to get tied up by one of two things: treasures on earth or treasures in heaven. And the teaching is just so clear, "Do not store up for yourselves treasures on earth" (Matt. 5:19a).

Stored up (*thesarizō*) and treasures (*thesauros*) come from the same basic Greek word, which is the source of our English word thesaurus, referring to a treasury of words. A literal translation would be, "Don't treasure up treasures on earth" (MacArthur 409). Jesus is saying, "Don't be seduced by the site of the temporary."

The Las Vegas *Review Journal* reported that some cows in Olympia, Washington, shook loose a pipe on their automatic feeding machine. Tons of grain spilled out on the ground. These cows thought it was great. It was like an all-you-can-eat buffet. They got into a feeding frenzy; and before it was over, thirty-two cows had eaten themselves to death.[2] They were seduced by the site of the temporary.

Jesus seems to be making a similar kind of point about the value of treasuring treasures on earth. "Do not store up for yourselves treasures on earth, where moth and rust destroy, and where thieves break in and steal" (Matt. 6:19).

It is as if Jesus is saying, "You know those Guess jeans you thought you had to have? Guess what's going to happen to them? Moths are going to eat them."

Then He says rust will destroy some of our stuff. Actually the word rust here literally means "an eating." Everywhere else this word is used in the New Testament it is translated "an eating of food, eating a meal" (MacArthur 411). Jesus seems to be saying all those earthly treasures are like pieces of grain that will eventually be eaten by rats, mice, worms, and insects.

Then Jesus says if the moths and rats do not get your stuff, a thief might just come in and take some of it. That happens all of the time. A Las Vegas man was arrested and charged with bilking over $26 million (he even had the $26 million cash in his house) from hundreds of local investors who believed they were going to get incredible returns on their money.[3]

Jesus' point is if you think treasures on earth are where you ought to be putting your treasure, you need to know it is not safe. It is vulnerable.

Yet the dark desire in all of us is to get more. Accumulate more. Indulge more. We are seduced by the site of the temporary, and it never fulfills.

Have you ever been unable to sleep, so you get up and walk out to the refrigerator for a late night raid? I am sure you know how this works. You get up, go to the refrigerator, and open the door. You do not know what you want, but you are hungry for something. You unwrap some aluminum foil and nibble on whatever is in there, even though you are not even sure what it is. Then you do what you tell your kids never to do—you drink some milk right out of the carton. You nibble on a few other things, but nothing really hits the spot or satisfies you. Eventually you close the door and you go back to bed, but you are still hungry. You are still not content. The refrigerator raid was not fulfilling.

I think a late night refrigerator raid is almost a parable of our lives. We say to ourselves, "I would be content if I could just get that house, land that job, get that raise, receive that commission, have that large screen TV, buy that boat, have that RV, make this amount of money, purchase that vacation condo. Then I would feel satisfied."

Jesus is trying to say you will never be satisfied when you treasure the treasures of earth, because moths will eat your clothes; bugs and rats and mice will eat your food; and thieves will steal your money. Instead, Jesus says, "But store up for yourselves treasures in heaven, where moth and rust do not destroy, and where thieves do not break in and steal" (Matt. 6:20).

Jesus is saying this is the only safe investment. It means investing your life in what God is doing, because that is the one thing that cannot be lost. It means putting your treasure into causes that matter forever. The only thing in this world that will last forever is God's Word and people. Everything we own, our stuff, our possessions, our money, is a treasure that we can use to help people find heaven. We can channel them to help people grow in Christ; to meet the needs of the poor, of children, and of young people.[4]

It seems Jesus is teaching there will be people who are in heaven because of the giving we have done to get the message to them. There will be people in heaven who say, "Thanks for giving to your church, because I found Christ in the student ministry of that church. I am in heaven because your generosity made that happen." There will be people in heaven who say, "Thanks for giving to build that building. You have no idea what a turning point it was in my 'forever' when I walked in there for the first time." There will be people from other countries who say, "Hey, thanks for supporting your church, because your support sent a missionary and trained a church leader that came my way. I heard the gospel because of where your treasure was."

Jesus' next statement is very sobering to me; one that continually causes me to re-evaluate my own finances: "For where your treasure is, there your heart will be also" (Matt. 6:21). It is as if Jesus is saying, "If you want to know what really has your heart, just look at your check book register; at your Visa bill. Look what is getting your treasure."[5]

Let me set your mind at ease by letting you know that this text is not prohibiting being prudent with your financial life. Elsewhere in the Bible we are taught to provide for our families and to make reasonable plans for the future. If you are a saver (an investor and setting some things aside for the future and contingencies), or if you are wealthy, Jesus is not condemning wealth any more than He is condemning all clothes, things, or possessions. We are even told that God has given us these things for our enjoyment. Jesus is prohibiting loving and treasuring things. This is prohibiting being a materialist who loves money and has an unhealthy drive for more. This is prohibiting your being stingy and miserly and hoarding it all for yourself.

Let me tell you what makes me uncomfortable about this. Sometimes I wonder if I am deceiving myself in my own financial management by saying, "I am just being prudent and a wise steward by the way I save and invest or take care of my family, as God has instructed me," when in reality I am holding on to more resources than I really need.[6]

Do you know what I think keeps this world from being evangelized more than anything else? I do not think we need more evangelism seminars, to train more people, to produce more gospel tracts, or have more crusades. Those are good and needed. However, I think the biggest roadblock above any other is just the sheer amount of materialism that gets its grip on people like you and me in the church. When we can break that, we will store up treasures in heaven; and our hearts will be in the right place.

WHERE IS YOUR VISION? (VV. 22-23)

Jesus uses an interesting metaphor. He says:
"The eye is the lamp of the body. If your eyes are good, your whole body will be full of light. But if your eyes are bad, your whole body will be full of darkness. If then the light within you is darkness, how great is that darkness!" (Matt. 6:22-23).
The eye is the only means of vision our body has. Without an eye we cannot see light. With a bad eye, our body is still full of darkness. If we have a good eye, our body will be full of light. This metaphor has to do with our spiritual vision. If it is cluttered by materialism and greed, we will be spiritually blind. If it is focused on what matters to God, we will be focused on what is really valuable. What we focus on is what we move toward.

When I worked on a farm and planted corn or soybeans, pulling an eight-row planter behind a tractor, do you know how I kept those rows semi-straight? I would pick out something on the horizon—like a telephone pole, a tree, a parked truck—and drive toward it, because what I focused on was what I moved toward. The same is true with spiritual vision. For instance, do you drive a little differently when you are driving next to a police car? Of course you do. One of the things that Jesus teaches is that God is always with us—always watching us. So, suppose God came down again in human form, as He did in Jesus; and He was with you all day so that you could see Him. Would you have done one or two things differently in the last few days? Of course you would have! So the question is, do we show by our actions that we really believe that He is with us? Are we focusing our spiritual vision and moving toward what matters to Him? Are we reflecting it in the way we channel our resources?

If you want to know where your treasure is, ask yourself if you have God's vision for people who need His love and grace. For example, when you look at lost, spiritually unconnected people, do you love them as Jesus loved them? Are you broken by their lost condition like He is? If so, you are walking in the light; and you have the right spiritual vision. The only investments of our lives, our resources, our time, and our talents that will last are the ones we ultimately make in other people. The truth is we all struggle to keep our vision focused on the right things. Sometimes we focus on a certain kind of house; and we get over-extended to get that house, hoping that one day our income will catch up. Some guys are driving big over-extensions of themselves. Some over-extend themselves on credit cards. Isn't it amazing? We will over-extend ourselves to get more stuff; but when it comes to God's kingdom, we say, "Well I wish I could do more. . . ." But the reason we cannot do more is because something else has our heart and our vision.

Imagine what could happen if we really got our spiritual vision right. What would it mean to reach thousands of children and teenagers? How many families would be restored through the power of Christ? How many churches could we start? How many fully devoted followers of Christ could we build? How many poor, struggling, and under-resourced people could we help? The key question is, Where is our vision? What we focus on is what we will move toward.

WHO IS YOUR MASTER? (V. 24)

Jesus continues in verse 24 acknowledging the obvious: "No one can serve two masters." The analogy is that of a slave. Jesus is pointing out that no slave can be the property of two different owners. The essence of slavery is single ownership and full-time service (Stott 158). There is an exclusiveness of devotion.

"No one can serve two masters. Either he will hate the one and love the other, or he will be devoted to the one and despise the other. You cannot serve both God and Money" (Matt. 6:24). Jesus indicates there is a contest going on between the God who made us—and entrusted us with all we have and who gave His only Son to save us from hell forever—and money. Every day there is this battle going on to see who is going to be in charge of our lives today. Who is going to lead our lives?

The thought is this: if we are dividing our allegiance between God and money, we have already given in to money. So, we have to learn how to own things without loving them. We have to learn how to possess money without it possessing us. We have to learn how to prize the donor instead of the gifts He has given us, because the supreme act of cosmic treason would be to prize the gift above the donor (Green 85).

How do we demonstrate who is our Master? We become like our Master and give by storing up treasure in heaven. I have had many interesting conversations with people about the subject of giving. For the most part, what the majority of people are trying to figure out is, "How little can I give and keep God happy with me? I don't want to be greedy, but I want to know where the line is. I want to get as close to greed as I can, without being greedy."

Hebrews chapter 11 contains those men and women in the Bible who possessed an unusual level of trust in God. It is interesting that the first person mentioned there is honored because he gave an offering. "It was faith that made Abel's offering to God a better sacrifice than Cain's. Through his faith he won God's approval as a righteous man because God approved of his giving" (Heb. 11:4 GN). Abel's brother Cain gave an offering that was safe. It did not take any faith. He did not have to trust God to provide. But Abel gave an offering that took a great deal of faith. It was an offering that stretched him, and he had to trust God.

Have you ever tested God's trustworthiness like that? Back in 1986, the church where I served asked its members to make a commitment over and above their regular tithes and offerings for a badly needed building expansion. I really wrestled with what God would want me to do. Was He my Master or was I just mouthing the words? I was twenty-six years old. My income was just over thirty thousand dollars a year. Out of that, I was already obeying God's Word by tithing. I was making a house payment and a car payment. I paid for all of my own health insurance and was attempting to contribute to a retirement plan. Honestly, after the bills were paid, there just was not a lot left. I barely had a savings account—one in name only to make me feel better—but there was nothing in it.

I prayed for my Master to lead me and went out on a limb of faith. I made a commitment that, over three years, I would give ten thousand dollars toward that project. I had no idea where the money would come from. And God used that period in my life to teach me something about sacrifice. I also learned who my Master was.

Eight years later, our church was facing a relocation project. My wife, Barbara, and I had just gotten married; and we had to wrestle with our contribution. It was uncomfortable. We prayed, we talked, and we had vocal disagreements with each other. We studied the Bible and finally both had a sense of God's guidance on the issue. We decided to make sacrifices, because of who our Master is. Our sacrifice was nothing compared to the woman who gave her last two copper coins at the temple. But we dipped into some retirement funds for part of it. We gave up health club memberships. We cut back on entertainment expenses and eating out. We sold our house, which had accumulated some equity. Our giving became the biggest single item in our budget—bigger than our house payment, bigger than our automobile budget. And amazingly we found that in addition to our tithes, God enabled us to give an amount many times greater than the size of that commitment made back in 1986.

Laying up treasures in heaven like that have been some of the most spiritually stretching, defining moments in my life. When I look at what God is doing in the church where I serve, I can honestly say there is nothing I have done with my money in the last ten years that even holds a candle to that. I need challenges in my life, because without them I can slip back into being comfortable and not even wrestle with who my Master is.

Is it clear by our giving who our Master is? We need to take those kinds of steps in giving that show us that God truly is our Master. It is hard to let go of our stuff, isn't it? I have a good friend who was frustrated with his wife when they were getting ready to move. She refused to depart with some of their stuff, which he knew they would never use or miss, but she would not let him give it away. So, he put it all in a box, sealed it with packing tape, and marked it, "Stuff my wife will never ever use." Six years later when they got ready for their next move, that stuff was still in the box, never opened. It is hard to let go of stuff; but when we do, we build up treasure in heaven and experience the blessings of a God who longs to give to us.

So, what do we treasure? What has our heart? Treasures on earth that can be eaten and destroyed? Or treasures in heaven? Jesus said where our treasure is determines where our heart is.

Where's our vision? Do we look at people and opportunities through God's lenses? Is it clear that reaching people who matter to God is the greatest thrill in life?

Who is our master? It is impossible to have two. We will hate the one and love the other; or be devoted to one and despise the other. Ultimately, the only way we know what we treasure is when we are willing to honor the Donor above the gift and give away chunks of it freely in order to advance His causes. Maybe more than anything that tells who our Master really is.[7]

NOTES

[1]Matthew uses the noun *thēsauros* three times (6:19,20,21). The word expresses the idea of a place of safe keeping. For a quick and concise overview of the word see W.E. Vine's *An Expository Dictionary of New Testament Words* (Old Tappan, NJ: Fleming H. Revell Co., 1966 reprint). Vol. IV, Set-Z, p. 152. See G.L. Archer's article, "Possessions," for a fuller treatment of the *thēsauros* and associated words in *Dictionary of New Testament Theology*. Vol. 2, 829-53. *Thēsauros* occurs sixteen times in the Synoptic Gospels, mostly on the lips of Jesus (for examples in Matt. see 2:11; 6:19,20,21; 13:52; and 19:2). The verb

thēsaurizō, "store up," occurs twice in this passage, once in 6:19 and once in 6:20.

[2]*Las Vegas Review Journal*, March 28, 1998.

[3]As reported by KLAS, channel 8, Las Vegas, 2002.

[4]One of the great Christian devotional classics is William Law's *A Serious Call to a Devout and Holy Life*. Law says we must seek to please God with all our possessions. "As the holiness of Christianity consecrates all states and employments of life unto God, requiring us to do and use everything as the servants of God, so are we more specially obliged to observe this religious exactness in the use of our estates and fortune. . . . There is no middle way to be taken, any more than there is a middle way between pride and humility and temperance and intemperance" (42, 46).

[5]No Gospel writer addresses the urgency of how we use the money and possessions entrusted to our care like Matthew. There are eighteen specific statements, 109 verses, devoted to this subject in his Gospel. See Matt. 2:1ff.; 4:1ff.; 6:1ff.; 6:19ff.; 6:25ff.; 9:9; 10:5ff.; 17:24; 18:21; 19:1ff.; 20:1-16; 22:15-22; 23:23-24; 25:1ff.; 26:6; 26:14; 27:4; and 28:11. Matthew is the only Gospel writer who begins his story of Jesus by having wise men bring Him gifts and conclude that story with Roman soldiers being bribed to lie about the resurrection. For Matthew money and possessions matter!

[6]Richard Foster offers ten controlling principles that can guide the Jesus-follower into practical, whole-life stewardship. See *Money, Sex and Power* (San Francisco: Harper, 1985).

–Buy things for their usefulness, rather than their status.

–Reject anything that produces an addiction in us.

–Develop a habit of giving things away.

–Refuse to be propagandized by the custodians of modern gadgetry.

–Learn to enjoy things without owning them.

–Develop a deeper appreciation for creation.

–Look with a healthy skepticism on all "buy now and pay later" schemes.

–Obey Jesus' instructions. . . .

–Reject anything that breeds the oppression of others.

–Shun any thing that distracts from following Jesus.

[7]The text pushes us into the very essence of discipleship. The primary question Jesus raises is: Who will be the boss of my life? Matthew uses the plural form of *kurios*, "Lord," to express this call to radical discipleship. Throughout the New Testament (717 occurrences) the word has a wide range of usages from that of master, to owner, to simply addressing another person with respect (i.e., emperor or king in Acts 25:26 or Rev. 17:14). "The Lordship of the messiah, Jesus, is a present reality. He is exercising in a hidden way God's authority and Lordship over the world and will bring it to completion in the eschatological future" (see H. Beintenhard, *Dictionary of New Testament Theology*. Vol. 2, 510-20).

15 ■ Worry

Matthew 6:25-34

Mike Breaux

²⁵Therefore I tell you, do not worry about your life, what you will eat or drink; or about your body, what you will wear. Is not life more important than food, and the body more important than clothes? ²⁶Look at the birds of the air; they do not sow or reap or store away in barns, and yet your heavenly Father feeds them. Are you not much more valuable than they? ²⁷Who of you by worrying can add a single hour to his life? ²⁸And why do you worry about clothes? See how the lilies of the field grow. They do not labor or spin. ²⁹Yet I tell you that not even Solomon in all his splendor was dressed like one of these. ³⁰If that is how God clothes the grass of the field, which is here today and tomorrow is thrown into the fire, will he not much more clothe you, O you of little faith? ³¹So do not worry, saying, "What shall we eat?" or "What shall we drink?" or "What shall we wear?" ³²For the pagans run after all these things, and your heavenly Father knows that you need them. ³³But seek first his kingdom and his righteousness, and all these things will be given to you as well. ³⁴Therefore do not worry about tomorrow, for tomorrow will worry about itself. Each day has enough trouble of its own.

Debbie just put some fresh-baked cookies on the counter and I'm grabbing a few as I start to write this. I love these things—warm, gooey, melt-in-your-mouth, chocolate chip—oh man!

So, as I begin to write this chapter and eat this cookie, I am thinking of one of the most successful advertising campaigns in years. The ads have been widely popular. They are in magazines. You have seen them on billboards, buses, and television. They depict various men and women, some famous, some not, who have obviously just taken a big gulp of milk, sporting those white mustaches. At the bottom of the picture is a two-word question, "Got Milk?"

I am guessing that as you read this, you are not sporting a white-milk mustache, but perhaps you have just taken a big gulp of life lately, and the more appropriate question would be, "Got Worry?"

Worry is a part of life and it affects us all, from the child to the parent, from the executive to the homemaker, from the college student to the retiree. It can seep into every fiber of our being, permeate all of our relationships, and steal all of our personal joy. So let me ask you again, "Got Worry?"

Do the following statements resonate with you? "The Dow Jones is down again!" "These kids are driving me crazy!" "I can't take one more day at this job!" "What do you mean overdrawn?!" "Please, just give me a little more time!"

Are you dealing with something, trying to process something, fix something, control something? And is that something just dominating your mind these days? What is it that is causing you to toss and turn all night, worry all day, and throw down mass quantities of TUMS? Proverbs 12:25 says, "An anxious heart weighs a man down." You read that and say, "Man, that's so true! I feel like an elephant is sitting on my chest!"

And into all that Jesus speaks, "It doesn't have to be that way!":

So I tell you, don't worry about everyday life—whether you have enough food, drink, and clothes. Doesn't life consist of more than food and clothing? Look at the birds. They don't need to plant or harvest or put food in barns because your heavenly Father feeds them. And you are far more valuable to him than they are. Can all your worries add a single moment to your life? Of course not (Matt. 6:25-27 NLT).

In my very first ministry at South Fork Church of Christ, deep in the cornfields of Rochester, Illinois, I had an old farmer give me his simple definition of worry: "Worry is getting all worked up over a bunch of stuff you ain't got no control over no-how!" Perhaps a bit grammatically challenged, but right on the money!

There are several things I have learned about getting all worked up with worry.

WORRY IS UNPRODUCTIVE

Can all your worries add a single moment to your life? Of course not. Jesus and my farming buddy were right: "Ain't no use getting all worked up!" There is nothing productive about worry. It does not make your relationships, finances, or job any better. It does not make you look any better or smile easier. It does not increase your contentment level. It does not make you more fun to be around. And you know what? It does not keep that something from happening either.

Now being prayerfully concerned about something and worrying about it are two different things. Worry is all about me, trying to fix, control, solve, and manipulate. Prayerful concern (unless it is just a spiritual sounding disguise for what in reality is worry) is recognizing that there is only One who sees the bigger picture and is in control of my life.

The Apostle Paul knew a lot about worry and anxiety. A lot of people in the Bible dealt with pressure, but Paul dealt with it on another level. Read 2 Corinthians 11 sometime and see how your worry-filled life stacks up! One day he found himself chained to a Roman guard in a prison cell, and he writes this to a bunch of worried people in the city of Philippi.

Look what he says to them in Philippians 4:6-7:

Do not be anxious about anything, but in everything, by prayer and petition, with thanksgiving, present your requests to God. And the peace of God, which transcends all understanding, will guard your hearts and your minds in Christ Jesus.

"Do not be anxious about anything. . . . I tell you, don't worry about your life." Hmmm, kind of sounds like Paul and Jesus had been talking! Both encountered enormous worrying situations. That's life. But both knew just how unproductive internalizing worry and anxiety can be.[1]

The word anxious[2] means "to be pulled in different directions." That sure describes my life at times. How about yours? We are pulled in one direction by our priorities, another direction by our pressures, another direction by our schedules, and yet another by our dreams.

One of the popular toys when my kids were little was a guy named Stretch Armstrong. Remember him? He was kind of like Gumby on steroids! You could just stretch him all kinds of different ways. A lot of us are like ol' Stretch. We look strong and cool and calm and tanned and relaxed, but really we're being stretched and pulled apart a hundred different directions. And that is so unproductive.

WORRY IS UNHEALTHY

I have a friend who is fond of saying, "It's not so much what you eat that kills you, but rather what eats you."

Worry will literally eat you alive. Acid reflux, chest pains, mental meltdowns, ulcers, sleep disorders, high blood pressure—all produced by worry. Worry has reached epidemic proportions in our culture. The U.S. Center for Disease Control estimates that half the deaths in our country between the ages of one and sixty-five are due to our worrying lifestyles. We Americans consume eight hundred million dollars worth of anti-anxiety pills annually. Worry, anxiety, and panic attacks drain us mentally, physically, emotionally, and spiritually.[3]

WORRY IS UNNECESSARY

Jesus says, "Look at the birds. Check out the lilies of the field. Does God not take care of them? We are talking feathers and flowers. You are much more valuable than they are!"

> Said the Robin to the sparrow
> I would really like to know
> Why those anxious human beings
> Rush about and worry so.
> Said the sparrow to the robin,
> Well, I guess that it must be
> That they have no heavenly Father
> Such that cares for you and me.[4]

With a Father capable of providing for all of our needs and the price tag He has placed on us, worry is absolutely unnecessary.

WORRY IS UNSPIRITUAL

Matthew 6:31-32 says, "So don't worry about having enough food or drink or clothing. Why be like the pagans who are so deeply concerned about these things?" (NLT).

He is saying, "Why live your life like there is no God? That's what pagans believe and that's how they act, chasing this and that. Worry takes God off His throne and substitutes other gods, and those other gods are not worthy of your worship and service."

Can you add a single moment to your life by worrying? Can it enhance your health? Do you or do you not matter to your Father? You see, worry is this unproductive, unhealthy, unnecessary, unspiritual way of getting all worked up over a bunch of stuff you "ain't got no control over no how!"

LETTING GOD BE GOD

When Jesus said to seek first the kingdom of God and all these things will be added to you, He was not only giving us a prescription for worry, He was giving us the one essential of life—live in God's hands.[5]

I read a few years ago about two single adults who decided to go on a creative date to top all creative dates. Romantic dinner? Nope—old school! Movie? Dark and boring! Bowling? Miniature golf? Laser-tag? Not even close! These two people, Stephen Trotter and Lori Martin, decided to have an X-treme Games kind of date together. Do you know what they did? They spent twenty-five thousand dollars (I said the date was creative, not cheap!) building a ten-foot long, six-foot diameter capsule whose steel interior was wrapped with fiberglass, covered with Styrofoam, and equipped with air tanks. You know why? Because this couple wanted to be the first man and woman team to ever go over Niagara Falls together inside a barrel.

Talk about some bonding time. I think you would pretty much figure out right there whether you were meant for each other or not! Only a dozen people have ever gone over Niagara Falls and lived to tell about it in the history of man, as far as we know. But no man and woman ever did it together before. So—whatever possessed them—they built this barrel, took their lives in their hands, and got inside.

Now as I read this story, I started asking the question, "Once inside the barrel, how do you get in the water? Do you get in the barrel in the parking lot and just start rocking until finally the barrel starts rolling down the hill and into the river?" Well, the article simply said something like: "Trotter's brother, Dan, and five friends pushed the capsule into the water about 100 yards from the falls on the Canadian side of the river. About fifteen seconds later, they had safely drifted to an eddy below Scenic Tunnel, a popular tourist attraction." As I read that, my heart started to beat pretty fast. I do have just a little bit of a risk-taker in me and he is thinking: good barrel, good company—that might be a rush! But the thing that really got my heart beating was those three words "fifteen seconds later"!

You see what I love about this picture is that there was a place where this man and woman let go of everything, totally yielding their lives to the flow and current of that mighty river. And for fifteen seconds their lives were completely out of their hands. And I thought that's the way I want to live—not in some irresponsible, going-over-Niagara kind of way, but totally and radically surrendered to God! I want my life to be completely out of my hands saying every day:

> God I really trust You for everything, and I want to throw my life
> into Your river. I want to get off the shore, step off of the banks,
> jump off the dock, and say my life is in Your hands. Wherever the
> flow and the current of Your mighty wisdom takes me, let it be so![6]

I have such a long way to go in so many areas of my life. God is still working on me. In fact, He is clocking some pretty heavy overtime in a few areas! But I look back at my life, and I can really see how He has been teaching me to trust Him and to walk away from worry. I do not run after stuff anymore. I do not chase the approval of others as before. I do not worry and wig-out about little things nearly as often. I have been reducing the noise of my life. Instead of wringing my hands and turning into some cynical basket case, I talk to Him more these days. I am learning to be still and know that He is God and I am not. I am saying no to some very good things that could fill my schedule, so that I may say yes to the vital things that must fill my life. And do you know what has been happening? The transcendent, unexplainable peace of God has been guarding my heart and my mind! I love living life this way—this day, this moment—in His hands.

Now that I think about it, those are the very lessons that Dr. Marion Henderson taught so many of us by word and by example in the class-room, on the basketball court, and in the church.

So as I finish this chapter and this chocolate chip cookie, I'll ask you again, Got worry? I can honestly say today, "Not me." But I sure could use a glass of milk!

NOTES

[1] Paul in Phil. 4:6 and Jesus in Matt. 6:25 use the same word *merimnate* to convey the pro-hibition, "Stop worrying."

[2] According to J. Goetzmann ("Care, Anxiety." *Dictionary of the New Testament Theology,* Vol. 1., Ed. by Colin Brown) this word family covers a range of responses from the sim-ple, "to care for," or "to be concerned about," (as in Paul's concern for the churches in 2 Cor. 11:28) to the more intense, "to be anxious about." Obviously it is the latter that is being prohibited by both Paul and Jesus.

[3] For further insights on the effects of anxiety see Rollo May's classic, *The Meaning of Anxiety*; and for study of the effects of stress, see Hans Selye's *The Stress of Life.*

[4] "Overheard in an Orchard" by Elizabeth Cheney.

[5] As Larry Chouinard observes, "The imperative 'seeks' (*zēteite*) calls for a persistent wholehearted devotion to the realization of God's reign in one's life. . . . When his 'king-

dom and his righteousness' are given ultimate priority, the disciple can be assured that God will provide the necessities of life (i.e., food, drink, clothing). Anxiety is therefore incompatible with a life devoted to the pursuit of God's kingdom" (*Matthew* 135-36).

⁶Though not all of us are thrill seekers John R.W. Stott (*Christian Counter-Culture* 160) rightly observes in his commentary on the Sermon on the Mount, "Jesus took it for granted that all human beings are 'seekers'.... We need something to live for, something to give meaning to our existence, something to 'seek,' something on which to set our 'hearts' and 'minds.'"

16 ■ Judging Justly

Matthew 7:1-6

Joe Grana

¹Do not judge, or you too will be judged. ²For in the same way you judge others,
you will be judged, and with the measure you use, it will be measured to you.
³Why do you look at the speck of sawdust in your brother's eye and pay
no attention to the plank in your own eye? ⁴How can you say to your brother,
"Let me take the speck out of your eye," when all the time there is a plank in
your own eye? ⁵You hypocrite, first take the plank out of your own eye, and then
you will see clearly to remove the speck from your brother's eye. ⁶Do not give
dogs what is sacred; do not throw your pearls to pigs. If you do, they may
trample them under their feet, and then turn and tear you to pieces.

In May, 1995, my father-in-law passed away. After the funeral we
stayed a few days in Indiana. One day I decided to mow their two-acre
yard on the riding lawn mower. The speeds vary. It was fun to go forward
and backward. It was challenging to weave between the trees and get close
enough to the tree trunks to minimize the trimming. The challenge was to
do this while driving as fast as possible.

For a while precision steering demonstrated excellent results. But
then, suddenly, in the twinkling of an eye, something went wrong. The
trees are a weeping willow-type with many branches hanging down in
umbrella-like fashion. From these little twigs protrude.

While making a sharp fast turn, one of these twigs jumped out at me.
I turned my head, but not quickly enough. As I raced past the limb, a twig
stuck in the side of my eye! I stopped the lawn mower as quickly as possible. Seeing the four-inch twig extended from my eye, I freaked. My first
reaction was to pull it out, which I did. Calmly I asked my brother-in-law
how to contact a doctor. Fortunately, the twig did not hit the pupil of my
eye. The intrusion left a hole; my contact was ripped. Thankfully, the eye
heals quickly; and the contact is easily replaced.

With the twig in my eye, my view was distorted. I could see, but not
clearly. Mostly, I could see the twig. Even with the twig removed, my

sight was hindered. My contact was ripped and needed to be taken out. Now my eyes were focused differently. I still did not see clearly until the hole healed and the contact was replaced.

The earliest commentary found on this passage is from *Didache* 9:5. Here an explanation of the overall text is not given, but simply an application. The comments explain the proper way to participate in the Lord's Supper or Eucharist. Prayers for the cup and broken bread are given. Then this commentary is included: "But let no one eat or drink of your Eucharist except those who have been baptized into the name of the Lord, for the Lord has spoken concerning this: 'Do not give what is holy to dogs'" (Holmes 154).

This appears to be a "narrow definition of a general principle" (France 142). To just apply this text to the Lord's Supper does not do justice to it. For our purposes, this explanation begins at the end of our study. Therefore, let us return to the first part of this text.

JUDGMENT

Emphatically, the passage starts *mē krinete*—"Not judge" or "do not judge." A minor debate starts here. The *Parsing Guide* (Han 10) states the verb can be indicative or imperative. The Complete Biblical Library (124) opts for the present, while Lenski and Chouinard (132) lean toward the imperative. The former could construe the meaning to be a prohibition of continuous judging, not judgment itself. The imperative "may mean to assist a course of action or to desist from such a course" (Lenski 288). "The present imperative (*krinete*) preceded by '*mē*' suggests a general rule of conduct best understood as 'don't get into the habit of being judgmental' or 'don't make judgmentalism a part of your lifestyle'" (Chouinard 138).

The wording is very emphatic, using repetition: "Judge not that you might not be judged: for with the judgment you judge, you will be judged and with the measure you measure you will be measured." Jesus is definitely demonstrating the importance of the concept judging rightly and its ramification in one's life.

Of course, the issue is: what does judge mean? One's understanding of judge determines the whole passage. Here are some ideas worth evaluating:

1) "... they span the scale from an aesthetic discerning to a legal act of a judiciary" (Guelich 349).

2) "...carries the connotation 'condemn' ... fault-finding, condemnatory attitude. ..." (France 142).

3) "... not only false judgment is forbidden, but a censorious habit of mind" (McNeile 901).

4) "... condemn, discern. It cannot refer here to law courts ... still less does this verse forbid all judging of any kind" (Carson, *Matthew* 183).

5) "condemn not, come to no formal decision, do not usurp the throne of judgment, or pass a sentence, or find a final verdict" (Morgan 72).

6) ". . . Nor must we judge of their eternal state. . . ." (Henry 1233).

7) "The LXX mostly has *krinō* for legal terms . . . the NT . . . in either an official or personal sense (Büschel, Bromiley 469).

8) "Separate, distinguish, then select, prefer" (Bauer 451).

More opinions could be added to this list. However, these will suffice. The consensus, although not unanimous, is that Jesus is speaking of an attitude that is continually critical and condemning. One cannot help to evaluate. In fact, evaluation or discernment is continually necessary regarding decisions, actions, motives of self and others. A condemning attitude, however, is a whole different matter. "But Jesus is here talking about the self-righteous, egotistical judgment and unmerciful condemnation of others" (MacArthur 433).

Stott seems to be correct when he writes:

To begin with we must reject Tolstoy's belief, based on this verse, that "Christ totally forbids the human institution of any law court," and that he "could mean nothing else by those words" (175). . . . If then Jesus was neither abolishing law courts nor forbidding criticism, what did he mean by *judge not*? In a word "censoriousness" (176). . . . To sum up, the command to *judge not* is not a requirement to be blind, but rather a plea to be generous (177).

Jesus gives a reason to watch one's attitude: it will come back. What goes around, comes around. A person reaps what he sows. If a person judges and is judged, who does the judging? D.A. Carson writes:

They may mean that the measure we use on others will be the measure others use on us; the person with the critical spirit is inviting a lot of criticism. Alternately, verse 2 may mean that the measure we use on others will be the measure God himself will use on us. . . . I think it is the latter meaning that is in view; . . . we should abolish judgmental attitudes lest we ourselves stand utterly condemned before God (*The Sermon on the Mount* 100).

The prospect is a serious one. It demands an attitude check. Furthermore, it demands insight.

What Jesus here forbids is self-righteous, officious, hasty, unmerciful, prejudiced, and unwarranted condemnation based on human standards and human understanding. He gives three reasons why such judgment is sinful: it reveals an erroneous view of God, an erroneous view of others, and an erroneous view of ourselves (MacArthur 433).

SUPERIORITY

Jesus' use of hyperbole here may well have been humorous to His audience. Even though the subject matter is extremely serious, Jesus uses examples that are extremely outrageous. The grammar makes an interesting shift from verse one to verse three. The command of "judge not" is second person plural—you all. But when He asks, "but why do you look at the speck . . .", He changes to second person singular. The general command has a personal application!

The speck is usually viewed as something small: splinter (McReynolds 22); chip, small piece of straw, chaff, wood, foreign object in a wine cup (Bauer 405). The log is a beam, "the branch of a tree, or a massive piece of timber" (Morgan 72). These terms are not used anywhere else in the New Testament. It is most difficult to see anything, let alone a speck, when one has a beam in the eye! The image is obvious.

However, none of this means the speck does not need removal. It does. Anyone wearing contacts especially understands this physical reality. Yet, in the circumstances, one desires the helper to see clearly to get the speck or eyelash out of the eye. "We may say that the man with the beam in his eye will knock out both of the eyes of the other man who has a splinter in his eye. A grand eye specialist he would be!" (Lenski 280). The same is true spiritually.

The problem with the helper is his blindness to his own shortcomings. The problem is one of attitude, taking God's place to judge. The problem is one of superiority to help. It may, however, be a cover up. Jesus' use of notice the log is *katanoeis*. It means "observe carefully" (Bauer 415) or "think carefully" (McReynolds 22). The *kata* adds intensity to the thinking. That intense awareness and thought is missing from the undiscerning, judgmental person.

This individual (you, me) must first be aware of his own (your, my) shortcomings (or, in this case, longcomings) and intentionally remove them. Then we are in a position to help others without destroying them.

DISCERNMENT

Jesus goes on, "Hypocrite, [ouch] throw out [imperative] your log." It should be noted that the word "hypocrite" is only found in the Synoptics and always used by the Lord (Vine 242). Hypocrite is only here applied to a disciple rather than to Jesus' Jewish opponents (France 143).

In fact, the verses are again interesting. "Why do you see (*blepeis*) the speck" transitions to "then you will see clearly (*diablepseis*) the speck." The addition of *dia* shows the intensity of the clarity. The concept shows:

1) "respect for others . . . we can be discerning without being judgmental. The approach of love to use personal power or privilege is to benefit another" (Augsburger 95).
2) ". . . the hypocrite's error is not his diagnosis, but his failure to apply to himself the criticism he so meticulously applies to his brother" (France 143).
3) "'Correct him,' said Chrysostom . . . 'but not as a foe, nor as an adversary exacting a penalty, but as a physician providing medicines'" (Stott 180).

At first read, a transition in thought is missing. How can Jesus go from specks and logs, being non-judgmental, to dogs and pigs, making judgments? John Stott quotes Charles Spurgeon, "The saints are not judges, but 'saints are not simpletons' either" (Stott 180). Not being condemning does not mean Jesus' disciples are not to make judgments. Perhaps a better way to think of it is we are to evaluate but not be judgmental.

Verse six goes back to the second person plural. After individualizing His command not to judge, Jesus broadens the possibility (subjunctive) of giving and throwing as another principle to follow.

Again, there are differences of opinion about what is even originally said here. For example, William Barclay:

With the exception of one word the parallelism is complete. Give is paralleled by cast; dogs by swine; but holy is not really balanced by pearls. . . . The word for holy is kadosh [kdsh]; and the Aramaic word for ear-ring is kadasha [kdsh]. . . . Still further, in the Talmud, 'an ear-ring in a swine's snout' is a proverbial phrase for something which is entirely incongruous and out of place. It is by no means impossible that the original phrase ran:

Give not an ear-ring to the dogs neither cast ye your pearls before swine (Barclay 271).

Although this has a ring of possibility, the textual evidence does not warrant it. "Holy" fits in especially when thinking about holy meat sacrificed at the altar. This meat is reserved for God and the priests, not dogs. These dogs, by the way, are not likely domesticated, since few were in Israel at the time. Jesus is referring to wild dogs. By paralleling dogs to swine, Jesus is thinking of the same group of people.

At any rate, the dogs and pigs do not appreciate the value of what is given them. They will trample (treat with disdain—Bauer 415) the holy truths and maul (NRSV) the one trying to share the truths. Jesus is stating "we must exercise discrimination and discretion" (Morgan 73). "And so, after warning us against judgmentalism, Jesus warns us against being undiscriminating" (Carson, *The Sermon on the Mount* 104).

CONCLUSION

The words of Jesus here are very strong. As Dallas Willard states, this is a "warning against 'condemnation engineering' as a plan for helping people" (*Divine Conspiracy* 138). We must watch our attitude. We are not to take God's place of judging. Not only is it His right, but we have more than enough faults of our own. We need to focus first on ourselves. Then we can help others. Yet, even then, it should be as a brother or sister, not a judge. We are fellow strugglers. We can become wounded healers, but we are not better than they are.

If we choose a condemning attitude, we are in jeopardy of receiving a similar judgment from God. The risk is not worth the attitude. We are to find the "right balance of humility and helpfulness" (MacArthur 436).

On the other hand, we are to be discerning. Not everyone is willing or ready to receive the holy truths of God. They will not appreciate them. In these cases, we must evaluate the risk of sharing. In a sense, we must judge the receptivity of others. It may be better to wait for a more opportune time. We may have to be discerning about "wasting time on the hardened" (Green, *Matthew for Today* 87). "In other words, use discretion as you share the truth of God with others" (Mounce 62).

17 ▪ Ask, Seek, Knock

Matthew 7:7-12

Denny Slaughter

> ⁷Ask and it will be given to you; seek and you will find; knock, and the door will be opened to you. ⁸For everyone who asks receives; he who seeks finds; and to him who knocks, the door will be opened. ⁹Which of you, if his son asks for bread, will give him a stone? ¹⁰Or if he asks for a fish, will give him a snake? ¹¹If you, then, though you are evil, know how to give good gifts to your children, how much more will your Father in heaven give good gifts to those who ask him! ¹²In everything, do to others what you would have them do to you, for this sums up the Law and the Prophets.

Did you ever wonder how you could connect with the Creator of the world? Well, Jesus tells us how we are to relate to God. Interestingly, He seems to be saying that the main way we get close to God is through prayer. That is right—prayer! Not worship, praise, stewardship, reading the Bible, or going to church, but prayer. They say confession is good for the soul, so let me confess to you that prayer is not my strong suit. I am convinced that there is no more intense time of spiritual warfare than during a time in the prayer closet alone with our heavenly Father.

I have always felt we have missed something when it comes to prayer. Oh, I pray and I am sure you do, too; but is prayer the basis of our relationship with God? Or is prayer something we just do out of a sense of duty? We pray before meals, in public when the occasion demands, and, of course, at the end of the day; but is prayer the heartbeat of our faith? Do we long for those wonderful moments we can spend alone with our heavenly Father? Or, let's be honest, is prayer time something to get through so we can continue with the really important stuff of the day?

For Jesus prayer was much more than a function or thing of duty. There must have been an aura when He prayed. Maybe the disciples could not see it, but they knew it was there—a feeling, a mood, something that caused all who listened to Him pray to know that they were in the very presence of holiness. There must have been a sense of reverence and love overflowing, so that they were touched to want that for themselves. After listening to Jesus' prayer to His heavenly Father, they requested that He teach them to pray. Remember the verse in Luke 11:1, "One day Jesus was praying in a certain place. When he finished, one of his disciples said to him, 'Lord, teach us to pray, just as John taught his disciples.'"

Jesus turned water into wine, walked on water, healed the sick, even raised the dead to life. Yet, the one thing that these men who knew Him best wanted to learn from Him was how to pray. This, of course, is just one of many sections where Jesus teaches us about prayer, but it is a passage that will help us understand the basics of communication with God in heaven.

A PROGRESSION (VV. 7-8)

You quickly notice the progression: ask, seek, knock.[1] Anyone who has ever been a parent or even a son or daughter (and that pretty much covers us all) has watched this progression unfold at home. Children soon learn the benefits of persistence.

My children learned this lesson when they first began to talk. "Daddy, can we go, too? Can we see that? Can we play here? Will you take us over there?" Most of the time I said yes. It was just easier, because if I said no, I knew they would take it to the next step. To say yes meant the issue was over; my only cost was time and some energy. But to say no did not always end it.

Down the hall they would come, seeking me with a "Why not? I'll bet Grandma would let us!" They followed me all around the house with their plea. They sought me out in the bathroom, the garage, everywhere I went! Finally, exhausted, weary, and unable to recall why I had said no in the first place, I would say okay! Their seeking me out paid off. However, if I again turned them down, they would go to the next step.

There is a knock at the door,[2] and a timid voice asks, "Can I can come in?" You cannot resist, so you say all right! This pitiful piece of humanity you call a son or daughter tearfully comes into your inner sanctuary, crawls up onto your lap, and begs in a trembling voice, "Daddy please, please let me go." You are done. You could have saved yourself all this grief if you had just said yes at the beginning, but you did not. Now your energy is spent. You are beginning to feel that you are an unloving parent and so you rush to say yes, yes, yes! There, it is done; and you feel better! Your child leaves happy, and you're left wondering how the tears evaporated so rapidly.

So Jesus says, "Do you want to know how to pray? I'll tell you. Be direct. Go right to your Father and ask.[3] If that doesn't work, chase Him down the hall and seek[4] Him until you find Him and ask again. If that doesn't work, wait until He is alone and knock[5] on the door. Crawl up on His lap and speak in your softest voice and ask again. No loving father can resist!"

Jesus, God in the flesh, is telling us how to talk to Himself. It is amazing to me that God would want even to be bothered, but He does. "We know that God does not listen to sinners. He listens to the godly man who does his will" (John 9:31). When I read that verse and others like it, I see God on His throne just waiting for His children to call. He longs to hear our voice, to feel our touch, and to answer our requests.

A PROMISE (VV. 9-11)

In his parallel passage, Luke defines the good gifts as just one very special gift, the gift of the Holy Spirit: "how much more will your Father in heaven give the Holy Spirit to those who ask him" (Luke 11:13). The plural gifts suggests the Holy Spirit and more.[6]

God is much more understanding than my earthly father, who more times than not denied my petitions.[7] Who would not like to have a dad who would answer every request with a yes? "Dad, can I have the car tonight?" "Sure, son, I know how responsible you are. Take it and stay out as long as you like!" In your dreams! Or, "Dad I'm tired of hanging around the house. I want my inheritance now so I can go into the far country while I'm young enough to enjoy it." "All right son, I was young once and understand how you feel. Go and have a good time." NOT LIKELY!!

So what is the promise? If God is granting carte blanche, how do we explain the times when He obviously says no? Some would say He never says no to His true children. I disagree, because I have heard Him say no several times. So how do we explain the fact that sometimes we ask and God says no when He said, "Everyone who asks receives"?; or when in faith we seek for answers or solutions and there are none, when God said, "He who seeks finds"?; or when we knock and knock at the door of the Almighty and He seems to ignore us, when He said, "To him who knocks, the door will be opened"?

These are questions all of us have asked from time to time. Did we miss something? Is there a footnote written in print so small we did not see it? Is there a time limit on the promise so that now the time has run out and the promise no longer applies? Or, worse still, has God reneged on His promise? Was He pulling a fast one on us and promising something He never intended to grant? Although God always gives good gifts to His children, I am not sure I can answer all the questions to your satisfaction or mine. I think there are some things that we are going to have to wait until we get to heaven to know. But let me try.

(1) First we sometimes ask the wrong way. James is pretty clear about this. Read his words again. "If any of you lacks wisdom, he should ask God, who gives generously to all without finding fault, and it will be given to him" (Jas. 1:5). That sounds consistent with the words of Christ in Matthew chapter seven. Read on. "But when he asks, he must believe and not doubt, because he who doubts is like a wave of the sea, blown and tossed by the wind" (Jas. 1:6).

Are there times when you wish you could edit the Bible? If I could, I would edit out this verse. I do not question its truthfulness; it just strikes so close to home with me. Now be really honest with yourself; when you pray, really pray, do you honestly expect something to happen? Or, rather, are you surprised when something does happen?

When called to the hospital room of a terminally ill church member and you pray fervently for that dear one to be healed, do you really expect him to be healed? Would you not be more surprised if he were healed than if he died?

James again comes to prick our conscience in the fifth chapter. "Is any one of you sick? He should call the elders of the church to pray over him and anoint him with oil in the name of the Lord. And the prayer offered in faith will make the sick person well; the Lord will raise him up" (vv. 14-15). Those words are followed by these: "The prayer of a righteous man is powerful and effective" (v. 16b).

I have, many times, gone with the elders of our church to do exactly what James says we should do. A sick person calls and requests the elders to come and pray and anoint with oil. It was always my job to bring the oil and read the Scripture and after prayer to anoint the sick person with olive oil.

One time especially remains in my memory bank. She was a young mother of three lovely daughters and was dying of cancer. Her beautiful face was pale, and her body had wasted away so much that she looked like a victim of starvation. We prayed with her that night, and I anointed her with oil. I lingered for awhile after the others had gone, and we talked. She said to me, "I'm really glad we did this, because I truly believe that Scripture in James that says, 'the prayer of a righteous man availeth much.' I believe I'm going to get better now." She died in a few weeks.

Why? Was it because we would all have been surprised if she got well and so we prayed doubting? Was it because we used the wrong kind of oil? Was it because none of us, elders or preacher, are truly righteous men and thus God did not hear? When I find the answer, I will write a book, not just a chapter of a book. Maybe the answer is yes to any and all of the above and perhaps more questions that have not been mentioned. I just know that James says, "He who doubts is like a wave of the sea, blown and tossed by the wind." We can ask the wrong way; and when we do, the answer is always no.

(2) We sometimes ask for the wrong reason. "When you ask, you do not receive, because you ask with wrong motives, that you may spend what you get on your pleasures" (Jas. 4:3).

This is not intended to be a commentary on James, but rather on the Sermon on the Mount as it is recorded in Matthew's Gospel. Perhaps you are beginning to think that I got the wrong assignment. I did not, and I plan to get back to Matthew soon. Dr. Henderson taught us that the best commentary on the Bible is the Bible itself, and these passages in James are a good commentary on Matthew chapter seven.

Do we ever ask for things for the wrong reason? Sure, all the time. "Lord let me win the lottery, even though as a Christian I can't buy a ticket." Maybe you would not pray that prayer, but have you ever thought about what a good steward you would be if God would make you rich? It isn't fair, is it? All that money wasted on the pagans! If God would just redistribute the wealth in favor of the Christians, He would be guaranteed ten percent right off the top. "If I were a rich man," we sing with Tevye, the church would never lack sufficient funds again. Sometimes we ask for the wrong reason, and the answer is usually no.

(3) Sometimes we ask for the wrong things. One of the main functions of parenting is to make sure your children do not have access to the wrong things. This is not an easy task today. So we busy ourselves and worry ourselves sick about what kind of movies they are seeing, what kind of books they are reading, what kind of stuff they are looking at on the Internet, and what kind of company they keep. Even though we are one hundred percent human, we care about our families. Fathers and mothers stay up at night waiting for their offspring to come home, partly because of the dangers we know are out there and partly because we remember what we did when we were their age.

My wife and I were not perfect parents—far from it! We loved our kids and tried to let them know it. Sometimes love is expressed through giving. That is a lesson today's world knows only too well. The television deeply plants that thought in our minds every time it is turned on. A young girl anxiously awaits her Christmas present. Her father announces that it is a new CD. The curtain is pulled back to reveal a Lexus complete with a CD player in the dash, I assume. The girl shouts, as she circles the car, "I'm not believing this!" Well I'm not either. Is that the way love expresses itself?

Does love not sometimes say, "I love you," by saying no? "No, you can't have the car tonight because the roads are slick, and I love you too much to see you hurt." We put covers over electrical outlets to keep little fingers from being shocked. We force-feed vegetables down little throats because they are good for them. We make our children go to school and church, take showers, get their hair cut, do their homework, and go to bed. We teach them to tie their shoes, brush their teeth, and look both ways before crossing the street. These are all things, and the list is far from complete, that they neither want to learn nor do. They would rather "pig out" on candy, never take a shower or brush their teeth, and homework is not even in their vocabulary. But sometimes we say no because we know that is the right answer. We know that much, and we are only people. How much more God must know. He is the perfect Father who only gives good gifts to His children (Matt. 7:11).

So, even though we are just people, we know enough and love enough to say no when our children ask for something they should not have—like a snake. "I just came from the pet store, and they have the neatest rattlesnake down there. Can I have him, Dad, please, please?" The answer is no, not because we do not love our child, but because we do. Sometimes love says no.

Sometimes love says wait. When our oldest daughter was a teenager, we discovered that she had scoliosis (curvature) of the spine. The doctors prescribed special shoes and exercise, neither of which seemed to help. We, of course, prayed that her spine would be straightened. We had faith that God could do that and would do that if we prayed in faith. Yet her spine remains curved today.

A few years after she was married, she and her husband were involved in a serious automobile accident. The other driver was intoxicated and driving in the wrong lane on a two-lane road. It was a head on collision. Our daughter and her husband were driving a large RV, or it is likely they would have been killed, too. Our son-in-law was seriously injured and had to remain in the hospital in Houston, Texas, for several weeks. Susan, our daughter, received back and neck injuries. The doctors said she had a chipped vertebra and that the chipped bone was dangerously close to the spine. We were to take her home and get her to a specialist as soon as possible. X-rays were taken, and then the doctor met with us to explain his findings. As we sat there, he put the X-rays on the lighted board and carefully pointed out the bone fragment. He then showed us how close the bone chip was to the spine and explained that if the bone had wedged itself in her spine, the result would have been devastating. "Notice the curvature of the spine," he said. "If her spine had been straight, the bone fragment would have lodged between her vertebra, and she would be paralyzed. In my opinion, this girl can walk today because of her curvature of the spine!"

Did God cause her spine to be crooked because He knew what was going to happen to her years later? I don't know. Did God say no to our prayers because He did not want our daughter paralyzed? I don't know. What I do know is that her slightly curved spine goes unnoticed today as she walks through the door of our home. I also learned that God sometimes says "I love you" by not giving us that for which we ask. We cannot know God's perfect planning. We must be very careful about the things for which we ask.[8]

THE PRIZE (V. 12)

There are two themes that are always connected in the Bible. The first is to "Love the Lord your God with all your heart, and with all your soul and with all your mind" (Matt. 22:37). The second is to "Love your neighbor as yourself" (Matt. 22:39). Everything hangs on these two themes. If we can master these two commandments, life will be fulfilling and complete. If we never master them, we will always be looking for something more.

Therefore, we should not be surprised when Jesus closes this section with the words of verse 12[9]: "Do to others what you would have them do to you." We call it the Golden Rule, and it is the basis for people living together in harmony and peace.

Jesus is saying that if we treat others the way we would like to be treated ourselves, we will also find it easier to develop a solid relationship with God. Again the duel themes of the Sermon on the Mount are relating to God and relating to people. You cannot have one without the other.

The connection is always there between relating to God and to people. If things are not right with people, then things are not going to be right with God. That timeless truth speaks volumes to our time in history. Terrorist acts, suicide bombings, and all-out war in the very land where the Prince of Peace was born are indicative of our failure to love God and to love our neighbor.

So what is the answer? Good question. The answer, of course, has not changed. It is still, "Do to others what you would have them do to you." That kind of love cannot be found apart from God, because unconditional love is fruit produced by the Holy Spirit. We cannot just clinch our teeth and say, "I'm going to do it this time. I'm going to treat everyone else the way I want them to treat me." Oh that we could!

The truth is that only when I allow myself to be loved completely by God with His unique brand of love, can I begin to learn how to love my neighbor as myself. Read again the paraphrase of Peterson:

"This is my command: Love one another the way I loved you. This is the very best way to love. . . . As fruit bearers, whatever you ask the Father in relation to me, he gives you. But remember the root command: Love one another" (John 15:12,16-17 *The Message*).

The final word is "for this sums up the Law and the Prophets" (v. 12b). Most of the time, the Law is against us it seems. It keeps pointing out our mistakes. It is impossible to keep, so we are all guilty and condemned before God because of the Law: "For all have sinned and fall short of the glory of God" (Rom. 3:23).

But there is good news! We are saved by grace not by works (Eph. 2:8-9a)—God's riches at Christ's expense! We are sure of our salvation only because we are sure that Jesus Christ died on the cross for our sins and was raised from the dead by the power of God. We claim the victory of Jesus Christ over death as our own, and it is ours as a free gift.

But there is another truth here that might be missed. That truth, that the Law put simply, is just this: Treat other people the same way you would have them treat you. That sums it all up. We can do that. Not by ourselves, to be sure, but with God's Holy Spirit living within, we can love even our enemies. Think how the world would change if we took these words seriously. For too long we have dismissed them by saying, "It's impossible, so why try?" Think of the marriages that could be saved, the church splits that could be avoided, the lives that could be spared, and souls that could be saved.

There is also comfort here. When you know you are obeying the law, you do not have to worry about the punishment that comes when you disobey the law. Have you ever driven over a hill only to discover a policeman with a radar gun clocking your speed? Your first thought is, "I've been caught!" Because most of us do not always drive within the law, we assume we have been caught speeding. But then you look at your speedometer and discover to your amazement that you are within the limits of the law. You are safe. Now the law becomes your friend because it keeps all those other reckless drivers at bay; you wave politely to the police officer—your newfound friend.

Here is my take on all of this. We cannot be good enough to earn heaven. You already knew that. On judgment day, if we hear God say, "Well done, good and faithful servant. Enter into the joy of the Lord," we will all know that is a stretch because we have not been good enough or faithful enough; but Jesus was and is both. So we get in because Jesus lived the Christian life for us, and He died for that part of us that was not very Christian.

That does not excuse me from trying to be the best I can be for God. God wants us to become new creations. So I begin by spending time with the Lord in prayer and devotion. It will be hard because Satan does not want me to get close to God. However, as I spend more and more time with the Lord, the easier it gets, because the more I learn about Him, the easier it is to love Him. So I make myself at home with His love. The more I grow in my love for Him the easier it is to love you.

If I am at home with His love, then I find it easier to treat people the way I want them to treat me. That may not be the whole Law, but it is the sum total of the Law. It may not get me into heaven, but it sure will help me get through all the speed traps of life. Just over the hill, He is waiting. He has no radar gun, only open arms of love. He waits for you to come to Him. So ask, seek, knock. He promises to hear and to answer your petitions. He also promises the Holy Spirit to help you develop a heartfelt relationship with Him. It all begins with a meaningful prayer life that always produces the ultimate prize of living in love with our neighbors. What a prize!

NOTES

[1]Regarding the key words ask, seek, knock Stott observes that "all three verbs are present imperatives and indicate the persistence with which we should make our requests known to God" (184).

[2]In his article on the word knock (*krouō*), Angel (qtd. in Brown, vol. 2 881) provides some helpful background: "The saying 'Knock and it shall be opened to you' (Matt. 7:7 par. Luke 11:9) is probably a proverb since it is found in Judaism (Pesikta 176a with reference to studying the Mishnah, 'If a man knocks, it will be opened to him')."

[3]Matthew employs the word ask fourteen times. He uses it several times in relation to prayer (e.g., Matt. 18:19; 21:22) as well as making requests of other people (e.g., Matt. 5:42; 27:20).

[4]The seriousness of this seeking is supported by the only other use of this verb in the Sermon on the Mount. In 6:33 Jesus urges His disciples to seek first God's kingdom.

[5]The word knock appears only nine times in the New Testament. Two of these occurrences are in Luke 11:9, 10, the parallel passage to Matthew 7:7-8. This figurative use of the word is found elsewhere in the New Testament. One well-known passage is Rev. 3:20 in which the risen Lord invites the lukewarm Christians of Laodicea to renew their relationship with Him.

[6]Hagner lays out three interpretative possibilities. "These 'good things' can be thought of as the eschatological blessings that accompany the presence of the kingdom (cf. Luke's 'Holy Spirit'), so that the work of the disciples in proclaiming the kingdom is primarily in

view, or alternatively the more ordinary and ongoing needs of the disciples (cf. 6:32-33). Less likely is the suggestion (e.g., Carson) that the qualities of character and life demanded by the sermon (i.e., righteousness, humility, purity, love) are intended" (174).

[7]D.A. Carson focuses attention on the central issue of God's fatherly love and care. "What is fundamentally at stake is man's picture of God. God must not be thought of as a reluctant stranger who can be cajoled or bullied into bestowing his gifts (6:7-8), as a malicious tyrant who takes vicious glee in the tricks he plays (vv. 9-10), or even as an indulgent grandfather who provides everything requested of him. He is the heavenly Father, the God of the kingdom, who graciously and willingly bestows the good gifts of the kingdom in answer to prayer" (*Matthew* 187).

[8]Filson aptly states, "Any problem about answer to prayer is not due to lack of goodness or ability in God; he is ready to give; he does give. If prayer seems to win no answer, the one praying may be at fault, or, as Gethsemane shows (xxvi. 36-46), God may have a wise purpose not yet understood" (105).

[9]According to Davies and Allison, structurally this verse concludes the central section of Jesus' Sermon. "Although the so-called 'golden rule' sums up in brief the right conduct towards others and therefore appropriately closes 6:19-7:11, a section on social behaviour, 7:12 is not simply the conclusion of 6:19-7:11 (or of 7:1-11). Rather it does bring to a climax the entire central core of the sermon on the mount, 5:17-7:11" (685). Jesus finishes where He started, with a general statement about the righteous conduct God expects in fulfillment of the Law and the Prophets.

18 ■ Choices

Matthew 7:13-14

Gary D. York

¹³*Enter through the narrow gate. For wide is the gate and broad is the road that leads to destruction, and many enter through it.* ¹⁴*But small is the gate and narrow the road that leads to life, and only a few find it.*

THE CALL TO CHOOSE

The free enterprise and capitalistic mindset of American culture creates a wide-open environment for choices. Without choices it is not America. Whether you choose cable television or a satellite dish, the range of options and costs with each requires some study. What about wireless phone companies? The plans for minutes and features are multiple, so broad, in fact, that it makes comparative shopping quite difficult. Internet access is a challenge, especially for those of past generations whose computer skills are limited at best. Once on line, the sites to visit, things to buy, programs to sign up for, ideas to investigate, material to read, and statistics to gather are so prolific, one tends to be somewhat paralyzed.

In the early nineties, two friends of mine returned from a year of mission work in India. The living conditions during their time away were quite Spartan. Adjustment was not easy. About the time they became somewhat accustomed to those austere surroundings, their assigned tour ended and they made their way home. A few days after arriving and getting settled in their home, a trip to the grocery store was needed. As they walked the aisles, they stared at the choices of canned goods, dairy products, vegetables, cuts of meat, and bread. Somewhat paralyzed and in serious need of mental floss, they were unable to decide on anything and left the market without a single purchase. John MacArthur is right:

> Our lives are filled with decisions—what to wear, what to eat, where to go, what to do, what to say, what to buy, whom to marry, what career to follow, and on and on. Many decisions are trivial and insignificant, and some are essential and life-changing (449).

Whenever we work with the Lord, choices are life-changing. From the moment we are old enough to make them, life is a constant flow of decisions. We have Adam and Eve to thank for this challenge. God said to them, "You are free to eat from any tree in the garden; but you must not eat from the tree of the knowledge of good and evil, for when you eat of it you will surely die" (Gen. 2:16-17). What they ate gave them a case of spiritual indigestion so severe it required an earthly visit from the Great Physician. And we have been saddled with hard-hitting choices ever since.

This point is further illustrated by a survey of the Proverbs. Solomon's wit and wisdom makes this letter one of my favorites in the Bible. To paraphrase a humorous thought from comedian Steven Wright, the first time I read Proverbs, I thought it was a poem about everything. Seriously, Solomon underscored our journey through life when he said, "Live right, and you are safe! Choosing sin will destroy you" (Prov. 13:6 CEV).

My job in this chapter is to remind you that living a life of fellowship with God is based on a series of choices; and they begin with a fundamental one, soundly stated by Jesus in Matthew 7:13-14. He challenges His disciples to be consistent in their choices and practices (Fisher 145). Read it carefully. Watch the imagery closely. "Enter through the narrow gate. For wide is the gate and broad is the road that leads to destruction, and many enter through it. But small is the gate and narrow the road that leads to life, and only a few find it."

Michael Green called it "an awesome choice" (90). John Stott described it as "the inescapable choice" (193). It is all about the destinations of heaven and hell. It is about being in or out of God's family. Two choices are offered. The narrow gate (Jesus) leads you in, and the broad gate (anything but Jesus) keeps you out. In the end, we are not allowed to merely respect the teaching; we are asked to submit to the only Teacher (Green 90) who grants entrance. Sociological voices scream with objection when confronted with that conclusion. In the name of tolerance, they demand many more choices. In fact, the pursuit of multiculturalism in America today would be quick to treat all cultures as morally equivalent, each merely reflecting its own history and experience, therefore a viable choice (Colson 21) and usable gate. But let me be quick to point out that as Christians who believe in a sovereign God, whose truth is revealed in the Bible, we are not given the privilege of specifying the number of acceptable ingresses. The heavenly Father declares that entrance into His family, life eternal in heaven, only comes through His Son Jesus.

TWO GATES

Let's not be misled. Heaven's gate is not narrow because it is disguised or hidden. It is not obscure or imaginary. Finding it is not a trek through some well-crafted maze or a sequence of appropriately executed clicks of a computer mouse. Discovering it is not based on a skillful negotiation through a life-size form of Tony Hawk on Play Station 2 (see your children for an explanation and demonstration). It is narrow because "truth is always narrow" (Fisher 146). "It is the gate of self-denial, through which one cannot carry the baggage of sin and self-will" (MacArthur 453). It is crossing the line of faith with Jesus Christ and Him only.

Only a few find it because it is the hard way, demanding, requiring self-denial. The word Jesus uses comes from a root that means "to groan," as from being under pressure (MacArthur 455). Maybe it is from the discipline the Christian life requires. The writer of Hebrews hinted at it when he wrote, "No discipline seems pleasant at the time, but painful. Later on, however, it produces a harvest of righteousness and peace for those who have been trained by it" (Heb. 12:11). Choosing this gate is counter-cultural. It is choosing to be a minority. It is choosing to be unpopular. It is choosing to walk against the trends of human thought. It is choosing to stand against the swelling pressures of multiculturalism and moral relativism. It is choosing to value life rather than submitting to an accelerating depreciation of it expressed through abortion, infanticide, euthanasia, or forms of genetic engineering. Let me repeat myself. It is a disciplined life.

Choosing the narrow gate is not just seeing the benefits of heaven and selecting it off the shelf of eternal dwelling places at Destinations in a nearby strip mall either. Rather, it is seeing the challenges of living and choosing everything about Jesus as the means of dealing with them successfully because the evidence for faith and trust in Him are long-standing, tried, and proven. He has worn well over time, and so it makes reasonable sense to choose Him.

Conversely, the broad gate has destruction written all over it: ". . . definitive destruction, not merely the sense of the extinction of physical existence, but rather of an eternal plunge into Hades and a hopeless destiny of death" (Carson, *Matthew* 189). But the print is small and ignored by those who opt to pass through it. By human standards this point of entrance is the most appealing. It appears comfortable, easy, fulfilling, and joyous to the majority because it is self-proposed—humanly designed. For that reason alone, the majority of human beings choose it in the name of freedom and tolerance. John Stott calls it the "road of permissiveness." It has "plenty of room for laxity of morals." Those who travel this road "follow their own inclinations, that is, the desires of the human heart in its fallenness" (194).

JESUS ALONE IS THE GATE TO HEAVEN

I agree strongly with Michael Green who asserts that Jesus is the gate, the door of the sheepfold, the way that leads to the heavenly Father, the true vine, and only by incorporation in Him can we be acceptable to the Father and granted entrance into heaven (*Matthew for Today* 89). With a humble confidence and declared joy (some relief, too, I might add), I declare my choice of Jesus. Without reservation, I have walked through the narrow gate and am winding my way through life and its challenges empowered by the Holy Spirit Jesus promised to send and now indwells me daily.

But it is not safe for me to assume that simply because you are reading this book—even own an autographed copy of it—and respect deeply the person in whose honor it has been assembled, that you have chosen Jesus and share fellowship with me. Just because you pursued a career in ministry, enrolled in Bible college, studied under Dr. Marion Henderson, aced your way through Gospels, Johannine Literature, and third-year Greek, does not mean that you received Jesus as your Savior and Lord.

There are numerous false motives floating around. You could have been infected by one of them and therefore been deceived into thinking that opting for a career through the local church puts you on the straight and narrow. You may think this decision somehow gives you an inside track with God, that it puts you in the preferred category when it comes to the good stuff God dishes out, or that it enters you in the secured column of heaven's assets.

The scribes and Pharisees, many of whom were probably listening to Jesus deliver this Sermon, had fooled themselves into believing they were in the starting lineup for God's eternal Super Bowl simply because they could recite all the right terms and observe all the right customs. It is easy for people to learn and use Christian lingo, have an intellectual grasp of the right doctrines (even convincingly teach them), outwardly do all the right stuff (even sincerely), yet not have chosen Jesus.

I was standing at the counter in a bagel shop in Bloomington, Illinois, where I live. The lady who kindly waited on me said, "You don't know me, but I started attending your church. Do you ever have appointments with people who attend the church?" I answered affirmatively and suggested that if she wanted one, to call me and I would arrange it. Several weeks later, she called. She came in and, after we exchanged some pleasantries, she got to the point of her visit. Following a rather lengthy trip through the jagged edges of her life, she tagged her biography with this statement, "I believe in God and I think I'm going to heaven. But you said I need to receive Jesus as my Savior. But I have no idea what that means."

The way is narrow because it is through Jesus, an alliance of faith with Jesus alone. You do not stumble into a relationship with Him. No one wanders into a friendship with Him accidentally. It is not a product of chance. The choosing is deliberate and intentional. In Luke 13:24 Jesus said, "Make every effort to enter through the narrow door." The term Jesus used indicates that entering God's kingdom takes conscious, purposeful, and intense effort (MacArthur 455).

Listen carefully. You may be able to quote the books of the Bible, even backwards, along with all the authors and main themes. You may be equipped to discuss in detail the authorship theories for the book of Isaiah. You may be ready to explain with great detail and passion your eschatological view, why you are or are not dispensational, and why you should or should not be Calvinistic in your systematic theology. You may have great compassion for hurting and broken people or a strong passion to work with children. But have you intentionally and personally chosen to embrace Jesus by faith? No matter how good your moral, intellectual, or humanitarian achievements may be, it is still the broad gate if you have not chosen Jesus.

Let us go deeper. Is it Jesus only? I think that is the deeper implication and application of Jesus' analogy here in Matthew 7:13-14. I hold that conviction because the scribes and Pharisees were masterful at rule keeping. They took great pride in creating rules in an effort to pridefully keep more and arrogantly push themselves above all others. That rubbed off on others. Even negative leadership can have followers. Not long after the church was started, groups of Jewish Christians formed, whose expressed purpose was to force new believers in Christ to become Jews—to become rule keepers before their faith in Christ could be valid. Specifically, they were seeking to require every new Christian to embrace, and observe faithfully, all the dietary regulations and liturgical ceremonies required under the Mosaic Law. These people became a significant threat to the expansion of the church as it spread its wings beyond Jerusalem.

While we may not fight the strict requirements of the Old Testament Law, we do have the same tendency as those influenced by the scribes and Pharisees. We have a huge temptation today to require faith in Jesus Christ, plus a rigorous endorsement of some unwritten rules; but they are just as burdensome and restrictive as those enacted by the Judaizers.

We might not say it, but some practice faith in Jesus plus a daily check of their horoscope. Some profess faith in Jesus Christ plus a commitment to use only a certain version of the Bible. Some claim faith in Jesus, but would never be without the work of their counselor or psychiatrist. Still others declare faith in Jesus plus a pledge to stay away from playing cards, going to movies, wearing jewelry, adorning themselves with trendy clothing, cutting their hair, competitive sports, all versions of the Bible except the King James, all games involving the use of dice, restaurants where alcoholic beverages are served, or listening to rock music.

But the narrow gate is Jesus only! Not Jesus and The Book of Mormon, as if it were another testament of Jesus. Not Jesus plus the Koran. Not Jesus plus the tradition of my church or group of churches. Not Jesus plus a prescribed list of rites and sacraments, creeds or dogmas. Not Jesus plus a series of moral or intellectual achievements. Not Jesus plus a noteworthy resume of financial advancements or savvy business strategies. It is Jesus plus nothing. "Salvation is found in no one else" (Acts 4:12). "For there is one God and one mediator between God and men, the man Christ Jesus" (1 Tim. 2:5). "If righteousness could be gained through the law, Christ died for nothing" (Gal. 2:21). Here in Matthew 7:13-14, Jesus draws a doctrinal line in the sand that says, "If you are going to stand with God, you have to stand with Me, and Me only."

Let me be compassionate and gentle, but push the envelope with you. You do not have a life worth living; you do not have a spiritual calling to do ministry; you do not have a guaranteed future in heaven (the destination of the narrow gate) if you have not chosen Jesus and Him only. Please, if you have not done it, bend the knee of submission to Him today.

In the words of the Apostle Paul, I close this chapter:

... we constantly pray for you, that our God may count you worthy of his calling, and that by his power he may fulfill every good purpose of yours and every act prompted by your faith. We pray this so that the name of our Lord Jesus may be glorified in you, and you in him. ... (2 Thess. 1:11-12).

19 ■ Warnings

Matthew 7:15-23

Ken Idleman

¹⁵Watch out for false prophets. They come to you in sheep's clothing, but inwardly they are ferocious wolves. ¹⁶By their fruit you will recognize them. Do people pick grapes from thornbushes, or figs from thistles? ¹⁷Likewise every good tree bears good fruit, but a bad tree bears bad fruit. ¹⁸A good tree cannot bear bad fruit, and a bad tree cannot bear good fruit. ¹⁹Every tree that does not bear good fruit is cut down and thrown into the fire. ²⁰Thus, by their fruit you will recognize them. ²¹Not everyone who says to me, "Lord, Lord," will enter the kingdom of heaven, but only he who does the will of my Father who is in heaven. ²²Many will say to me on that day, 'Lord, Lord, did we not prophesy in your name, and in your name drive out demons and perform many miracles?" ²³Then I will tell them plainly, "I never knew you. Away from me, you evildoers!"

The Word of God, in both Testaments, is laced with references in contrasts: obedience and disobedience; life and death; blessings and curses; Spirit and flesh; light and darkness; truth and lies; righteousness and wickedness; heaven and hell; wisdom and folly, to name a few. As Matthew closes his account of the Sermon on the Mount, he records the words of Jesus in the final section (vv. 13-28) with contrasts consisting of two gates/roads/destinations, two trees (prophets and claims are included), and two builders. Each of these metaphors represents a contrast of choice. The wide gate/broad way leads to destruction; the small gate/narrow way leads to life. The good tree bears good fruit; the bad tree bears bad fruit. The wise man builds his house upon the rock; the foolish man builds his house upon the sand.

A masterful sermon calls for decision. It impresses truth with a call for commitment. As Jesus ends His discourse, He presents the listener/reader with three pairs of options. They are simple and direct. He compels the listener/reader to apply all that He has revealed as He has preached and taught about the core values of the kingdom of God. The options are not diversified. There are only two ways to go. Mark Moore says:

Our syncretistic society is offended by Jesus' black and white options. We demand a smorgasbord of ethical choices. We describe such teaching as narrow-minded, overly simplistic, and even bigoted. Is it possible, however, that some have become so open-minded that their brains have fallen out? (214).

Jesus uses a sequence of mind-sticking word pictures to reveal that there are but two gates by which a person may enter life; two ways by which a person may journey toward life; two kinds of fruit a person can bear in life; and two foundations on which a person may build a life. Jesus presses His claims in the concluding parable of the wise and foolish builders. If a person hears His words and puts them into practice, he is wise. If a person hears His words and does not put them into practice, he is foolish.

In an age of tolerance and permissiveness, the claims of Jesus seem narrow and confining. He would not agree with the statement, "It doesn't matter what you believe as long as you are sincere." He would not affirm that we are all climbing up to God by our own routes. He would not sanction that everyone is striving for the same thing and that is what counts. Jesus would not relate well to our shallow pluralism. Instead, He says that there are but two gates, two ways, two fruits, and two foundations. Christians who uphold the standard of limited personal choice represented in these three closing illustrations are not being arrogant or exclusivistic. They are being fair and faithful to the truth, which is powerfully punctuated at the close of the Sermon on the Mount in the words of the Co-creator Himself.

His warnings at the close of the Sermon on the Mount are not extended in cool detachment. They are desperate pleadings by the Lord of life for His disciples to embrace a completely radical approach to life and living, to deny popular appeal as the basis for our beliefs and ethics, to expose the lack of morality in the root structure of our culture, and to assert that there is but one reliable spiritual foundation on which a human life and destiny can be constructed.

Michael Green says:

How does a Christian justify this exclusivism which seems to be so arrogant? . . . Religion, if conceived as a man-made attempt to become acceptable to God by whatever system of beliefs and practice, is a beggar's refuge. It will not keep out the wind and the hail. What Jesus offers is totally different. It begins not from our reaching up, but from God's reaching down. It is not religion at all, but a revelation. Jesus is the revelation of what God is like; never has there been such a true likeness. The King has come to bring in the Kingdom (*The Message of Matthew* 109-10).

WARNING ABOUT FALSE PROPHETS (V. 15)

For four hundred years before the time of Christ, it was generally believed that prophecy had ceased. The period between the two Testaments is sometimes called the silent years. The heavens were as brass. With the appearance of John the Baptist on the landscape, the first prophetic voice in four centuries was heard. The historical and contemporary impact would be impossible to overstate. When John the Baptist was imprisoned, Jesus came preaching. To the crowd that gathered on the day of Pentecost, Peter explained that the phenomenon of tongues was the fulfillment of Joel's promise that in the last days God would pour out His Spirit on everyone, so that young men would see visions, old men would have dreams, and both men and women would proclaim His message (Acts 2:17-18).

As the infant church grew, the problem of false teachers became acute. Jesus had warned against the rise of false prophets who would deceive the people (Matt. 24:11, 24). John the apostle also warned his followers (1 John 4:1-3; Rev. 2:20). How were they to be recognized? In earlier days, a prophet was discredited if what he proclaimed in the name of the Lord did not come true (Deut. 18:20-22). The *Didache* had two simple tests to identify a false prophet. If he stayed more than two days or asked for money, he was to be red-flagged as insincere and self-serving. It states that, "from his behavior then, the false prophet and the true prophet shall be known" (qtd. in Mounce 68).

The scourge of false prophets has always existed. A prophet is fundamentally a messenger for someone else, and these false prophets claim to be speaking for God. The acuteness of the danger they present is that they are accepted at face value, they "appear and deceive many people" (Matt. 24:11). We should not be surprised, if we remember the archetype behind these false prophets. Paul, writing of certain men with whom he had to deal, unveils their model:

For such men are false prophets, deceitful workmen, masquerading as apostles of Christ. And no wonder, for Satan himself masquerades as an angel of light. It is not surprising, then, if his servants masquerade as servants of righteousness. Their end will be what their actions deserve (2 Cor. 11:13-15).

John MacArthur:

. . . there has always been a large market for false prophets, because most people do not want to hear the truth. They prefer to hear what is pleasant and flattering, even if it is false and dangerous, over what is unpleasant and unflattering, even if it is true and helpful (461).

Under the blotter on my desk at the college where I have served as president for the past twenty-five years I keep my favorite quote by C.S. Lewis:

If the divine call does not make us better, it will make us very much worse. Of all bad men, religious bad men are the worst. Of all the created beings, the wickedest is one who originally stood in the immediate presence of God (*Reflections on the Psalms* 32).

The fact is that functioning as God's spokesman has some occupational hazards. You can begin to treat holy things as common. You can develop a hard heart. You can become callous. You can expect deference. You can come to regard the applause of men as your due. You can lose your identity as a spiritual leader. You can incur the judgment of God. False prophets are not born; they are made. It happens over time, by installments. Self-interest is inevitable if we stray far from the ethic of the Lord Jesus revealed in Mark 10:45: "For even the Son of Man did not come to be served, but to serve, and to give his life. . . ." This attitude is radically different than that of the false prophets described by the Lord in the Sermon on the Mount.

Jesus describes them as coming in "sheep's clothing, but inwardly they are ferocious wolves" (v. 15b). We learn from this metaphor that the false prophets are both dangerous and deceptive. The danger is that in reality they are wolves. In first-century Palestine, the wolf was the natural enemy of the sheep, which was defenseless against it (Stott 198). Wolves roamed the hills and valleys, looking for a sheep that strayed from the flock or lagged behind. When a wolf found such a sheep, it quickly attacked and tore it to pieces. Even a grown, healthy sheep was utterly defenseless against a wolf. Wolves are known to be merciless and ferocious. False prophets and wolves are clever and wily, and are always on the lookout for new victims. False prophets and those who follow false prophets are as dangerous to God's people as ravenous wolves are to sheep.

One of the greatest tragedies on the historical religious landscape happened when a man by the name of Jim Jones, a self-appointed prophet, and nearly one thousand of his followers committed mass suicide at Jonestown, a remote church settlement in the jungles of Guyana, South America. Mel White tries to determine why so many people could be so fatally misled. Among the reasons he suggests are:

> He [Jim Jones] knew how to inspire hope. He was committed to people in need; he counseled prisoners and juvenile delinquents. He started a job placement center; he opened rest homes and homes for the retarded; he had a health center; he organized a vocational training course; he preached about God. He even claimed to cast out demons, do miracles and heal. But, on the other hand we find the marks of a false prophet. He promoted himself through the use of celebrities; a very common vehicle for false prophets to gain credibility. He manipulated the press; he wanted certain favorable stories . . . and he used the language and the forms of faith to gain his power (Mel White qtd. in MacArthur 462).

John McArthur further says:

> He [Jim Jones] replaced Jesus Christ as the authority and more and more garnered loyalty to himself. He began demanding money for every service he offered and was preoccupied with sex, in both its normal and deviant forms. He would lie convincingly about anything in order to gain the admiration and praises of countless church leaders, governors, senators, congressmen, and even the president of the United States (463).

The Christian community in every generation must be vigilant with respect to spiritual leadership. False prophets are deadly to the health and growth of the true church in any age. They should be exposed, confronted, and resisted. They should be shunned and starved out in order to avoid the victimization of many in the flock of God.

WARNING ABOUT FRUIT (VV. 16-20)

False teachers are to be known, not simply by their teaching, but by the practical effect of their teaching both on them and others close to them. Jesus teaches what to watch for in identifying pseudo-Christian leaders. Because they are extremely deceptive and dangerous, the Lord identified the means of determining who they are. Here the Lord changes His metaphor from sheep and wolves to trees and their fruit. After saying the false prophet cannot always be easily recognized (a wolf in sheep's clothing), He instills confidence regarding the ways by which they may be identified: by their fruit you will recognize them (vv. 16 and 20). The point is that a wolf may disguise itself, a tree cannot. Jesus said, "Examine the fruit."

John R.W. Stott identifies the three kinds of fruit by which false prophets reveal their true identity as: 1) character, 2) teaching content, and 3) influence (201-2).

The primary identifying mark of a genuine spiritual leader is character. Of the character traits that are required of church leaders in the Pastoral Epistles, all have to do with character, except being able to teach. All other aspects of a godly leader's life are related to his conduct and the reputation that flows from that conduct over time. Some false prophets are so noticeably deceitful and duplicitous that only the most gullible person would be taken in. Others conceal their true nature with remarkable verbal and acting skills. But, given enough time, their fruit blooms and reveals their true nature. Jesus observed, "A good tree cannot bear bad fruit, and a bad tree cannot bear good fruit" (v. 18).

An excellent checklist of what constitutes good and bad fruit is the passage in Galatians 5:16-26. Lay this text alongside the life and leadership of anyone who claims to represent the truth of God and the Spirit of Christ. The Apostle Paul writes, "The acts of the sinful nature are obvious . . . but the fruit of the Spirit is. . . ." The fruit associated with false prophets would be "sexual immorality, impurity and debauchery, idolatry and witchcraft, hatred, discord, jealousy, fits of rage, selfish ambition, dissentions, factions and envy, drunkenness, orgies, and the like." The fruit associated with true prophets would be "love, joy, peace, patience, kindness, goodness, faithfulness, gentleness, and self-control."

It is stunning how often decisions are made about the calling of a ministry leader or the appointment of an elder on the basis of what he has accumulated or what he can accomplish, rather than on the basis of his character. When this course is pursued, the results in the church body are always stagnation at best and division at worst. The vitality and unity in the body of Christ depend on the careful choice of genuine spiritual leaders, not false prophets.

In 1999, my wife Kaylene and I visited the Holy Land, and while there I had the opportunity to give a devotion at the place called Mount of Beatitudes. To prepare, I dug out my wife's class notes from Dr. Henderson's Sermon on the Mount lectures he gave in Gospel's class. I experienced waves of nostalgia as I read and reflected on the life-transforming impact that exposition had on me three decades earlier. Doc lived what he taught; so thousands in his Bible college classes, as well as in the churches, could see what Jesus meant when He talked about the good tree. This has always illustrated for me how character with good fruit makes a difference.

The second area in which a false prophet can be judged is doctrine. Generally he may invoke the right words and phrases, but closer examination reveals ideas that are self-serving and unscriptural. Important truths will be omitted. Jesus confronted the Pharisees in His day with the words:

> "You brood of vipers, how can you who are evil say anything good? For out of the overflow of the heart the mouth speaks. The good man brings good things out of the good stored up in him, and the evil man brings evil things out of the evil stored up in him" (Matt. 12:34,35).

So then, if a person's heart is revealed by his words, as a tree is known by its fruit, we have a responsibility to test a teacher by his teaching.

> "Cling to the pure Word of God," cried Luther, "for then you will be able to 'recognize the judge' who is right." Calvin made the same emphasis: "All doctrines must be brought to the Word of God as the standard," for "in judging false prophets the rule of faith (*i.e.* Scripture) holds the chief place" (qtd. in Stott 202).

Influence is power. It is the power to shape the thinking and conduct of others. What effect has the behavior and teaching of a prophet had on those who are aligned with him? Typically he will attract and retain followers who are or will become like him in his superficial and sensual ways. He tends to attract a following because he teaches and practices what others want to hear and pursue. His followers will be like him—egotistical, proud, self-absorbed, self-promoting, self-indulgent, self-willed, and self-satisfied. The fact is that the faithful can also be seduced by doctrines of demons and fall into the snare of false teachers. The attraction of false prophets and the corruption of their followers exist in the twenty-first century in much the same way as the first century. The warning about false teachers is as up-to-date as tomorrow's newspaper.

WARNING ABOUT JUDGMENT (VV. 21-23)

Jesus begins the Sermon on the Mount with blessings (Matt. 5:3-12) and ends it with warnings. To heed the warnings is to open the door of blessing. The Apostle Peter would later make it clear that false prophets are doomed. Some of the strongest and most indicting language in the

New Testament is found in 2 Peter 2, as Peter pronounces the ultimate destruction of false prophets. Statements like, "They will be paid back with harm for the harm they have done" (v. 13a) and "Blackest darkness is reserved for them" (v. 17b) impress the severity with which they will be dealt with on judgment day.

The clear reference in the words of Jesus here is to eternal punishment. "Every tree that does not bear good fruit is cut down and thrown into the fire" (Matt. 5:19). This saying is reminiscent of the words of John the Baptist in Matthew 3:10 and John 15:6. While the application is primarily to false teachers, the principle will be extended to include all that are not faithful to the Lord's teaching. Fred Fisher points out that the implication would seem to be that a prophet who does not produce pure teaching or who lives a life that is inconsistent with divine truth should be rejected by the community of saints, since he is under the judgment of God (149-50). Those who passively or actively embrace them must share in their fate.

One of the most sobering passages in the Sermon on the Mount begins with the words, "Not everyone who says to me, 'Lord, Lord,' will enter the kingdom of heaven, but only he who does the will of my Father who is in heaven (v. 21)." The profession of Jesus as Lord constitutes the heart of true conversion. It is indicated in 1 Corinthians 12:1-3 that the evidence of the work of the Holy Spirit in a person's life is bound up in being able to say, with content and meaning, "Jesus is Lord." Jesus here impresses that reality. He is not interested in lip service. He is not impressed with religious exhibitionism. The history of the nation of Israel revealed the besetting sin of mere lip homage. Isaiah 29:13 says, "These people come near to me with their mouth and honor me with their lips, but their hearts are far from me." Jesus also asked His disciples then and now, "Why do you call me, 'Lord, Lord,' and do not do what I say?" (Luke 6:46). The evidence of the Lordship of Christ is not in a glib profession of faith; it is in a surrendered life of demonstrated conformity to His Word. We can never claim salvation because we have made an orthodox confession. Confession must be followed by a changed life; it has no validity until it is translated into obedience. Sonship means obedience.

It is stunning that false prophets and those who have bought into their teaching and practices expect to gain entrance into the kingdom. These people consider themselves to be genuine believers. In fact, they appeal their sentence by appealing to their good works. Three activities are claimed—prophecy, exorcism, and miracles. Jesus does not deny their claims. Paul suggested in 1 Corinthians 13:1-4 that it is possible to preach, prophesy, have all knowledge, and remove mountains by faith without having love; that is, without having Christ. Origin said, "Such curative power is of itself neither good nor bad, but within the reach of godless as well as Godly people" (qtd. in Fisher 151). Miracles are insufficient as documentation of real faith. The confirmation of genuineness and authenticity in the heart of a person is a submitted life of consistent obedience.

D.A. Carson says:

It is true that men are saved by God's grace through faith in Christ; but it is equally true that God's grace in a man's life inevitably results in obedience. Any other view of grace cheapens grace, and turns it into something unrecognizable. Cheap grace preaches forgiveness without repentance, church membership without rigorous church discipline, discipleship without obedience, blessing without persecution, joy without righteousness, results without service. In the entire history of the church, has there ever been another generation with so many nominal Christians and so few real, obedient ones? And where nominal Christianity is compounded by spectacular profession, it is especially likely to manufacture its own false assurance (*The Sermon on the Mount* 131).

The words of an engraving from the cathedral of Lübeck, Germany, beautifully reflect our Lord's teaching at the close of this section of the Sermon on the Mount:

Thus speaketh Christ, You call Me master and obey me not, you call Me light and see Me not, you call Me the way and walk Me not, you call Me life and live Me not, you call Me wise and follow Me not, you call me fair and love Me not, you call Me rich and ask Me not, you call Me eternal and seek Me not, if I condemn thee, blame Me not (MacArthur 480).

We who claim to be Christ-followers in this generation must especially heed the teaching in this passage. Ours is a suspicious age . . . with good reason. Disillusionment and disappointment with spiritual leaders has been replaced with the demand for accountability and integrity. Rightly so. There has been a constant parade of scandals among professed Christian leaders for a quarter of a century now. The exposure of numerous high-profile televangelists in the early 1980s right up to the present proliferation of pedophile priests and cover-up cardinals has given us bad fruit. We must heed the words of gentle Jesus, Who would not bruise a reed and Who attends the funeral of every sparrow. They sound so uncharacteristic, don't they? "I never knew you . . . away from me!" What can it be like to incur the wrath and rejection of Christ? He died that we might be saved and empowered by the Holy Spirit in such a way that we would never know.

20 ■ Obedience

Matthew 7:24-27

Charles McNeely

²⁴Therefore everyone who hears these words of mine and puts them into practice is like a wise man who built his house on the rock. ²⁵The rain came down, the streams rose, and the winds blew and beat against that house; yet it did not fall, because it had its foundation on the rock. ²⁶But everyone who hears these words of mine and does not put them into practice is like a foolish man who built his house on sand. ²⁷The rain came down, the streams rose, and the winds blew and beat against that house, and it fell with a great crash.

A PARABLE OF TWO BUILDERS

Jesus concludes His Sermon on the Mount with a parable. After speaking of two ways (7:13-14) and two trees (7:15-20), He tells a story of two men who build houses on different kinds of foundations. One builds on solid rock and the other on shifting sand. You can imagine the result. When the storms come, only one house survives.

The word parable is the transliteration of a Greek word meaning "to throw alongside." It is a story placed alongside a truth in order to reveal the truth more clearly—or sometimes to conceal the truth from those whose hearts are hardened and whose ears are closed (13:10-17). Unlike the parables that are, in part, meant to conceal, the meaning of this one is crystal clear: obedience to Jesus' teaching is the only sure foundation for life. It is not just what a man hears, believes, plans, or professes that counts, but what he does. Martin Luther may have written off the book of James as a "right strawy" epistle, but what the author penned in James 1:22 sounds very similar to Jesus' parable of the two builders. He wrote, "Do not merely listen to the word, and so deceive yourselves. Do what it says." And in 2:14, "What good is it, my bothers, if a man claims to have faith but has no deeds? Can such faith save him?" Does that not sound a lot like Jesus' warning about the house that "fell with a great crash"?

In His infinite wisdom, Jesus knows that one of the most deadly temptations His followers will face is the temptation to hear but not do, to understand but not obey. If there is any lesson needed by Christians today, it is the implication of this parable that just knowing Scripture, showing perfect attendance in Sunday school, and getting a Bible college degree is not enough. We must obey the Lord! As we quote the Great Commission from Matthew 28 and emphasize going, making disciples, and baptizing, we must also remember Jesus' mandate to teach them "to obey everything I have commanded you." We must never forget that Jesus said, "If anyone loves me, he will obey my teaching" (John 14:23) and "You are my friends if you do what I command" (John 15:14). What Jesus expects, then, is for us to say, "I understand . . . and I'll do it!"

Although it has been several years, I will never forget the rebellious attitude of a Christian woman in a marriage counseling session. Her husband was a minister. She was a Sunday school teacher and a youth group sponsor. They had four children, and she was in love with her oldest daughter's boyfriend. After a lengthy session of establishing rapport and learning about her frustrations and her unfaithfulness, I encouraged her husband to be forgiving but firm. I suggested that she repent of her affair, confess to those she had hurt, and go back to her family. I told her that the Bible says adultery is a sin, divorce is not in God's plan, and that she had an obligation not to be a stumbling block to others, especially the young ones. I will always be haunted by the look of defiance in her eyes when she said, "I know what the Bible says, but. . . ." With a hardened heart she left her family. Her husband left the ministry. Her children left the church. And the young man was eventually left confused and lost.

Less than two weeks later, I met with an elder who openly confessed that he intended to get his preacher fired over a personality conflict. We talked about the context of the problem and the potential of the church. I predicted a real setback for the congregation if he went through with his plans, not to mention the harm done to the minister and his family for no good reason. I urged the elder to reconsider; but in anger he restated his plan to get rid of the minister, "Even if it means dividing the church," he said. I referred to Ephesians 4:3 and reminded him that the Bible says to "make every effort to keep the unity of the Spirit in the bond of peace." The elder responded stubbornly, "I know what the Bible says, but. . . ."

No wonder Jesus insisted so strongly on obedience at the end of the Sermon on the Mount! When we hear, understand, and then intentionally disobey, everybody suffers! Jesus knew that. That is why He told this parable.

When Jesus began with the word therefore (v. 24), He connected the parable with the central teaching in the previous section. The story of the two builders helps illustrate His statement in 7:21, where we read, "Not everyone who says to me, 'Lord, Lord,' will enter the kingdom of heaven, but only he who does the will of my Father who is in heaven." Words are cheap. Jesus is looking for action. And the action He wants is, very simply, to put His words into practice.

At the outset, the wise man who hears (v. 24) is no different from the foolish man who hears (v. 26). They both have opportunity to know the will of God. But they respond differently. One obeys; the other does not. In the future, some of Jesus' hearers would include Pharisees who would not obey. Just two short chapters later, they hear, but accuse Jesus of blasphemy (9:3) and indict Him for eating with tax collectors and sinners (9:11). In Luke's Gospel, there is the contrast between Simon the Pharisee, in whose house Jesus was a guest, and a woman who had lived a sinful life (Luke 7:36-50). Both heard Jesus' teachings. But whereas the woman wept spontaneously over the feet of Jesus and was forgiven of her sins, Simon struggled throughout the whole encounter with Jesus' very acceptance of such a sinner. In fact, Simon probably identified with Jesus' critics ("Who is this who even forgives sins?" (v. 49b) when he should have identified with the woman.

The point for us today is that, having access to Bibles and hearing sermons and lessons, many have ample opportunity to know Who Jesus is and what He wants us to do. There are also more devotionals and study Bibles (including software) than ever before in the history of the church. Now we have the responsibility to do. It is called decision time. And the decision we make every day is whether or not to put His words into practice.

It helps, however, when we are first confronted with the claims of Christ or with a response to a particular command, if we make a decision up front to be obedient. A youth minister once called his junior high boys to a decision early in their development. (His wife did the same with the girls.) When they went into seventh grade, he taught them the biblical perspective on the Christian's body and how it is called the temple of the Holy Spirit (1 Cor. 6:19). He challenged them to say no to drugs, save sex for marriage, and keep their bodies fit and pure. His sage advice was, "If you make godly decisions now, you won't have to wrestle with what to do later when you're under pressure from peers. You'll just follow through with the decisions you've already made." A number of those boys heard and did not make a decision then. They have paid a price ever since. A few of them took the advice seriously and kept their bodies pure. They are the ones who have never regretted the foundation they have been building on ever since seventh grade. We must remember that decision making has always been at the heart of discipleship (Matt. 4:19).

CLAIM TO DEITY AND AUTHORITY

We should not move too quickly beyond Jesus' phrase "these words of mine" (vv. 24,26). That phrase carries with it a claim about Jesus' deity and authority that did not set well with the religious leaders of His day. Just as the parable illustrated His teaching in 7:21, so His emphasis on "these words of mine" identified His teaching with "the will of my Father." He was referring to His divine nature; and it was that divine nature that gave Him the authority to call people to repentance (4:17), heal various diseases (4:23), calm the storm (8:26), cast out demons (8:32), forgive sins (9:2), and raise the dead (9:25). Where did He get this kind of authority? What gives Him the right to insist that we obey His words? First, His authority was derived from His relationship with the Father. He is the pre-existent Christ, the Word that was God from the beginning (John 1:1-2) and later became flesh and lived among us (John 1:14). He is the image of the invisible God, by whom all things were created (Col. 1:15-16). He is the God-servant, who humbled Himself and became obedient to death—even death on a cross (Phil. 2:6-8). He is the radiance of God's glory, sustaining all things by His powerful word (Heb. 1:2-3). He had the authority from the beginning! No wonder His hearers were amazed at His teaching—"that he taught as one who had authority, and not as their teachers of the law" (7:29).

Secondly, He earned that authority by doing the will of the Father, by practicing what He preached, by submitting in total obedience. Remember Gethsemane? That was perhaps Jesus' greatest storm! That is where the Son of Man wrestled with the biggest decision of His life: whether to call legions of angels to rescue Him (Matt. 26:53) or to go through with the Father's plan for redemption of mankind. That is where He was in "anguish" and "his sweat was like drops of blood falling to the ground" (Luke 22:44). That's where He fell with His face to the ground and prayed, "My Father, if it is possible, may this cup be taken from me." But that is also where He made the final decision that took Him to Calvary: "Yet not as I will, but as you will" (Matt. 26:39). In other words, that is where Jesus said, "I know what God wants me to do—and I'll do it!"

As long as I live, I will remember Dr. Marion Henderson's teaching on Jesus in Gethsemane. He made it come alive. Even though it was 7:30 in the morning, I sat on the edge of my chair and hung on every word. Like everyone else in class, I realized for the first time what Jesus went through for me. It was the kind of life-changing experience that I thought every student should have. So I counted it a privilege to be able to call him back to Lincoln twenty years later to work as my assistant and to teach an entire class just on Jesus' last days—including especially Gethsemane.

LESSONS FROM THE PARABLE

The first builder was wise because he built on rock. Luke adds that he "dug down deep" (6:48) to bedrock in order to find a foundation that would be firm enough for that type of terrain. Building a house on rock (not on "a rock") is possible in many parts of Palestine. Hultgren writes:

> The topography of Galilee inland from the Mediterranean Sea to Upper Galilee in the north and to the Sea of Galilee in the east includes hilly and mountainous areas of sandstone, basalt, calcareous (chalky) rock, and limestone. . . . The Temple at Jerusalem stood securely on a rock base (cf. Isa. 28:16) (133).

In the Old Testament, rock is a metaphor for a solid, stable, immovable foundation (Ps. 40:2) and God is often portrayed as the Rock on Whom we can build our lives (1 Sam. 2:2; Ps. 18:2). It is the same word used by Jesus in Matthew 16:18 when He informed Peter that He would build His church on "this rock"—the fact that Jesus is the Christ, the Son of the living God!

By contrast, the second builder did it the fast and cheap way. He built on sand. Unlike rock, sand is loose, unstable, and extremely movable. Although it is not smart, there are many places in Palestine where a house can be built on sand, particularly along the coastal plain where sand and sand dunes extend inland for several miles. There are also other locations—gullies—which in summer appear as pleasant, sandy hollows—easy places to build quickly. But in winter, they become raging torrents of rushing water. Palestine is known for downpours that come up suddenly and turn dry wadis into raging rivers.

Both times when Jesus describes the storms, three elements of bad weather are cited: heavy rain, unexpected flash floods, and extreme winds. "These are the calamities that can befall inhabitants of Palestine during the rainy season (October to April, but especially from November to February, when seventy percent of the rain falls annually)" (Hultgren 133-34). Residents have described as much as forty inches falling, as the winds whip up off the Mediterranean Sea and the rains come down from the hills. Each house looks secure in good weather. But the storms reveal the quality of the work and the foundations laid by the builders.

Barclay makes an interesting point when he writes that Jesus was a carpenter—a craftsman who knew all about the building of houses. "When he spoke about the foundations of a house, he knew what he was talking about. This is no illustration formed by a scholar in his study; this is the illustration of a practical man" (Barclay 295).

The state of Florida has often been in the news because of its many sinkholes. It is bad enough when lavish homes and luxury cars are swallowed up because of where people have chosen to build and live. But recently an entire barn fell in a giant hole, and with it two prize horses. Worse yet, children and adults have sometimes been injured or killed. We realize then how critically important it is to build wisely.

The wise builder represents those who put Jesus' words into practice. They, too, are building for the future and need to prepare for the storms of life. On the other hand, "Those who pretend to have faith, who have a merely intellectual commitment, or who enjoy Jesus in small doses are foolish builders. When the storms of life come, their structures fool no one, above all God" (Carson, *Matthew* 194). Elsewhere Carson writes:

> In the Old Testament, and also elsewhere in Jewish writings, the storm sometimes serves as a symbol of God's judgment (see Ezek. 13:10ff), especially God's eschatological judgment. No power was more certain to evoke fear in pre-nuclear man than the unleashed fury of nature's violence—the symbol was therefore apt (Carson, *The Sermon on the Mount* 133).

Lightfoot asks the question, "How is it that we can hear and not obey?" (91). He suggests three explanations. First, we choose not to act when we should. We may thoroughly enjoy the sermon and leave the place of worship with every intention of doing what we have been neglecting. But Sunday is a day of rest, and Monday is a day of work. So by the time Monday evening arrives, we have lapsed back into the routine of another unproductive week (91).

Second, we do not want to be inconvenienced. Like the foolish man who did not bother about the extra expense and time necessary for a solid foundation, we take the easy way out. We are willing to obey Christ as long as it is pleasant and convenient. But when His will conflicts with ours, then we are ready to part company. "We forget that Christ's mission to earth was not to make it easy for man but to save man" (91).

Third, we do not look ahead. The world is full of people who wish that years ago they had taken a different view of education. They sought the pleasures of the moment, quit school, and took a job with no future. "Either we choose what is pleasurable for the moment and incur disaster later on, or we choose what is difficult for the moment but what will prove best when we stand before Him to render accounts" (92).

Much more devastating is when we make the same mistake on a spiritual level. And, of course, that is Jesus' whole point with the parable. Lightfoot claims that this is the strongest lesson Jesus ever gave on obedience. He writes:

These are words that ring through the centuries. They are not ordinary words. They are not the words of a preacher, a teacher, or a prophet. They are much more. They express the stupendous claim of Jesus to be the only guide for men's souls. Jesus laid it down as a positive and inescapable law that all men had to obey Him. Men must listen to Him and keep His words, or else their lives will crumble in defeat (90).

The Sermon ends with what has been implied from the beginning—the demand for radical submission to Christ. As Carson puts it, "Entrance into the kingdom, then, does turn on obedience after all—not the obedience which earns merit points, but which bows to Jesus' lordship in everything and without reservation" (*The Sermon on the Mount* 131).

The parable ends on a flat note. As the children's chorus says, "The house on the sand fell flat!" Jesus said, "It fell with a great crash" (v. 27). However you word it, the conclusion of the parable is meant to wake us up and shake us into action. Is it a bit surprising to find that not just the parable, but Jesus' whole sermon ends with a loud, crashing alarm? True, Jesus often ended in a positive way when He told stories or touched lives:

1) "But we had to celebrate and be glad, because this brother of yours was dead and is alive again; he was lost and is found" (Luke 15:32).
2) "Rise and go; your faith has made you well" (Luke 17:19).
3) "Neither do I condemn you. . . . Go now and leave your life of sin" (John 8:11).

A WARNING TO OBEY

There were even more times when Jesus concludes His stories with a warning. In fact, that was typical in the Sermon on the Mount. Note the following conclusions to major sections in the Sermon: "Blessed are you when people . . . persecute you" (5:1-12); "not enter the kingdom" (5:17-20); "not get out" of prison (5:21-26); "go into hell" (5:27-30); "commits adultery" (5:31-32); "comes from the evil one" (5:33-37); "not forgive your sins" (6:5-15); "enough trouble of its own" (6:25-34); "turn and tear you to pieces" (7:1-6); "only a few find it" (7:13-14); and, "Away from me, you evildoers!" (7:15-23). It may be surprising, in an age of tolerance, to discover that the majority of the sections of the Sermon on the Mount end with a severe warning.

Jesus is usually seen as a kind and gracious Teacher, overflowing with love and mercy. And He is. No one has ever loved the way Jesus loves. No one has ever cared the way Jesus cares. He is tender. But He is also tough. And when He gets tough, is when He wants us to face the seriousness of our decisions and His warnings about eternity. He wants us to understand fully the consequences of rejecting His claims or ignoring His teachings. Just as Jesus did not shy away from open confrontation with His enemies, so He was not afraid to end His great teachings with a warning.

In 2 Corinthians 5, the Apostle Paul takes the same approach when he concludes his encouragement not to lose heart, not to give up, but to be always confident. In verse 10, he writes, "For we must all appear before the judgment seat of Christ, that each one may receive what is due him for the things done while in the body, whether good or bad." As Carson concludes, "The Sermon on the Mount does not press men and women to despair, still less to self-salvation. Rather it presses men and women to Jesus" (Carson, *The Sermon on the Mount* 131).

And that is what happened when Jesus finished the Sermon. The crowds were "amazed at his teaching" (7:28) and they "followed him" (8:1). Jesus wants nothing less from us—with full obedience. And when the storms come, we will stand. When He comes back, we will be ready!

Conclusion to the
Sermon on the Mount

Matthew 7:28-29

J.K. Jones Jr.

*²⁸When Jesus had finished saying these things, the crowds
were amazed at his teaching, ²⁹because he taught as one
who had authority, and not as their teachers of the law.*

We have come to the conclusion of the Sermon, so what will we do
with Jesus? That is not only the question here, but it is also the fundamental question in all of life. When everything is said and done, the ultimate issue still remains: How do we respond to Jesus? Rafael, the mag-
nificent painter, was once working on one of his now famous Vatican fres-
coes. Legend tells us that there were several pompous and self-absorbed
cardinals watching the painter closely and scrutinizing his every stroke of
the brush. Customarily these onlookers would stand and stare. Without a
word from Rafael, the amateur art critics would begin to criticize the
painter's work. It is reported that one of the cardinals said, "The face of
the Apostle Paul is much too red." Rafael quietly and humbly responded,
"He blushes to see into whose hands the church has fallen."

Dear Christian reader and leader, the church has been entrusted to our
care. This is our watch. What happens in this initial portion of the 21ˢᵗ century falls under our kingdom responsibility. Jesus has preached His heart
out in this segment of Matthew's Gospel. Everything that He has wanted
to say, everything that He wants His disciples to know, and everything that
is necessary for the maturation of future disciples has been shared by this
Teacher. Who is this man? John Stott is insightful as always:

> He did not hum and haw, or hesitate. He was neither tentative nor
> apologetic. Nor again, on the other hand, was he ever bombastic
> or flamboyant. Instead, with quiet and unassuming assurance he
> laid down the law for the citizens of God's kingdom. And *the
> crowds were astonished,* even—for the Greek verb is a strong

one—"dumbfounded." "After nineteen hundred years," comments A.M. Hunter, "we are astonished too" (213).

So I ask again, what will we do with Jesus? It might be good and wise to pause for a moment, literally, and ask yourself: What have I done with Jesus thus far? If I was compelled to testify clearly and articulately my relationship with this man, what would I say? Better yet, how do I understand what Jesus wants to do with me? Even beyond that, what difference would it make? If you are a reader of the Psalms, you may have noticed that there is a little word that appears and reappears seventy-one times. It is the nearly unnoticeable term *selah*. We are not certain of its meaning. The word probably conveys the idea "to lift up" (Hayford 138). This small liturgical or musical notation may have been a reminder to the reader or the worshiper to pause and consider what had just been prayed about or sung. It may have been that strategic place where the Levites praised the Lord for being good and the people responded by prostrating themselves before Him (Bullock 251). Whatever *selah* denotes, it at minimum invites reflection. *Selah.*

Matthew's account of Jesus' message concludes in this fashion: "When Jesus had finished saying these things, the crowds were amazed at his teaching, because he taught as one who had authority, and not as their teachers of the law." D. Martyn Lloyd-Jones understood the critical importance of these concluding verses:

> These two verses are by no means an idle or useless kind of epilogue. They are of great importance in any consideration of the Sermon. I have no doubt that that was the reason why the writer was led by the Holy Spirit to record the effect of the Sermon, because we are directed here to the Preacher rather than to the Sermon. We are asked, as it were, having considered the Sermon, look at the One who delivered it and preached it. . . . When we consider the Sermon on the Mount, we are never to stop even with the moral, ethical, spiritual teaching; we are to go beyond all these things, wonderful as they are, and vital as they all are, to the Person of the Preacher Himself (Lloyd-Jones 326-27).

The fundamental word that must be grappled with is authority.

Matthew uses this word ten other occasions in his Gospel. In Matthew 8:8-9, a marvelous conversation between Jesus and a Roman army officer ensues. The centurion, not wanting to bother Jesus from His appointed task, says:

> "Lord, I do not deserve to have you come under my roof. But just say the word, and my servant will be healed. For I myself am a man under authority, with soldiers under me. I tell this one, 'Go,' and he goes; and that one, 'come,' and he comes. I say to my servant, 'Do this,' and he does it."

A chapter later Jesus heals a paralyzed man and the teachers of the Law have a fit because Jesus' kind of healing includes both body and soul. They accuse Him of blaspheming because He grants forgiveness to the needy man. Jesus' response to their criticism is simple and direct:

"... 'so that you may know that the Son of Man has authority on earth to forgive sins. . . .' Then he said to the paralytic, 'Get up, take your mat and go home.' And the man got up and went home. When the crowd saw this, they were filled with awe; and they praised God, who had given such authority to men" (9:6-8).

Matthew inserts the word again in chapter ten where the text says, "He [Jesus] called his twelve disciples to him and gave them authority to drive out evil spirits and to heal every disease and sickness" (10:1). Jesus then gives the disciples some final instructions and sends them out on kingdom business. They leave with His authority. Ten chapters later (21:23-27) the subject of authority shows up in a question-and-answer session between Jesus and another group of religious leaders. They ask:

"'By what authority are you doing these things?' 'And who gave you this authority?' Jesus replied, 'I will also ask you one question. If you answer me, I will tell you by what authority I am doing these things. John's baptism—where did it come from? Was it from heaven, or from men?'"

They form their unholy huddle and conclude they cannot answer His question. If they respond by saying that John's baptism is from heaven, then Jesus is going to ask them why they did not believe Him? If they say that John's baptism is from men, they are in deep trouble with the people. Jesus concludes the encounter by saying, "Neither will I tell you by what authority I am doing these things." The word does not show up again until the end of Matthew's entire account. His Gospel concludes:

Jesus came to them [the disciples] and said, "All authority in heaven and on earth has been given to me. Therefore go and make disciples of all nations, baptizing them in the name of the Father and of the Son and of the Holy Spirit, and teaching them to obey everything I have commanded you. And surely I will be with you always, to the very end of the age" (28:18-20).

Again, these disciples hear Jesus say that authority finds its ultimate source in Him. Because they are connected to Him intimately, they share in His all-encompassing authority. This is no traveling salesman hocking religious ware. To put it plainly, the disciples are under His sovereign Lordship. All subsequent disciples share that same position and commission. Though Jesus is a Jew, His message is not exclusively Jewish. The crowd recognizes this fact. This Preacher is authoritative.

Matthew says that the hearers of this Sermon realized in absolute amazement that the Preacher did not teach them like one of their rabbis. He was uniquely different! While teachers of the Law were finding their authority by quoting other rabbis, Jesus preached and taught with divine authority. So how does the word authority impact this text and us? Or to ask it in another way: Does my response to Jesus reveal my on-going spiritual formation or my spiritual failure? How would those closest to me respond to this last question? Would they say that Jesus' authority so rules and reigns over my life that I am being shaped by Him in every way? Would they say Jesus' authority does not seem to be making much difference in my loved one's life? Do not get in a hurry. Pause for a moment and ponder these questions. *Selah.*

In the New Testament Scriptures, the word authority occurs 108 times. It is most often found, not surprisingly, in 1 Corinthians, where Paul is struggling with an immature body of believers who are more concerned about their own agendas then that of Jesus; in Luke, where Jesus is constantly under attack from the Pharisees and other religious leaders; and in Revelation, where Jesus is the Lamb on the throne at the center of all reality.

Jesus is the issue. His authority makes it so. To put it into theological terms, Jesus' coming to earth, His reason for being here (to seek and save lost people), put Him on a collision course with the religious leaders of His day (Betz 610). Oswald Chambers, the beloved devotional writer of a previous generation, understood what was at stake in the Sermon:

> Its application for us is not, "What would Jesus do?" but, "What did Jesus say?" As we concentrate on what He said, we can stake our immortal souls upon His words. It is a question of scriptural concentration, not of sentimental consecration (1472).

Let us cut to the chase. What does Jesus' authority mean for us in the 21st century? Clearly, Matthew is concluding a section of his writing and wants the reader to know it. Perhaps you have noticed what others have. Matthew seems to structure his Gospel around the line: "When Jesus had finished. . . ." On four other occasions, Matthew inserts those words. We see them in 11:1; 13:53; 19:1; and 26:1. Each of these major sections includes large hunks of Jesus' teaching ministry. Matthew seems to be saying to the reader, "Take notice. I have just given you some unique insight into the life and words of Jesus." In the first part of Matthew's Gospel, Jesus is revealing how people are to live under God's reign. He concludes this in 7:29. In the second part of his account, he highlights Jesus' instructions to the disciples as He sends them out as missionaries under His supervision. This portion concludes at 11:1. In the third segment there are several controversies recorded. These controversies are grouped with seven parables that invite a clear response to the kingdom. This division concludes at 13:53. In the fourth part of Matthew's account, he portrays Jesus as teaching about the appropriate conduct of believers. This section is wrapped up in 19:1. In the final teaching slice of Matthew's Gospel, he tells the story of Jesus' journey to Jerusalem and the kingdom instruction offered in the final days. The division concludes in 26:1 and then quickly narrates Jesus' trial, crucifixion, resurrection, and commission. Do not lose sight of how the Sermon with its conclusion is the key to all of this material. It compels us to do something with and about Jesus. Virginia Stem Owens has come to understand this essential implication. In her superb reflection on the person of Jesus, she shares a gem:

> As soon as I could understand language, Jesus was handed to me on

a silver platter, like a fish already gutted, cooked, and garnished. People who loved me worked hard to prepare that dish, and it nourished me and made me strong. What it couldn't give me was what those same people called a "personal relationship with Jesus." For that, I needed a live fish. So I had to reverse the process that had first brought him to me—throwing out the parsley, retrieving the entrails, stitching up the slits—trying to get back to the original, elusive fish slipping through deep water. . . . Looking for Jesus is an undertaking fraught with danger. As I intimated earlier, the closer you get to finding him, the higher the stakes become. He is no mere passive object to be circled and appraised like a piece of sculpture. You look at him and he looks back. You may begin the search for Jesus with your own agenda, but be warned: he has one too. As the disciples discovered, you pay the price for finding Jesus (247, 256).

So how did you come to find Him? Better yet, how did He come to find you? How did you meet this authoritative Preacher? *Selah.*

The authority of Jesus is not simply a postscript to the Sermon. Throughout Matthew 5–7, Jesus discloses His authority. On six different occasions (6:21,27,31,33,38, and 43), Jesus uses the refrain, "You have heard that it was said. . . . But I tell you. . . ." This formula pits Jesus' correct understanding of the Law with that of the incorrect interpretation of that same Law by the religious leaders. He, again, is making claim to His divine authority. These are clear statements of His deity. This gigantic, universal authority is also seen in Jesus' keen insight into man's sinful condition, man's motives, and the judgment that will follow for those who reject the will of the Father (7:21-23). This is a clear call to discipleship. The Sermon is an invitation to authentic and lasting spiritual formation. The kind of obedience required is the kind that cannot be microwaved or hurried. It cannot be found through an Internet search or an eastern guru. This relationship is not brought about through legalistic effort and exercise. To be shaped and molded by Jesus' authority, requires dependency, the total kind, upon Jesus. That is the kingdom secret of sweet renunciation. In that renunciation, in that dependency upon Jesus, resides a life-changing storm of grace. The righteousness of the Pharisees and the other religious leaders was completely inadequate because they rejected the authority of Jesus. He was the only means through which these broken leaders could be put back together. So it is with me. So it is with you. Therefore, what will we do with Jesus?

The Sermon penetrates to the heart and to the very center of our attitude. John Stott reminds us of the all-encompassing nature of Jesus' authority. Christ's assessment calls to the deepest places of our soul. Stott speaks of Jesus' authority as the Teacher, as the Christ, as the Lord, as the Savior, as the Judge, as the Son of God, and most of all, of Jesus as God (212-20). What will we do with this Jesus? Stott is right:

We cannot escape the implication of all this. The claims of Jesus were indeed put forward so naturally, modestly and indirectly that many people never even notice them. But they are there; we cannot ignore them and still retain our integrity. Either they are true, or Jesus was suffering from what C.S. Lewis called a "rampant megalomania". . . . The only alternative is to take Jesus at his word, and his claims at their face value. In this case, we must respond to his Sermon on the Mount with deadly seriousness. For here is his picture of God's alternative society (222).

There is within the human spirit a longing for God. If the pre-Christian culture in which we live reveals anything to us, it is this hunger and thirst for the spiritual. Granted, it is the kind of spiritual appetite that is often misapplied and frequently antiauthoritarian. We live at the mercy of our ideas about God. Do we believe in Him or not? There is enough evidence to support the claim that He believes in us! Do we believe that He has our best interests at heart or not? It is the claim of Jesus that the answer to that question is an affirmative (John 3:16). The Preacher of the Sermon is abundantly clear about this one overriding fact: He is God! Therein resides His supreme authority.

This book is a tribute to a man who has lived his life in absolute allegiance to the authority of Jesus. Dr. Marion W. Henderson is a teacher and preacher in love with Christ. If *The Preachers' Teacher* has not evidenced that, then those of us who have contributed to its content have failed. Now and then, since our offices are just down the hall from one another, I am blessed by entering into conversations with this beloved man. Periodically he will just poke his white head into my office and greet me. Sometimes he will linger longer and enter into a hearty conversation about something he has read or something he heard in a recent chapel sermon that has been whirling around in his active mind. Like Jesus, Doc loves to ask questions. By asking those questions, he gives a gift that keeps on giving, even though many students hope and pray that Doc will not call on them to answer any of his questions! Whether the student knows it or not, he has been willed something that will far outlive Doc. A Jesus-intentioned life can be built on a good, healthy question. Marion Henderson knows this truth. In that same spirit, I would like to offer a series of questions that I sometimes ask my students. I think they are so vital to my own spiritual development that I have written them into the front of my Bible. These twenty questions seem appropriate to the whole issue of Christ's authority over every segment of our lives. I would encourage you, dear reader, to not hurry these questions. Taste and savor them one at a time. Pray over them. Meditate on them. Pack them up and carry them with you. *Selah.*

1) Am I closer to Jesus now than at my conversion?
2) Am I consistently striving to be more grace-centered and less legalistic?
3) Does my family see God in me?
4) Do I live in a way that it is clear that my life is ruled by His authority?
5) Can I be trusted?

6) Am I a slave to dress, friends, work, or habits?

7) Do I exaggerate, or am I honest in my daily words and actions?

8) Do I spend regular time in Scripture? Am I applying what I read there?

9) Are my passion, personality, and giftedness working together to bring glory to my King?

10) Am I self-pitying, self-justifying, and just plain "selfed" today?

11) Am I growing in awe and wonder of God?

12) Am I working toward praying without ceasing?

13) Am I being a trusted steward of what God has placed in my care?

14) Am I getting to bed on time and up on time? Does my life show a rhythm in response to His authority?

15) Am I maintaining a balanced diet both spiritually and physically?

16) When was the last time I spoke openly to someone about the claims of Jesus over my life and over their life?

17) Am I jealous, impure, or irritable toward anyone today?

18) Have I developed an unholy habit of grumbling or complaining?

19) Am I obedient in the little things?

20) Have I been anywhere, seen anything, done anything, or heard anything that is not God-honoring?

Each question seeks to elevate the authority of Jesus over my life. The response to this kind of real authority can make the difference between a life of spiritual formation and a life of spiritual failure. The "so what" of life is ultimately and only answered in the Preacher of this Sermon.

For some time I have been a lover of old Christian books and old Christian words. They have stood the test of time and are sure foundations for future construction. In the 4th century, Patrick, the missionary to Ireland, wore a breastplate over his heart that conveyed the authority for his life. Upon that breastplate were written these eloquent words:

Christ with me, Christ before me,
Christ behind me, Christ in me,
Christ beneath me, Christ above me,
Christ when I lie down,
Christ when I sit down,
Christ when I arise,
Christ in the heart of every man who thinks of me,
Christ in the mouth of everyone who speaks of me,
Christ in every eye that sees me,
Christ in every ear that hears me
(*A Little Book of Irish Verse*).

What will we do with Jesus? That remains the question for all time.

Appendix 1

PREACHING AND THE SERMON ON THE MOUNT
G. Charles Sackett

They call it the Sermon on the Mount. Yet the text says, "Now when he saw the crowds, he went up on a mountainside and sat down. His disciples came to him, and he began to teach them . . ." (Matt. 5:1-2) and "When Jesus had finished saying these things, the crowds were amazed at his teaching, because he taught as one who had authority, and not as their teachers of the law" (Matt. 7:28-29).

Two words intrigue me—"taught" and "authority." Jesus did not preach as we often envision it. There was no pulpit, no notes, no invitation at the end. Instead, He explained, expounded, corrected. And He addressed issues directly. He spoke plainly. He hid nothing. He corrected misunderstanding. He called for decisions. He used illustrations and direct speech. He used a variety of forms. But nothing was hidden.

I admit it—I am standing on my soapbox. In recent years there has been a consistent move among homileticians calling for indirect or inductive or narrative preaching. And no doubt there is a place for all of them in the preacher's arsenal. But most of the time the arguments of those proposing these forms revolve around Jesus' use of parables and stories. There are claims made that Jesus only used parables. Both explicitly and implicitly there is a denigration of classical, direct preaching. Exposition is caricatured as three points and poem.

Undoubtedly, poor expository preaching needs improvement. All expository preaching needs inductive elements. Without question, narrative texts and parables deserve to be treated as unique literary forms. But it appears many preachers have thrown baby and bath water (truth and form) out together. I am suggesting it is too extreme a decision. Some texts, like the Sermon on the Mount, call for direct exposition (complete with appropriate inductive elements).

For that reason, these sermons are direct in nature. They reflect the nature of the texts they exposit. They are reflective of what the Author did when it was originally presented. I hope they are clear and helpful.

The sermons represent the material included in the various chapters as they were presented by their respective authors (though edited for consistency, with apologies to the original authors for liberties taken). They are presented as models, not as final editions. They present a way to get at these texts. They form a unit that might become a series for use in a congregation (though admittedly it would be a long series).

Please, use what you can. Adapt all of what you use and preach them with vigor and passion. Dr. Henderson would want it that way. He is a lover of good preaching. He appreciates the creative, but he loves the direct explanation and application of the Scripture. He is submissive to Scripture and knows it is only a word about Jesus that makes any difference. *May Dr. Henderson rejoice in the legacy he has left, but may **Jesus** be the one who gets the glory!*

1 ■ LISTENING TO THE TEACHER
Matthew 5:1-2

Dominant Thought: Genuine disciples reflect the character of their teacher.
Objective: The listeners will determine to submit to the teachings of Jesus.

Walter Henrichsen says, "Disciples are made, not born." Today we might say, "Disciples are formed . . ."
➢ Jesus might have said, "Disciples are called."
● Note the context: Matthew 4:18-22
Matthew 5:1—He saw the crowds, but it was "His disciples" who "came to Him."
➢ Early in Matthew (before the Twelve are selected) we are told what disciples look like.

Genuine disciples reflect the character of their teacher.

Transition: What do called disciples look like? What might characterize us if we were disciples of Jesus? What in Jesus develops in us?

1) Genuine disciples recognize the difference between the Word of God and the words of men.
Restatement: Disciples of Jesus know what God means when He speaks. They are students of the truth, who obey the truth when they hear it.
Explanation:
    a) Matthew 5:3-16 reflects the disciples' character and influence.
    – Who we are determines what we can do.
    b) Matthew 5:17-20 clarifies that we are seeing a "new Word" from God.
       i) The perfect Jew has arrived. He came from the right family with the right birth. His baptism was proper. He had a successful wilderness experience. He now speaks from the mountain of God.
      ii) Later, He is affirmed in the transfiguration.
    c) Matthew 5:21-48
    – Six clear sets of opposites—"You have heard it said, but, I say to you. . . ."
    d) It is one thing to think we know what God means, quite another to actually know.
    – Traditional interpretations were giving way to divine insight.
    e) Disciples look carefully at the words of God. They want to know the truth.
Illustration: Fred Johnson chapel sermon (Matthew 4:1-11): Jesus was not only word-centered but also truth-centered.
    f) Disciples listen diligently to the words of God. They want to obey the truth.

Illustration: "I know that's what the Bible says, 'but. . . .'"

➤ Question: As we study the Sermon on the Mount, will you listen? Will you obey? Will I listen? Will I obey?

Transition: Like Jesus, we recognize God's Word when we hear it.

2) Genuine disciples reflect the difference between the *fact* of righteousness and the *act* of righteousness.

Restatement: Disciples of Jesus realize that we cannot do righteousness until we are righteous.

Explanation: Lots of people put on the right face. They look the part.

    a) Matthew 6:1-18 reflects the secret places where the motives lie.
       – "When you. . . ."
    b) Matthew 6:19-24 reflects the secret place where the masters vie.
       – "Can't serve two masters. . . ."
    c) Matthew 6:25-34 reflects the secret place where the mission drives.
       – "Seek first. . . ."
    d) Disciples are made right by their relationship with Jesus.
       – Their behavior and attitudes merely reflect what God has already done in them.
    e) Disciples do what they should: give, pray, fast and trust, but not because they want to earn something.

Illustration: Gift versus merit

➤ Question: As we study the Sermon on the Mount, will we evaluate our activity? Will we look to see what drives our actions? Is it an attempt to reflect righteousness or appear righteous?

Transition: Like Jesus, our actions reflect our character.

3) Genuine disciples realize the difference between God's judgment and man's opinion.

Restatement: Disciples of Jesus learn to see what God sees.

    a) Not everything is as it appears on the surface.

Explanation:

       i) 7:1-5 warns against being judgmental
       ii) 7:6-12 warns against being undiscerning
       iii) 7:13-14 warns against the seemingly simple (wide gate)
       iv) 7:15-20 warns against the outwardly safe (wolves looking like sheep)
       v) 7:21-23 warns against the foolishly disobedient (workers of lawlessness)
       vi) 7:24-27 warns against the subtly unstable (sand)
    b) Disciples recognize the need to make wise decisions based on what they understand of God.
       i) Judgment and discernment are not antagonistic.
       ii) We are to judge a righteous judgment.

Illustration: Confronting a brother versus "gossip" in prayer meeting
- c) Disciples realize they need to make wise, intelligent choices about life.

Illustration: Choosing a line in the store/filling station
- ➢ Question: As we study the Sermon on the Mount will we look at our current choices? Are we making wise decisions? Are our decisions being guided by a biblical understanding of God?

Jesus calls us to be disciples. But the call is not to instant perfection; it is to a journey. He calls us to a process of formation into His character.
- ➢ Join us in working through the Sermon on the Mount listening carefully how God speaks to you personally.
- ➢ Determine to listen and obey even when it appears the opposite choice may seem easier or more sensible at the moment.
- ➢ Respond with obedience and you will find yourself reflecting the character of Jesus more clearly every day.

2 ■ AS ONE WITH AUTHORITY
Matthew 7:28-29

Dominant Thought: Jesus is God, therefore fully authoritative.
Objective: The listeners will follow Jesus as His disciples.

"He did not hum and haw, or hesitate. He was neither tentative nor apologetic. Nor again, on the other hand, was he ever bombastic or flamboyant. Instead, with quiet and unassuming assurance he laid down the law for the citizens of God's kingdom. And the crowds were astonished. . . ." (John R.W. Stott).

Matthew 7:28-29

"These two verses are by no means an idle or useless kind of epilogue. They are of great importance in any consideration of the Sermon. I have no doubt that that was the reason why the writer was led by the Holy Spirit to record the effect of the Sermon, because we are directed here to the Preacher rather than to the Sermon" (David Martyn Lloyd-Jones).

➤ The fundamental word we wrestle with is authority.
- Ten occurrences in Matthew (7:29; 8:8-9; 9:6-8; 10:1; 20:23-27; 21:23-27; 28:18-20).
- Disciples are under the authority of the sovereign Lord.
- Disciples find their authority only in their relationship with Jesus.
- Jesus taught with authority, unlike the rabbis (29).

➤ The concept of authority pervades the New Testament.
- 108 occurrences.
  - 1 Corinthians—Where the struggle is over the agenda set by Jesus versus personal agendas.
  - Luke—Where Jesus is under attack from the Pharisees.
  - Revelation—Where Jesus is the Lamb on the throne.

➤ The authority of Jesus makes Jesus the issue.
- "Its application for us is not, 'What would Jesus do?' but, 'What did Jesus say?'" (Oswald Chambers).
- The key question is, "What does Jesus' authority mean to us?"
  - Matthew's organization surrounds "When Jesus had finished . . ."
    - Each time it says "Take notice! I've given you a unique insight into Jesus."
    - Matt. 7:28; 11:1; 13:53; 19:1; 26:1.
  - This conclusion compels us to do something about Jesus.

➤ The Sermon on the Mount focuses on Jesus' authority.

- "But I say to you . . ."
  - Matt. 6:21,27,31,33,38, and 43.
  - Jesus corrects the contemporary misunderstandings of the Law.
- The Sermon becomes a call to discipleship—submission to the Lordship of Jesus.

➤ The Sermon penetrates to the heart and center of our attitudes.
  - Jesus calls to the deepest places of our soul.
  - "We cannot escape the implication of all this. The claims of Jesus were indeed put forward so naturally, modestly and indirectly that many people never even notice them. But they are there; we cannot ignore them and still retain our integrity. Either they are true, or Jesus was suffering from what C.S. Lewis called a 'rampant megalomania.' The only alternative is to take Jesus at his word, and his claims at their face value" (John R.W. Stott).

Our pre-Christian culture reveals its hunger and thirst for the spiritual.
➤ Do we believe in Jesus or not?
➤ Will we believe that He has our best interests at heart?
➤ Will we submit to His authority or not?

The Preacher of the Sermon on the Mount is abundantly clear about this one overriding fact: He is God! All authority rests in Him. Our only acceptable response is to follow as His disciples.

3 ■ APPLAUSE FROM NAIL-PIERCED HANDS
Matthew 5:3-12

Dominant Thought: Jesus blesses the upside-down people who make up
   His disciples.
Objective: The listeners will choose to live against the tide of the world's
   values.

Many metaphors for the church exist in Scripture (body, flock, family,
etc.). Other metaphors for the church are not explicitly named in Scripture
but perhaps implied:
➤ The church is a woman in her wedding gown standing on top of a
   landfill.
➤ The church is a conduit taking the fresh water of life to the desert.
➤ The metaphor that I would like to develop in this message has to do
   with a river and a canoe. You are in the canoe paddling upstream.
   Everyone in the world is on one bank yelling that you are going the
   wrong way. There is only one person on the other bank. He has first-
   century Palestinian clothing on, has olive-colored skin and nailed-
   pierced hands. He is not saying a thing, but He has a smile on His face
   and is applauding you.
Allow that image to fill your mind as we study the first part of the introduction to the Sermon on the Mount from Matthew 5:3-12. The main idea
from this text I would like to stress is that Jesus blesses (applauds or honors) the upside-down people who make up His disciples.

1) Jesus blesses needy people (3,6,10-12).
   a)   The message of the bulk of the Bible is, "God helps those who
   can't help themselves."
   b)   The beatitudes portray three kinds of needy people:
      1)   Bankrupt people (3): These people have only one direction
           to look, and that is up because they are flat on their backs.
      2)   Starving people (6): These people cannot get enough of God.
           They are passionately trying to get closer to Him.
      3)   Hurt people (10-12): These people are being beat up and
           mocked, but they have a spring in their steps and a song in
           their hearts.

2) Jesus blesses kneeling people (4-5).
   a)   Prayer is an important part of the Sermon on the Mount (6:5-15;
        7:7-11), but there are other purposes for which to kneel.
      1)   Sometimes we are brought to our knees by tears (4).
      2)   Sometimes we are brought to our knees by humility (5).
   b)   Let the church go forward on her knees. She cannot stumble
        when she is on her knees.

3) Jesus blesses focused people (7-9).
   a) Focused people will be pro-active concerning expressing their loving kindness (7).
   b) Focused people will be pro-active concerning their moral excellence (8).
   c) Focused people will be pro-active concerning their reconciliation (9).
   d) The power of purpose is a wonderful thing. Consider Paul, "This one thing I do . . . " (Phil. 3:13).

Conclusion:
We have to decide whether we desire the applause of people or the nod of God. The applause of people dies quickly; the nod of God lasts for eternity.
➢ Christianity will always, by its nature, be counter-cultural.
➢ Anyone ready to paddle upstream?

4 ■ THE POWER OF INFLUENCE
Matthew 5:13-16

Dominant Thought: Disciples are God's way of changing things.
Objective: The listeners will seek opportunities to influence their world.

John Piper says, "The reason we have evangelism is because we do not have worship." He is right.
➤ We live in a fallen world that appears to be getting worse all the time.
➤ Yet John Stott reminds us that we should not blame the world.
  ● "Don't blame the house for getting dark; that's what happens when the sun goes down."
  ● "Don't blame the meat for getting putrid; that's what happens when bacteria sets in."

God calls disciples to influence the world; disciples are God's way of changing things.

Matthew 5:13-16

Transition: If the beatitudes are the disciple's character traits, the salt and light passages are his influence.

1) The purpose of our influence: turn the world to worship.
Restatement: Disciples exist to make a difference. They are used by God to change the focus of people's attention.
  a) Salt and light are both influences that cannot be ignored. Their presence is undeniable.
Illustration: Bright lights; salty food
  b) God has always desired to have people live in a relationship with Him, unselfishly.
    i) Isaiah 42:6: "light to the nations"
    ii) Isaiah 49:5-6: "too small a thing"
  c) If it was wrong for Israel to ignore the nations, it is equally wrong for the church.
    i) We must minister across ethnic divisions, age differences, and socio-economic strata.
    ii) Our goal, as disciples, is to turn those who worship themselves toward the only One worthy of worship.
    iii) We do not get to choose our purpose. That has already been chosen.
      – Matthew 28:18-20

Transition: Evangelism is not what we tell people, unless what we tell is totally consistent with who we are. It is who we are that is going to make the difference. If we do not truly enjoy our faith, nobody is going to catch the fire of enjoyment from us. If our lives are not totally centered on Christ, we will not be Christ-bearers for others, no matter how pious our words. [Madeleine L'Engle qtd. in *Christian Reader* (May/June 1998, p. 50)].

2) The power of our influence: turning character into action.

Restatement: Doing something is first contingent on being something.

Explanation: Metaphors at work—statements of fact

➢ You ARE salt and light.

➢ God has so made us.

    a) What we are must precede what we do.

        i) Context: The beatitudes come first as a picture of a disciple's character (5:3-12).

        ii) Context: Faithful obedience follows the beatitudes accurately reflecting truth (5:17ff.).

    b) At the center of the Sermon are metaphors showing what our character is to reflect.

        i) Absolutely essential that disciples work on their character.

        ii) Integrity (wholeness, consistency) is key to successful witnessing.

Who we are determines our effectiveness.

Illustration: Rebecca Manley Pippert's title: *Out of the Saltshaker and into the World*

➢ Salt must be applied to serve its purpose.

➢ A light should be placed on a stand, not under a bushel.

The challenge to the disciple:

➢ Develop character.

➢ Deploy into the world.

5 ■ LIVING ABOVE THE LAW
Matthew 5:17-20

Dominant Thought: Disciples choose a life that exceeds mere duty.
Objective: The listeners will choose to make righteousness a way of life.

Living above the law is not an unfamiliar statement today.
➤ Whether it is the President of the United States or a Fortune 500 company, too many people believe they are above the law.
➤ Even Christians fall into that trap.
- Breaking the speed limit
- Borrowing supplies from work
- Fudging on our taxes
- Dabbling inappropriately on the Internet
- Cheating on a spouse

➤ But what if living above the law meant something different—actually living on a higher spiritual plane?
➤ That is the call Jesus makes to His disciples in Matthew 5:17-20: Disciples choose a life that exceeds mere duty.

1) Jesus clarifies His relationship to the Law.
Restatement: He came to fulfill the Law, not destroy it.
Explanation: Jesus and the Law
➤ The Law defined (illustrate with scribal laws)
➤ The authority of Jesus—He can do what He wishes.
  a) The accomplishment of God's plan for saving mankind is the fulfillment of the Law.
    i) Jesus did what the Law could only prepare people for.
    ii) In Matthew, He is the perfect Jew (He is in contrast to Israel).
      (1) His pedigree goes to Abraham.
      (2) His birth fulfills prophecy.
      (3) He left Egypt.
      (4) He overcame temptation (did not fail).
      (5) He explains the Law and keeps it perfectly.
  b) In keeping the Law He accomplished God's intended purpose.

Transition: Nothing anyone could do was going to prevent God from carrying out His covenant purpose. The Law would serve its purpose.

2) Jesus clarifies our relationship to the Law.
Restatement: We live above the law and not in submission to it.
Explanation: Christians are not under the Law; we are not obligated to keep it.
  a) Christians, instead, live a life that reflects grace and gratitude.

    b)   For Christians, the Law becomes the means of understanding the heart and mind of God.
        i)   So we attempt to live even more righteously.
        ii) Not because such a life saves, but because such a life shows gratitude.

Illustration: Children should obey their parents because they love them, not because of their rules.

➢ A hard concept to grasp—we tend to fear license if there is no law.

Conclusion:

➢ The Law is our teacher—to bring us to Christ.
➢ The Law is our guide—to clarify God's heart and standards.
➢ The Law is our friend—to enable us to live a life worthy of the death of Christ.

6 ■ MANAGING ANGER
Matthew 5:21-26

Dominant Thought: The disciple seeks to live at peace with all men.
Objective: The listeners will take all appropriate steps to manage anger.

Jesus sets up this section of His Sermon on the Mount with this amazing declaration in verse 20: "For I tell you that unless your righteousness surpasses that of the Pharisees and Teachers of the Law, you will certainly not enter the kingdom of heaven."
➢ Followed by six teachings used as examples of what He means.
➢ Six authentic issues of the heart: anger, purity, marriage, truth, grace, and love.
➢ Jesus raised the bar from Law to grace.
➢ Jesus' model in these instances was to follow this pattern: What? So what? For instance.

What?
1) Anger is our attempt at self-preservation.
   a) **Explanation**: "Anger is defined as an interest to preserve 1) our personal worth; 2) our essential needs; 3) our basic convictions" (Les Carter).
   b) Even God displays these interests:
      i) The Father is angry with the Israelites—an issue of preserving righteousness (an essential need based in His character).
      ii) Jesus is angry with the Pharisees over healing a man's hand on the Sabbath—an issue of personal worth.
      iii) The Holy Spirit displays anger toward Ananias and Sapphira when they lie—an issue of basic convictions about truth.

So What?
2) Anger is our entrance into unholy attitudes.
   a) It is interesting that managing anger leads the list of misapplications of God's laws.
   b) Jesus teaches that anger can lead to murder.
      i) He was a victim of just such a development.
      ii) Anger is a pervasive problem in American culture that needs to be addressed.
   c) Jesus lifts the bar from codebook to heart.
      i) Not even "Raca" or "you fool" is acceptable.
      ii) **Illustration**: Hate-crime legislation
   d) Jesus raises three levels of anger:
      i) Anger in the heart—no words; yet can kill one's heart.

    ii) Anger in the heart that treats with disrespect—words spoken; relationships killed.

    iii) Anger in the heart that condemns another—may be manifest in physical acts.

    iv) All are considered unacceptable.

For Instance.

3) Anger affects our relationship with God and man.
    a) Jesus calls us to reconciliation before we worship.
        i) "Go and make amends" is our responsibility.
        ii) Unhealthy relationships require immediate attention.
    b) Jesus calls us to reconcile before we go to court.
        i) Winning is not the most important issue.
        ii) Anger can take the heart prisoner and could be worse than actual prison.

The key is managing the natural emotion of anger. Because so much is at stake in our relationship with God, the disciple seeks to live at peace with all men.

7 ■ A MATTER OF HEART, NOT HORMONES
Matthew 5:27-30

Dominant Thought: Christ, not culture, determines our sexual values.
Objective: The listeners will determine to remain sexually pure.

➤ "Today's Bible lesson is on sex," announces the teacher to the unsus-pecting class. Silence reigns as some fear what may become known.
➤ "Today's Bible lesson is on sex," announces the teacher to the unsus-pecting class. "I've committed adultery," he continues. "So have you!"

Transition: The heart of Jesus' teaching on sexual purity revolves around the truth that sexual purity is a matter of the heart.

1) Jesus teaches us to reject sexual perversion (27).
   a) The Bible is not prudish, nor pornographic in discussing God's design for sexual expression.
      i) Sex is a divine gift with specific parameters.
      ii) Sexual expression is restricted to one's marriage partner (Heb. 13:4; Gen. 2:18; Matt. 19:6).
   b) Adultery violates God's will for marriage (1 Cor. 16:9).
      – Unfaithfulness to one's spouse is adultery.
   c) All extramarital sexual activity violates God's will for marriage.
      – Any sexual expression outside of marriage constitutes unfaithful-ness and adultery (1 Thess. 4:3; Gal. 5:19; Col. 3:5; 1 Cor. 10:8).

Transition: Christians must understand and commit themselves to obey-ing God's standards concerning sexual purity.

2) Jesus calls us to control our sexual passion (28).
   a) God designed both sexual purity and sexual passion.
      i) Sexual desire is God ordained (Song of Sol. 8:5-6; 5:18-19).
      ii) But "look" must not turn to "lust" (Exod. 20:15; Deut. 5:18).
   b) In calling lust adultery, Jesus stresses the spiritual/heart nature of sexual purity.
      i) Obedience is both external and internal.
      ii) Christ calls for both holy deeds and holy desires.

Transition: Christians must acknowledge sexual purity as a matter of heart and action.

3) Jesus compels us to practice sexual purity (29-30).
   a) Jesus uses hyperbole to stress the importance of dealing with sex-ual temptation.

      i)   Sexual activity outside of marriage violates God's standards and ends in judgment.

      ii)   The most precious or cherished parts of our life are to be sacrificed to protect against failure.

  b) Christians may make no room for compromise, accommodation, concession, or negotiation.

Quotation: MacArthur (300)

Transition: Christians must respond to all sexual temptation with direct confrontation of both heart and body.

Conclusion:
Since sexual purity is primarily a concern of the heart, the decision to control one's sexual life is a matter of intention. The disciple intends to remain sexually pure and will do whatever is necessary to maintain that decision.

8 ■ BEFORE THE DIVORCE PAPERS
Matthew 5:31-32

Dominant Thought: A biblical perspective on marriage provides the best prevention for divorce.

Objective: Listeners will adopt a biblical view of marriage that honors God and upholds His character in a fallen world.

➢ John Stott's confession in *Christian Counter-Culture* (92).
➢ Like Jesus, we are weighing in on an issue close to God's heart—balancing grace and truth.
  ● All grace minimizes the costs and consequences of marital failure.
  ● All truth treats divorce as the unforgivable sin and the divorced as hopeless and helpless before God.
➢ The problem is not divorce but that people don't know how to be married. (Quote from Dallas Willard, *Renovation of the Heart* 190).

We begin where Jesus began. Before He would talk about divorce, He talked about marriage. Matthew 19:3-12 is the best commentary on Matthew 5:31-32.

Transition: Jesus teaches three truths about marriage that shape a biblical perspective on divorce.

1) The origin of marriage is rooted in creation not in culture.
Restatement: The source of our marriages is the mind of God.
  a) Jesus answers the questions about divorce by focusing on the origin of marriage in Genesis 2:18-24.
  b) When Paul speaks of the mystery of Christian marriage, he appeals to the origin of marriage in Genesis 2:24.
Illustration: A cartoon shows a previously promiscuous cave man dragging a woman to become foolishly monogamous.
  c) Marriage ceremonies and rituals are cultural, but marriage is God-ordained.
  d) Divorce, on the other hand, owes its origin to the hardness of men's hearts and is cultural in origin.
  e) Divorce practices vary from culture to culture.
  f) Divorce practices have evolved over time.
Illustration: Israel's adaptation of pagan practices were the causes which prompted Moses' requirement for a certificate of divorce.
  g) Jewish interpretation in first century
  h) Attitudes in America over the past 200 years

Transition: Marriage is God's design while divorce is man's idea.

2) The essence of marriage is a covenant not a contract.

Restatement: The substance of our marriages is the character of God.

    a) Marriage is a covenant involving three parties, not a contract between two consenting adults who can dissolve it at will if there is cause, and, in some cases, even no fault.

Illustration: Breaking of the covenant in Malachi 2

    b) Divorce is the legal act of dissolving a marriage contract—what man does to separate a union in spite of what God does to make a union.

Transition: Marriage is intended to be for a lifetime, not just for a while like other contracts which we may cancel at will.

3) The essential ingredient for marriage is commitment, not compatibility.

Restatement: The success of our marriages is the will of God.

    a) Years ago The Compatibility Game was used to test how compatible couples were for each other—backgrounds, interests, personality types, etc. The most common cause for divorce is incompatibility or irreconcilable differences.

Illustration: Low divorce rates in cultures of family-arranged marriages

    b) Love is a choice, not a feeling. Commitment to family and honor are more important than compatibility.

    c) The most important ingredient for marital success is commitment.

        i) Commitment to marriage

        ii) Commitment to your marriage partner

        iii) Commitment to Christ

    d) Divorce that is consistent with Jesus' teaching is the violation of the marriage commitment expressed in marital unfaithfulness (Matt. 5:32; 19:9). Such an act of unfaithfulness breaks the bond of marriage and the one-flesh union (1 Cor. 6:16-20).

Conclusion:

The model for Christian marriages is the relationship of Christ and the church—planned by God before creation, expressed in covenant, and lived out in mutual commitment to one another. This model reflects God's unfailing love in spite of Israel's unfaithfulness (Hosea) and Christ's perfect love in spite of the church's imperfections (Eph. 5:23-32).

9 ■ TRUTH-CENTERED SPEECH
Matthew 5:33-37

Dominant Thought: Our words reveal our character.
Objective: The listeners will determine to speak the truth in all situations.

➢ **Illustrations** of key words that relieved Jews of their obligations (e.g., Corban)
- Jesus' exhortation on oaths was made because of the perversion of God's law by Jews to avoid being truthful.
- Jesus taught that our words were always to be the truth.
- Peter was betrayed by his speech as he denied Jesus (Matt. 26:73); let our speech portray Christ as we serve Him.

Transition: Jesus teaches us that our words reveal our character.

1) Our words reflect whose we are (33).
Restatement: We are Christ-followers who identify with Christ.
    a) God's Word tells us who He is:
        – In the beginning God (Gen. 1:1); "I am that I am" (Exod. 3:14); "Be still, know that I am God" (Ps. 46:10) are all descriptions of God.
    b) Jesus is identified by the Word and His words.
        – John 1:1-14; John 14:6
    c) We are identified by His Word and our words.
        – I am a kingdom person (Matt. 5:3-12); I have put on Christ (Col. 3:1-11).

Transition: God's Word, coupled with our words, reflect our relationship with God as His children.

2) Our words reflect what we are (34-36).
Restatement: We are Christ-followers who depend upon grace.
    a) The Word tells us God is ruler of the universe.
        – This is illustrated in His response to Job (chapters 38–39); yet full of grace and mercy.
    b) The Word tells us Jesus is redeemer of the universe.
        – He came to seek and save the lost (Luke 19:9) and brought salvation to all men (Titus 2:11-14).
    c) The Word tells us we are sinners saved by grace.
        i) All have sinned (Rom. 3:23); saved by grace (Eph. 2:8-9); heirs with Christ (Rom. 8:12-17).
        ii) Our words confirm or deny the truth of what the Word teaches about us.

Transition: God's Word, reflected in our words, demonstrate we are sinners saved by grace.

3) Our words reflect where we are (37).
Restatement: We are Christ-followers who speak the truth.
    a) The Word reveals that God always was and always will be.
       – And He's always on our side (Rom. 8:31-38).
    b) The Word reveals that Jesus is on the side of truth (John 18:37).
       – He is the same yesterday, today, and forever (Heb. 13:8).
    c) The Word, confirmed by our words, reveals we are to be people of the truth.
       i) A man's word is his bond (the power of a handshake).
       ii) A person's dignity and reputation are maintained by his words.
       iii) Christ-followers concentrate on TC (truth-centered) instead of PC (politically correct) speech.

Conclusion:
A person's heart is revealed through his mouth. His character is demonstrated in his truthfulness. As disciples we have identified with Christ by depending upon grace. The world will never believe that, unless we demonstrate the change through truthful speech and a truth-filled life.

10 ■ MORE
Matthew 5:38-42

Dominant Thought: Disciples practice self-sacrifice rather than self-preservation.
Objective: The listeners will choose to demonstrate a sacrificial spirit, especially in the hard situations.

All our lives we have been taught that "more is better" and "less is for some unfortunate person who does not quite have what it takes." Jesus' take on "eye for eye" and "tooth for tooth" runs counter to this notion in its insistence that real disciples give away more than anyone could ever anticipate. Rather than looking to entitlements and rights for their sustenance, disciples of Jesus are forever finding ways to demonstrate compassion by giving whatever they have been given by God: a cheek, a coat, a mile, and/or money.

Matthew 5:38-42

Transition: There are at least four circumstances that illustrate the point well. We follow Jesus by:

1) Giving more—when we are treated as victims of shameful acts (39).
Restatement: Meet violence with surprise—offer the other cheek!
   a) The setting of 39a was a legal one.
   b) Christians, watch the four R's: retaliation, retribution, revenge, and resentment.
   c) Being generous is giving without thought of personal consequence.
Illustration: The life of George Dawson in *Life Is So Good* (with Richard Glaubman, Penguin USA, 2001)

Transition: Christians give more than is expected by meeting violence with surprise, but we also follow Jesus by:

2) Giving more—since we are people under God's Law (40).
Restatement: Giving more than God Himself requires!
   a) Explain the concept of tunic and cloak in Exodus 22:26-27.
      i) A law rooted in compassion.
      ii) Offering the cloak is more than the Law demanded.
      iii) Consider what this principle teaches us about radical forgiveness.
Illustration: The actions of Reginald Denny, who was attacked following the Rodney King verdict in Los Angeles. After recovering, Denny returned to those who mugged him and forgave them.

Transition: Both when treated as victims of shameful acts and as people under God's Law, disciples give more. But that is not all, we further demonstrate compassion by:

3) Giving more—since we are people under human authority (41).
Restatement: Giving more than the state demands!
   a) This is a hard pill for some to swallow.
   b) Remember Simon of Cyrene (Matt. 27:32)? He practiced the principle of submission to the conscripting state.
       – Cf. Romans 13:1ff.
   c) "The first mile renders to Caesar the things that are Caesar's; the second mile, by meeting oppression with kindness, renders to God the things that are God's" (T.W. Manson).
Illustration: Specific voluntary relief efforts since 9/11 demonstrate extraordinary civic compassion.

Transition: Outrageous giving in every area of our lives includes:

4) Giving more—since we are to be compassionate caregivers (42).
Restatement: Offering more than beggars ask!
   a) The Old Testament made provision for gifts and loans (Exod. 22:25; Deut. 15:7-8).
   b) But, in keeping with the context, Jesus is calling for more.
   c) This requires a new orientation for Americans:
       i)   Rather than finding out how much we are able to borrow, we need to examine how much we can give.
       ii) Rather than focusing on what we can get, we should rather center on what we are able to give.
Illustration: Wayne Smith tells the story of two high school boys who each gave their entire personal savings to the church building program, giving up their hopes of buying cars.

Transition: Giving more catches the attention of everyone. True, it is risky, but is it not riskier to hoard all you have, or even to give only what is required?

This is no easy text, but whoever said discipleship was easy by human standards? If anything, it is "non-discipleship" (Dallas Willard) that costs us our lives and our souls. In asking His followers to give more, Jesus is in reality liberating them from the damning tyranny of riches and material goods. He is offering release from the very consuming self-interest that has stolen the heart of this nation. There is a better way!

In 1966 Private Milton Olive received the Medal of Honor, the highest honor awarded anyone in this country. In a war that for many made no sense, in a time of paralyzing national indecision, right in the midst of a rebellious drug culture and a shameless sexual revolution, this young African-American, thousands of miles from home, lunged to his death on a live grenade in order to save the lives of his four comrades. President Lyndon Johnson said, "to put others first and self last is the hardest but highest decision any man is caused to make," and an entire nation stood transfixed. For a moment we were forced to ask fundamental questions: Why are we here? For whom have we come? What will we do with our lives? What will be said of us when we have left? Is there any instinct higher than self-preservation? In those chaotic years, defined by a war many thought uncalled for, no one thought Private Olive's actions were insignificant.

11 ■ TAKING THE HIGH ROAD
Matthew 5:43-48

Dominant Thought: Disciples love like their Father loves.
Objective: Respond with love and not revenge.

It is a pretty easy command . . . unless you have been hurt by someone.
Illustration: Response to daughter's rape and murder
Illustration: Common theme of movies: Karate Kid; Superman; Batman
. . . Revenge, cast in the framework of nobility
"You take the high road and I'll take the low road . . ."
The high road, in this case, is a tough climb, but worth it.
Disciples love like their Father loves.

Matthew 5:43-48

1) We demonstrate a higher standard than the world.
Restatement: Our mandate is to love our enemies.
   a) **Explanation**: Love versus hate; neighbor versus friend.
   b) Anyone can love a neighbor who does good things for him or her.
   c) Question is—can we love those who hurt us?
   d) The little issues sometimes get us.
      i) A neighbor who does not mow his lawn or pick up his trash bugs us.
      ii) Someone irritates us when he takes our parking spot or our favorite seat.
   e) The big issues often overwhelm us.
      i) We are lied about, slandered.
      ii) Someone embarrasses us in public.
   f) The serious issues drown us.
      i) Someone we love is raped, robbed, or murdered.
      ii) Someone in the professional field sues us out of his or her personal revenge.
   g) The Christian response is love.
      "A committed concern for another person's well being, whether physical or spiritual, without thought of what you'll get in return" (Kenneth Beckman, BBC, 1969).
   h) We do what is good for the other people.
      i) We serve them, pray for them and seek their best.
      ii) We forgive them and forbear.

It is a pretty easy command . . . unless you have been hurt.

2) We imitate a superior model in contrast with the world's.
Restatement: Our model is greater than the world can offer.

Explanation: The Father sends rain and sunshine on all. Even the sinners love each other.

    a) Our model is the Father Himself.

        i) He treats all equally including sending His Son to die for all (Rom. 5:6-8).

        ii) He is perfect.

           – There is no unwholeness, inconsistency, or lack of integrity in His response.

    b) Our response must be to seek the good of all, even those who mistreat and abuse us.

    c) Our greatest goal must be for others to find a relationship with the same Father we have.

Disciples love like their Father loves…and that includes loving the unlovely.

➢ Elizabeth Elliot and Rachel Saint went back to the very tribe that killed their husbands.

➢ Corrie Ten Boom saw a German guard in a church service. This guard was a guard in the concentration camp where Ten Boom was placed. He had become a Christian, and she was able to forgive him.

➢ Florence Dace gave her husband's Bible to the man who killed him. She prayed and visited the killer while he was in prison, and rejoiced when he gave his life to Christ.

Who do you need to love? What will you do today to demonstrate that you love like a disciple?

12 ■ GIVING THAT GLORIFIES GOD
Matthew 6:1-4

Dominant Thought: Genuine generosity pleases our Father.
Objective: The listeners will choose to glorify God through their giving.

Have you received any appeals for money for the poor this week? What did you do with the requests? Did you send them straight to the wastepaper basket? Did you think, "I wish I could help, but . . ."? Did you send a check? Our text speaks today to the issue of the Christian's concern for the poor.

Matthew 6:1-4
Genuine generosity pleases our Father.

Transition: What characterizes giving that honors and pleases God?

1) We share our Father's compassion (2a,3a).
Restatement: We follow the right example.
   a) God's concern is evident through the Bible.
      i)   Generosity is present in our text as Jesus assumes His disciples will contribute to relief funds.
      ii) Various passages instruct Israel to provide assistance for those in need.
         – God is frequently seen as the champion of the poor.
      iii) Generosity is present in the New Testament, which reports the efforts of the early church to care for its own and others.
   b) We should share this same concern today.
      i)   There are many opportunities to assist others right in our own community, either directly or through our church or local charities. We can contribute time as well as money.
      ii) There are also numerous opportunities to assist needy people in our own country and through the world through a variety of organizations, especially Christian relief agencies.

Transition: But not only do we share our Father's compassion, we imitate our Father's motives.

2) We imitate our Father's motives (1-3).
Restatement: We give for the right reasons.
   a) God is not pleased when we give for the wrong reasons.
      i)   Jesus condemns the Pharisees and teachers of the Law for their hypocrisy. These hypocrites (actors) were actually concerned about receiving human attention and applause. They had the fleeting reward they sought but forfeited any reward from God.

   ii) Ananias and Sapphira (Acts 5:1-11) illustrate the importance of right motives.

   iii) We should examine our own hearts to make sure our giving is free from pride and the desire to be recognized for our generosity.

  b) God is pleased when we give for the right reasons, which are to meet genuine needs and glorify Him.

   i) Our left hand is not to know what the right hand is doing.

    (1) Not a command to hide our giving. Good works cannot be hidden (Matt. 5:16; 1 Tim. 5:25).

    (2) A disciple's character is seen in his action.

   ii) The key issue is that our motives should be pure.

    (1) Jesus refers to self-forgetful giving (Matt. 25:37-40).

    (2) Jerusalem Christians (Acts 2:44-45) and Macedonian believers (2 Cor. 8:1-6) are excellent models of selfless giving.

Transition: We share our Father's compassion and we imitate His motives. Also:

3) We anticipate our Father's pleasure (Matt. 6:4).

Restatement: We are rewarded in the right way.

  a) The promise of a reward for righteous living and service is found throughout the Bible.

  b) Matthew includes several by Jesus; others are found in both the Old and New Testaments.

  c) God does not reward us because we deserve it, but because He is such a gracious and loving Father.

  d) The reward involves both the present and the future.

   – Our reward in this life is focused on spiritual, not material, blessings.

    (1) We have the joy of knowing we are pleasing God by caring for others.

    (2) Unimaginable joy awaits us on judgment day when the Lord praises His faithful servants (Matt. 25:34-36).

13 ■ A DISCIPLES' PRAYER
Matthew 6:5-8

Dominant Thought: Disciples pray to be heard by the Father.
Objective: The listeners will pray with renewed reliance on God.

It is always a temptation to desire attention, acclaim, approval. If you do not believe it, go to the toy store (where children clamor for mom's ear); to the high school (where clothing styles shout for attention); and to some churches (where plaques indicate that giver may be more important than gift).
Illustration: Wynona Ryder is going to ride her felony conviction all the way to the publicity bank.

But, when you have the acclaim, you have all the substance you will ever get. Jesus, in the Sermon on the Mount, describes three areas of temptation for the disciple. First is giving—using large, heavy, noisy coins. Prayer is second—using public, open arenas. Third is fasting—using torn clothing and unwashed faces.

Transition: The second of Jesus' three concerns is the center of our text.

Matthew 6:5-8
Disciples pray to be heard by the Father.

Transition: What can we learn from these few short verses?

1) We pray to be heard, not seen (5-6).
Explanation: Pharisees made it a habit to be conveniently in the public center when prayer time occurred.
Illustrations:
➣ Ostentatious public prayers; the "prayer voice" is used
➣ Praying at a meal when it was only my boss and me. His response was, "Are you okay? You're not getting sick are you?"
    a) We are not being told that public prayer is wrong. In fact, it appears that public prayer is common.
       – 1 Corinthians 11; 1 Timothy 2
    b) We are encouraged, however, to have a private place of prayer.
       i) This was the primary model of Jesus; at least it is the model of Jesus that Scripture calls to our attention.
          (1) Luke 5:16; Mark 1:15; Matthew 26:36ff.
       ii) The closet is where no one sees us except the One who needs to see us—the Father.
    c) We are promised a hearing in either case.
       i) If we pray in public, the public will hear us, but the public cannot help us.

    ii) If we pray in secret, the Father will hear us, and He can help us.

Transition: We pray, in secret, to be heard by someone who really counts.

2) We pray with our understanding, not merely our mouths (7).
Explanation: Jews had set prayers, like the Shema. They prayed them often. And, like us, they fell into the habit of merely mouthing words, and not capturing the heart and imagination before God.
Illustration: A friend has often said, "All of us have one routine prayer in our system; and once we get rid of it, then we can really start to pray!"

    a) We are not being told that repeating ourselves in prayer is wrong. It is apparent Jesus, Paul, and others did so.
        i) Matt. 36-46; 2 Cor. 12:7-8; Luke 11:5-13; Luke 18:1-8
        ii) We might often take our prayer to the Father.
Illustration: Mr. and Mrs. Rinard prayed for me for eleven years.

    b) We are encouraged, however, to pray with our minds, our understanding.
Illustration: Seneca ridiculed those who fatigued the gods with many words.

        – Having our minds engaged in our prayers keeps our repeated words from becoming vain repetition.

Transition: So, we pray in secret, with sincerity. But that does not exhaust this brief text.

3) We pray without answers, but with hope (8).
Explanation: God already knows what we need. His sovereignty may be as apparent in prayer as it is anywhere.
Illustration: Sermon from a student—"If God answers every prayer just the way we pray it, He is no longer God."

    a) We come to the Father, not because He needs information, but because we need transformation.
        i) Nothing demonstrates our dependence upon the wisdom and power of God like prayer.
            (1) Matt. 17:14-21 (compare Mark 9:14-29; esp. v. 29 "this kind only comes out by prayer").
            (2) It appears the disciples attempted to do this without praying, a temptation we all face.
        ii) We have the promise of God to hear us and we have the assurance He will answer us.
            – What we sometimes lack is the wisdom to know that His answer may not be the same as ours.

So, what will it be? Will we seek the approval of men? Will we disengage our minds? Will we tell God what to do? Or will we find our way into the closet and share our hearts with our Father, in the full confidence that we may come forth from the closet more changed than when we entered.

Illustration: Elijah in the cave listening to the still small voice of God and then being sent back to his ministry.

Disciples pray to be heard by the Father.

14 ■ KEY COMPONENTS OF AUTHENTIC PRAYER
Matthew 6:9-15

Dominant Thought: For the disciple, true prayer centers on God's glory.
Objective: The listeners will seek to align their agenda with God's will.

The trivialization of words:
➤ Model prayer is fifty-seven words. Contrast that to Gettysburg Address or modern legal documents.
➤ Martin Luther—"The right method is to use few words . . . the fewer the words the better the prayer. . . . Few words and much meaning is Christian. Many words and little meaning is pagan."
➤ God does not like the complex prayer; whereas humanity often makes prayer complex.

Matthew 6:9-15
For the disciple, true prayer centers on God's glory.

Transition: Jesus was responding to both the request of His disciples to be taught how to pray and the misdirected prayers of the Jewish and pagan cultures. This model prayer points the disciples in four directions when considering appropriate prayer.

Our prayers should include:
1) The anticipation of the Lord's coming kingdom—"Your kingdom come"
   a) This prayer refocuses our self-centeredness to His kingdom-centeredness.
      – The already and the not yet.
   b) This prayer removes our existential obsession with the present and urges us to think about *God's* future.
   c) This prayer reminds us of the need to make His name Holy.
Illustration: The recent curiosity in America with the end times in the *Left Behind* series and the reality of terrorism in America

Our prayers should include:
2) The expectation of God's provision—"Give us today our daily bread"
   a) Since the kingdom of God is under His reign, He will make provision for His will and purpose.
   b) It is the responsibility of the Christian to be an appropriate steward of that provision.
Illustration: An occasion of God supplying the needs of Christians

Our prayers should include:
3) Reconciliation between the Father and His people—"Forgive us our debts as we forgive our debtors"

a) This new kingdom will be marked by a new, superior ethic of grace and forgiveness.
  – Contrast law and legalism with a kingdom of grace
b) Our forgiveness of others frees God to forgive us.

Illustration: "It's not as if God won't forgive you unless you forgive those who have wronged you . . . He can't. How can we receive His gracious pardon with open hands, if our hands are clinched tightly against those who had wronged us" (Michael Green)?

Our prayers should include:
4) Preservation from the evil one—"Lead us not into temptation, but deliver us from the evil one"
  a) The pervasive challenge of the evil one must be recognized and responded to quickly.
  b) God provides a way out of temptation.

Illustration: The picture of a servant-child of God seeking desperately the deliverance from the evil one by a willing and able Father.

Two fundamental concerns are expressed in this prayer: 1) the glory of God and 2) the needs of men. It is always a mistake to get caught thinking about the latter, before addressing the former. The disciple always centers prayer on the Father's glory.

15 ■ NOT IF, BUT WHEN
Matthew 6:16-18

Dominant Thought: Jesus calls His disciples to appropriate experiences of fasting.
Objective: The listeners will begin to incorporate fasting into their spiritual practices.

Interesting, but irrelevant. "In a culture where the landscape is dotted with shrines to the Golden Arches and an assortment of Pizza Temples, fasting seems out of step with the times" (Richard Foster).
➤ **Illustration**: Bill Bright led a gathering for three days of prayer and fasting
➤ A definition is in order: "*Fasting* is a total abstention from food. It can be legitimately extended, however, to mean going without food partially, or totally, for shorter or longer periods. Hence of course the naming of each day's first meal as 'breakfast', since at it we 'break our fast', the night period when we ate nothing" (John R.W. Stott).
➤ So the question becomes, should Christians fast today, and, if so, why?:

Matthew 6:16-18
Jesus calls His disciples to appropriate experiences of fasting.

1) Jesus assumes we will fast (16-17).
Restatement: It is not a matter of *if*, but *when* we fast.
Explanation: Context is verses 1-15 where Jesus leads the disciples to avoid the abuses of the Pharisees. They prayed, gave, and fasted for public recognition and reward. Yet no one today would suggest Christians are not to pray and give.
    a) Jesus clearly implies fasting in the life of His disciples (Matt. 9:14-15).
    b) New Testament precedent includes fasting (Acts 13:2; 14:23).
Illustration: David Smith concludes, "Early law was but a type of that which was to be written on the hearts of believers, after they had experienced the new birth . . . although fasting is not commanded in the New Testament, it is a duty which Christians do perform."

Transition: It is not a matter of if Christians will fast. They will. Rather the issue is how? In what attitude will we fast?

2) Jesus corrects the attitude in which we fast (18).
Restatement: It isn't a matter of *if*, it is a matter of *how* we will fast.
Explanation: Jewish fasting among Pharisees (e.g., Monday/Thursday; sackcloth; ashes)

Illustration: Martin Luther wrote, "It was not Christ's intention to reject or despise fasting. It was His intention to restore proper fasting."
   a)   Attitude is more easily kept correct when the real purposes for fasting are clearly seen.
   – We do not fast for the applause of men.
   b)   Fasting serves three fundamental purposes:
      i)   Fasting humbles us before God.
         – Ezra 8:21; 2 Chr. 20:12; Dan. 9:3
      ii)   Fasting focuses our attention on God.
         (1)   Removes our distractions
         (2)   **Illustration**: Steve Hawthorne (seven-day fast for wisdom): "Did you receive the guidance you were seeking?" "Probably not . . . but I do know the Guide better now."
         (3)   Fasting empowers us for service.
            (a)   Mysterious release of spiritual power results from fasting
            (b)   Acts 13-14: Saul and Barnabas sent on missionary journey illustrate the need for fasting

Transition: Not only does Jesus assume fasting will be done with a right attitude, but:

3)   Jesus assures us of His attention (18).
Restatement: It is not a matter of *if* they will notice, but *when He* notices.
Explanation: Our attention to spiritual discipline gets God's attention and appreciation.
   a)   In this life men seem to thirst for men's applause.
Illustration: Current popular TV series: *Fear Factor, Survivor*, etc.
   b)   The disciple is interested in only one person's attention— the Father's.
   c)   God always honors the surrender and subsequent service of His followers.

John Stott says, "Whatever our reasons, Jesus took it for granted that fasting would have a place in our Christian life." The question becomes— what place will you give it?

16 ■ TREASURES: A MATTER OF THE HEART
Matthew 6:19-24

Dominant Thought: We reveal our hearts by what we treasure in life.
Objective: Listeners will begin to give more freely of their time, talent, and treasure.

We reveal our treasures by what we try to protect, secure, and selfishly keep for ourselves.
Illustration: Ski rack; blanky

Matthew 6:19-24
We reveal our hearts by what we treasure in life.

Transition: Three questions reveal our true treasure.

1) What has our heart (19-21)?
Restatement: We all value something.
- a) We treasure things with eternal value or things with only tempo-rary worth.
  - i) Word study—treasure
  - ii) Las Vegas *Review Journal*—cow story
- b) Earthly treasures are temporary.
  - – Moths, rust, thieves
- c) We should invest in that which has eternal value.

Transition: What we value indicates what possesses our heart. A second question might be:

2) Where is our vision (22-23)?
Restatement: We all focus on something.
Explanation: Metaphor for spiritual vision
Illustration: Planting with a tractor, setting sights on a target
- a) People are the only part of creation in which we ought to be investing.
- b) We will overextend for *things*; will we for people?

Transition: What we focus on reveals what has captured our imagination. There is yet another question to consider.

3) Who is our master (24)?
Restatement: We all serve someone.
- a) We own things without loving them; we possess things without being possessed by them.
- b) Conversations on giving; people playing the edge.

    c)   Hebrews 11: Cain and Abel
    d)   Campaign contributions

So, what do you treasure?
➤ That is who has your heart!

17 ■ DON'T WORRY—BE TRUSTING
Matthew 6:25-34

Dominant Thought: Disciples trust whole-heartedly in God's provision.
Objective: The listeners will seek ways to demonstrate confidence in
    God's promise of daily care.

➤ In 1988, Bobby McFerrin released the instantly popular *Don't Worry,
    Be Happy*.
➤ In June 1994, Disney released *The Lion King* with the popular
    Hakuna Matata tune by Tim Rice and Elton John.
➤ We live in a world that longs to have no worries—yet we worry
    constantly.
➤ Apparently the world has always had that problem as Jesus addressed
    it in the Sermon on the Mount.

Matthew 6:25-34
His conclusion: Disciples trust whole-heartedly in God's provision.
Restatement: Those who seek after God trust Him to take care of them.

1) We are tempted to seek what seems important: Assurances about
    today.
Restatement: We worry about food and drink and clothes.
Explanation: "Do not worry" is a strong imperative statement not a glib
tune (vv. 25,31,34).
    a) We want to know that our everyday needs will be met.
Illustrations:
➤ Israel faced the dilemma in the wilderness. They had to pick up just
    enough manna for one day.
➤ During World War II children were sent to bed with a slice of bread
    so they would know they could eat tomorrow.
    b) Jesus teaches us to look around at the universe and see that God
       cares for it.
       i) We are more valuable than the creatures in the world.
       ii) We have significance simply because we are made in His
         image.
    c) Some are tempted to work too hard, invest too riskily, gamble
       foolishly, and accumulate too much.
       – The challenge is to be sensible.
    d) Some are tempted to work too little, invest nothing, and spend
       foolishly.
       – Jesus does not condemn work, investment, and planning.

2) We are tempted to seek the impossible: Assurances about tomorrow.
Restatement: We worry about tomorrow and its impending disasters.

Explanation: v. 34—tomorrow will be here . . . tomorrow
- a) We want to know what is around the corner.
  - i) We worry about the difficulties and the potential problems.
  - ii) In so doing, we have to live them unnecessarily as many never happen.
  - iii) In so doing, we have to live them twice. The few that do happen then plague us a second time.
- b) God is wise enough not to tell us what tomorrow will bring.
  - – Who would want to know about getting cancer, Alzheimer's, or being in a traffic accident?
- c) God in His kindness tends to tomorrow for us.

3) We are called to seek the significant: The will of the Father.
Restatement: There is only one thing worth really seeking—to know the will of the Father.
Explanation: v. 33: We seek two things—His kingdom and His righteousness.
- a) John Stott points us to two significant concerns that legitimately occupy the heart of a disciple.
  - i) Evangelism/mission: advancing the kingdom of God
    - – We are sometimes tempted to individualize this text, that is, to be concerned about our place in the kingdom. It is a worthy concern, but much too limited and small.
  - ii) Social justice: seeking God's righteousness for all humanity
    - – The church must step forward and address issues of hunger, homelessness, injustice, etc.
- b) When we seek after these significant issues which have size to them, we will not have time to worry about the insignificant issues of food, housing, clothing.

It is a huge text—do not worry, trust Me.
➢ Simple manifestations which can move us forward:
- Give liberally to the church
- Daily prayer (like the line in the Lord's Prayer—this day . . .)
- Adopt a simple lifestyle (fewer possessions; keep things longer)
- Empty your closet of both unused and used clothing/toys
- Work in a soup kitchen
- Counsel at a crisis pregnancy center
- Speak to your neighbors about the church
- Invite them to a Bible study
- Tell them about Christ

But, most significantly, look in the mirror to see if you see one whose eyes are glued to the Father and His will.

18 ■ JUDGING DOGS & PIGS & PEOPLE
Matthew 7:1-6

Dominant Thought: Disciples practice appropriate judgment.
Objective: The listeners will choose to guard against improper condemnation of others.

Illustration: Lawn mowing story
It is impossible to be around people and not make discernments. Disciples of Jesus must be careful to guard against inappropriate condemnation.

Matthew 7:1-6
Disciples practice appropriate judgment.

Transition: How do we prevent inappropriate judgment without lacking genuine discernment?

1) We develop an accurate view of God.
Restatement: Judgment belongs to God, not us.
Explanation: Judging is different from practicing discernment.
    a) The judgment we use will be turned back upon us.
        i) Either by others whom we have judged, or by God Himself
        ii) Word studies
    b) Only God is qualified to judge in a final sense.

Transition: As important as an accurate view of God may be, it alone, is insufficient.

2) We develop a healthy view of others.
Restatement: Judgment tempts us to feel superior.
Explanation:
    a) Others are not inferior just because they do or see things differently.
    b) We come to discernment as fellow pilgrims. We have the desire to see all God's children in relationship to Him.
        – Proper discernment helps us help them.

Transition: Not only must we see God and man correctly, but . . .

3) We develop an honest view of ourselves.
Restatement: Judging requires that I first look at myself very carefully.
    – I must be willing to see myself as God sees me.
        i) I am not, in myself, capable of making right judgments.
        ii) However, for the sake of the kingdom, I must be willing to make discerning decisions.

Transition: An accurate view of God, a healthy view of others and an honest view of myself are the dimensions necessary to practice appropriate judgment. However:

4) We develop the right balance within ourselves.
Restatement: There is more to judging than meets the eye.
   a) We are called to be humble.
   b) We are called to be helpful.
   c) We are called to be discerning.

Our unwillingness to judge means some will never be held accountable for their lives. Our unwillingness to discern means the gospel will be wasted or withheld from others. Neither is an acceptable alternative. Therefore, we must learn to judge wisely.

19 ■ ASK, SEEK, KNOCK
Matthew 7:7-12

Dominant Thought: Prayer forms the foundation of the disciples' relationship with God.

Objective: The listeners will commit to growing in the discipline of prayer.

Illustration: Lunch with spinach on your guest's tooth; only to find you have spilled something on yourself
➢ Context of speck and plank
➢ Matthew 7:1-6

Matthew 7:7-12
Prayer forms the foundation of the disciple's relationship with God.
➢ Confession: I find it difficult to pray
➢ Luke 11:1
  • Jesus did miracles, healed, and taught, yet the disciples wanted to learn to pray.

Transition: The characteristics of Jesus' prayer may inform us how to be better equipped to pray.

1) We notice a progression in our prayers (7-8).
   a) Ask, then seek, then knock
      – Asking parents for things.
   b) Jesus tells us to be direct. Go straight to the Father and ask.
      – John 9:31

Transition: He longs to hear our voices, feel our touch, and answer our requests.

2) We receive a promise to answer our prayers (8).
   a) Ask-receive; seek-find; knock-open
      i) Yet sometimes the answer is no.
         (1) Sometimes we ask the wrong way (Jas. 1:5-6).
             – **Illustration**: Terminally ill patient
         (2) Sometimes we ask for the wrong reason (Jas. 4:3).
             – **Illustration**: Dreaming of winning the lottery
         (3) Sometimes we ask for the wrong things (9-11).
             (a) Luke 11:13
             (b) Parental care of families illustrates how God may answer prayer.
                 (i) Sometimes love says "no"
                     Illustration: No car tonight
                 (ii) Sometimes loves says "wait"
                     Illustration: Car accident

Transition: We do not know God's answer, but we can trust God's timing.

3) We receive a prize at the end of our prayers (12).
   a) Connect the two great commands and life is fulfilling.
      i) Matt. 22:37-40
      ii) Therefore, no surprise in the golden rule (12)
      iii) 1 John 4:20-21
   b) Prayer is the avenue to loving people.
      i) Lucy—"I love mankind; it's people I can't stand."
      ii) Peterson's *The Message* (Matt. 5:21-24)
      iii) Jesus was born Prince of Peace.
      iv) Peterson's *The Message* (John 15:9-17)
   c) Prayer is our connection to loving God.
      i) This sums up the Law and the Prophets.
      ii) The Law seems against us.
         – Rom. 3:23; Eph. 2:8
      iii) Through the Holy Spirit we can even learn to love
         our enemies.

When I am at home in the love of God, it is easier to treat people the way I should. God waits for us to come to Him and there is no greater prize waiting than being in His presence.

20 ■ CHOICES
Matthew 7:13-14

Dominant Thought: Discipleship means being consistent in our choices.
Objective: The listeners will ask how Jesus fits into every choice.

The free-enterprise mindset of American culture creates a wide-open environment for choices.
➤ Cable or satellite; wireless phone plans; Internet sites
➤ Missionaries to India—return from Spartan life to American marketplace
John MacArthur—"Our lives are filled with decisions—what to wear, what to eat, where to go, what to do, what to buy, whom to marry, what career to follow, and on and on. Many decisions are trivial and insignificant, and some are essential and life-changing."
➤ Gen. 2:16-17—saddled us with hard-hitting choices ever since
➤ Prov. 13:6

Matthew 7:13-14
Disciples must be consistent in their choices and practices.

Transition: We have two options from which to choose.

1) We can choose the narrow gate.
➤ America cries for tolerance and more choices.
➤ Christians, who trust the Bible, recognize these are the only choices.
   a) Heaven's gate is narrow.
      i) Not because it is obscure or imaginary.
      ii) It is a gate of self-denial through which one cannot carry the baggage of sin and self-will.
   b) Only a few will find it.
      i) Choosing it is unpopular, counter cultural.
      ii) It is a disciplined life.

2) We can choose the broad gate.
➤ It appears on the surface to be the most appealing.
➤ It has "plenty of room for laxity of morals" (John Stott).
   a) Many false motives for being a disciple
      – An inside track with God like the Pharisees
   b) No one wanders into a relationship with Jesus. You must choose to follow Him.
      i) Luke 13:4
      ii) No matter how good your moral, intellectual, or humanitarian achievements may be, it is still the broad gate if you have not chosen Jesus.

c) Is it Jesus only?
    i) Pharisees had a list of rules as well as their belief in God. This can be a trap into which we sometimes fall.
    ii) The narrow gate is Jesus only.
        (1) Not Jesus plus the Book of Mormon or Koran
        (2) Not Jesus plus a list of rites, sacraments, creeds, or dogmas
        (3) Acts 4:12; 1 Tim. 2:5; Gal. 2:21

You do not have a life worth living if you do not have Jesus. You do not have a spiritual calling to ministry, you do not have a guaranteed future in heaven, unless you have chosen Jesus.

21 ■ DISCIPLES' CHOICES
Matthew 7:15-23

Dominant Thought: Disciples choose to know Jesus personally.
Objective: The listeners will seek to develop and maintain a personal relationship with Jesus.

Gates, trees, and houses are pretty common objects. Yet they are the stuff
of Jesus' teaching on making choices. Verses 13-27 present us with three
clear sets of choices: the right gate, the right fruit, the right foundation. We
might apply John Stott's description of the gates as "inescapable" to all
these choices we make.

Transition: Paying attention to the details of the text before us will lead
us to a simple conclusion as to its meaning.

Matthew 7:15-23

Please note verse 23—"I never 'knew' you."
It becomes apparent that "doing the will of God" (21) is what allows
entrance into the kingdom, yet verse 23 makes it clear that doing the will
of God is knowing Jesus.

Disciples choose to know Jesus personally.
Knowing Jesus leads us to make some wise choices, which in turn leads
us to know Jesus.

1) Disciples choose carefully to whom they should listen (15-20).
Explanation: There are going to be false teachers who will come to the
church. Traveling teachers were the norm and nearly every writer addresses
this concern (John in his epistles, Paul in his hospitality talk, Jude, and
Peter). For Jesus it was their fruit—the activity that revealed their character.
    a) It is imperative that disciples practice discernment when listening
       to the voice of those who claim to speak for God.
Illustration: Guyana/Jim Jones; Waco, Texas/Branch Davidians
    b) We are called to know the truth vis-à-vis the accepted religious
       voice.
       i) This paragraph in the Sermon on the Mount sets the stage for
          another mountaintop experience.
       ii) Matthew 17:1-13—the Mount of Transfiguration. In verse 5
          the disciples are instructed to hear Jesus above Moses and
          Elijah who represent the Law and the Prophets.
       iii) From this point onward it is the voice of Jesus that is heard.
          – Note the context of chapter 5: ". . . but I say. . . ."
    c) We are also called to teach the truth so our sheep will know the truth.

– Ephesians 4:11-16—Church leaders are to prepare the body to discern false teaching.

    (1) Truth and falsehood are mutually exclusive.

    (2) That is the dilemma for our postmodern audience.

Illustration: Stott calls false teaching both "dangerous and deceptive." The question is will we willingly look at all our favorite voices to see if they tell the truth. This would include authors, composers, singers, and preachers.

Transition: Disciples choose wisely. They choose carefully the voice they hear.

2) Disciples choose wisely what they depend upon (21-23).

Explanation: Religious activity is the natural outcome of religion. We are all involved in doing what seems the natural expression of our faith. It is the fruit of activity that determines whether a prophet is a real prophet. It is only natural that we do the things that seem natural.

    a) We are called to do the will of the Father.

      – Vis-à-vis doing the accepted religious practice

Illustration: Everyone knows the accepted practice of a specific congregation: pie, no pie; traditional music, contemporary music; communion first, preaching first.

    b) We are called to know the true religious activity that indicates genuine relationship with Jesus.

      i) Like the first paragraph set the stage for the Mount of Transfiguration, so this text sets the stage.

      ii) Nearly every Sabbath text calls into question the accepted religious practice.

        – Jesus constantly challenged the norm with the truth.

Explanation: Doing the will of God seems to challenge us to answer at least these two questions.

➢ Do we do what we say? That is, is there consistency in our way of life? Do our actions agree with our words?

➢ Do we do what He says? Are we willingly obedient to the Word of God as it comes from Him?

Illustration: A young man sat in my living room as we discussed baptism. "If I show you a text that says 'baptism saves you,' will you believe it? "It doesn't say that" he insisted. I said, "That's not what I asked." "If I show you a text that does say it, will you believe it?" After two more nearly identical exchanges he finally conceded, "I guess I'd have to." When I showed him 1 Peter 3:20-21, he said, "I don't believe it."

That is the question—will you do what He says? Even when it means challenging long-held, cherished beliefs.

The bottom line to getting into the kingdom, being a kingdom person is making the right choices. We choose the right gate, we choose the tree that bears the right fruit, and we build on the right foundation.

In every case, we are simply doing one thing. We are choosing to develop and maintain a living, personal relationship with Jesus. That is what disciples do, they know Jesus and do whatever is necessary to enhance that relationship.

22 ■ OBEDIENT DISCIPLES
Matthew 7:24-27

Dominant Thought: Disciples prepare for judgment by being obedient to Jesus.

Objective: The listeners will determine to obey the teachings of Christ.

Illustration: A man and his children boarded the evening subway. He sat with little apparent awareness that his children were running wild in the train car and disrupting the commute of the passengers. One particular passenger watched until he could no longer tolerate the inattention and ill behavior. He roused the father from his lethargy and asked if he had noticed the commotion his children were causing. The father quickly apologized and offered a brief word of apology. They had just left the hospital, he said. His wife, the children's mother, had just passed away and he was distracted as he wondered what was to come next. Suddenly, filled with compassion, the fellow traveler asked if he could entertain the children during the remainder of the journey.

Suddenly, the man's perspective was changed and the whole meaning of the situation changed. It is like that in viewing scripture. How we see the context in which a text occurs can make all the difference.

There are many who view our story, neatly packaged parable that it is, as a message about facing the difficulties of life. There is truth to that approach. Undoubtedly, those who build their lives on Jesus face the difficulties of life differently than others.

Matthew 7:24-27
One could rightly say that the disciple who obeys Jesus can stand in the storms of life.
➢ I cannot imagine facing sudden death without Christ (Mehaffeys).
➢ Or, choosing to maintain life support for your child (Clevengers).
➢ Or, facing long-term battles with murderous cancer cells (Peerys).
➢ Or, dealing with the abduction and murder of your daughter (Osborns).
Certainly, Jesus spoke a word that would help us deal with life's tragedies. And while we may not be able to explain all the pain we feel, or answer all the questions we have, at least with Jesus, we can stand.

Romans 8:28

Transition: But is that the point of the parable? Would we not be wise to investigate the context a bit more?

The Sermon on the Mount appears to call believers to action. It introduces us to the lifestyle of a disciple.

In fact, looking at the context leads one to reach a more specific conclusion.
> 7:15-23—This text concludes with final judgment talk.
> 7:22-23—"Away from me" sounds like a final decision.
> 7:28-29—This text calls attention to the authority of Jesus. He taught with authority, as if He should be heeded.

Transition: Might it be better to look again at this text?

Matthew 7:24-27

Sometimes we concentrate on what is common. At other times, we concentrate on what is different.

What is interesting in this closing parable of the Sermon on the Mount are the similarities.
> We find two houses of similar quality.
> We find two builders with similar interests.
> We find two builders facing similar circumstances.

But that is where the similarity ends. The one fundamental difference is where those two similar men choose to build, and that one difference makes all the difference.

The wise man built his house on solid rock. He chose the foundation wisely.
> St. Louis Arch—multi-story concrete and steel-reinforced foundation allows the 660-foot arch to sway in the wind, but never fall.
It matters what you build your life upon. More correctly, it matters whom you build your life upon.

The Sermon on the Mount calls the disciple to build a house on Christ and Him alone.

In building one's life on Christ, according to the context, one not only prepares to meet the storms of life, but far more important, prepares for final judgment.

Surviving what this life brings has value. Life is tough. Jesus' offer to help us through it is wonderful. Who would want to live without Matthew 11:28-30?

But, according to 7:21ff., you could survive this life, and still not be prepared for the next. That would be tragic indeed.

So, what this text reminds us of might be summarized: Christ is the Rock and if you build your life on Him you, too, will survive the storms of life.

But that would be to miss the bigger picture. What this text really tells us is this: Prepare for judgment by being obedient to Christ.

Listen to the words of Jesus, and do them. Hear what He says, and obey. For it is the obedient disciple who prepares for judgment by obeying the words of Christ.

Appendix 2

TEACHING AND THE SERMON ON THE MOUNT
J.K. Stevens

Many have called Jesus "the Master Teacher" and rightly so. Even a quick read of the Gospels reveals that the content of Jesus' lessons always fit the needs of His hearers while the authority of His presence caused them to stand in awe. Nowhere is that seen more vividly than in the Sermon on the Mount. The weaving of themes and applications are intensive and intentional. The truth of each lesson penetrates every day life and captures every listener in some way.

No one has ever taught like Jesus even though many have tried. Of course, He had a distinct advantage in His ability to see into a person's heart—combined with the wisdom to teach to the problem, Jesus could cut through any student's resistance to confront what needed to be learned.

While those of us who teach cannot fill Jesus' shoes, we can certainly follow in His footsteps. I know a few men and women who have done so, but few as well as Dr. Marion Henderson. Because he spent so much time at the feet of Jesus, those of us who sat at his feet came to know the person of Jesus as well as His teachings in a dynamic way. It is our hope that the lessons that follow will lead you along the path that Doc Henderson has lead so many of us—lessons that we have found popping up in our lives and ministries every since the first day we walked into one of his classes.

These lesson outlines are, by necessity, brief and to the point. They are designed to build upon the material in the parallel chapters with a balance between Jesus' content and the modern day application. They are patterned after the simple "Hook-Book-Look-Took" approach that Dr. Larry Richards presented so well in his book, *Creative Bible Teaching* (Moody Press)—I encourage you to refer to it as you prepare and present these lessons.

A number of years ago, Dr. Bruce Wilkinson studied the teachings of Jesus and those Christian teachers he felt best emulated Jesus' content and style. He concluded that the teachers who were most effective divided their presentations evenly so that they were 50% content and 50% application. We have tried to model that balance in these lesson outlines with the belief that too much content leaves out personal impact while too much application robs the lesson of its foundational meaning. We encourage you to keep that balance in mind as you guide others in this study.

As my colleague wrote about the sermon outlines, I say the same about these lessons: "Please, use what you can. Adapt all of what you use." It is our desire that you take the outlines and make them your own, teaching the words of Jesus with "vigor and passion." The goal is to build a learning experience that brings your students to the feet of Jesus.

I remember being a college freshman and hearing about a professor whose teaching was so enthralling that upper classmen would schedule visits to his freshman classes just to hear him teach again what Jesus taught. Little did I understand what they meant until I heard Dr. Henderson for myself. However, he would never let us point to him as our goal . . . he wanted us to join him in pointing to Jesus! As you study and use these materials, we call you to do what Doc taught . . . whether you are in a classroom or a small group or just living life every day, always point to Jesus and let His words guide you to eternity!

Lesson #1: INTRODUCTION
TO THE SERMON ON THE MOUNT
Text: Matthew 5:1-2

Key Issue: What would you expect in a sermon from Jesus?
Key Verses: Matthew 5:1-2

Hook: Ask your class the following questions—When you arrive at church, what do you expect in a sermon? How do you know when the sermon was or was not what you expected? *(Provide just a few minutes for discussion before moving to the next point.)*

Let's be more specific—What would you expect if Jesus were preaching in your church this Sunday? *(Provide a few more minutes for discussion.)*

Transition Sentence*: The content of Matthew 5–7 is called the Sermon on the Mount, but it is not the kind of sermon we would necessarily hear when going to church today. This is because Jesus was no ordinary preacher and His teaching came from an extraordinary source.*

Book: Jesus' Sermon on the Mount is different for a number of reasons. *(See the chapter for specific statements and illustrations.)*
1) Jesus was different than any other teacher of His day.
    a) Matthew 1-2 tells us that He had a unique birth.
    b) Matthew 3-4 tells us that He had a unique mission to perform.
    c) This background set the stage for a very different message.
2) Jesus' content was different than anything being taught in His day.
    a) His teaching was focused on His hearers having a personal relationship with a forgiving God.
    b) The application of His teaching targeted how that relationship worked itself out in daily life.
3) Jesus' goals were different than the goals being taught in His day.
    a) He was establishing a kingdom of people transformed by God's forgiveness.
    b) He intended that this kingdom be shared around the world so that all of mankind could be transformed in the same way.

Transition Sentence*: Jesus' teaching was built around a call for all people to think differently and then live differently because of their change in status based on God's forgiveness.*

Look: The Sermon on the Mount begins with a description of the person who follows Christ, then moves quickly through various areas of daily living, all of which are affected by a new relationship with God. In preparing to "hear" this sermon, what is your reaction to the following statements found in the Sermon on the Mount? How do these statements indicate the purpose of Jesus' teaching? *(This activity can be done with a large group reacting to only a few of these statements or in small groups who are each assigned one of the following statements for discussion.)*

1) "Let your light shine before men, that they may see your good deeds and praise your Father in heaven" (5:16).

2) "Be careful not to do your acts of righteousness before men, to be seen by them" (6:1).

3) "The eye is the lamp of the body. If your eyes are good, your whole body will be full of light" (6:22).

4) "Do not worry about your life, what you will eat or drink; or about your body, what you will wear" (6:25).

5) "Ask and it will be given to you; seek and you will find; knock and the door will be opened to you" (7:7).

6) "Every good tree bears good fruit, but a bad tree bears bad fruit" (7:17).

Going Deeper: *Interview Your Preacher (another activity for the "Look" section)*

How would your preacher prepare to listen to the Sermon on the Mount? Why not ask him? If he is available, have him come to your class to discuss this question. If he is not available, have someone interview him and bring his thoughts to share with the class.

Transition Sentence: *We are about to study the best-known sermon presented by the best-known Teacher in the history of the world. Will you become a daily disciple of Jesus because of what you "hear" in this sermon?*

Took: The Sermon on the Mount climaxes with this statement, "Therefore everyone who hears these words of mine and puts them into practice is like a wise man who built his house on the rock" (Matt. 7:24). This fits with the description of a disciple: someone who, as a student not only learns, but accepts the impact of what he or she learns so that life is different from that moment on. Are you ready for the challenge? If so, how do you know? If not, what will you do to prepare? *(Have the class offer suggested answers to these questions. Then provide enough time for them to pray with each other toward a personal preparation to hear Jesus' words.)*

Lesson #2: BLESSINGS
Text: Matthew 5:3-12

Key Issue: What does it mean to be blessed by God?
Key Verse: Matthew 5:12

Hook: The word "bless" and its family are familiar to us. We often hear people say, "Bless you!" or a common greeting of the day is, "Have a blessed day!" Have you considered what it means to bless someone? What is it that we are hoping for when we wish blessings on another person? *(As a class, make a list of definitions and/or wishes that we bring to bear when we call for a person to be blessed.)*

Transition Sentence: *Jesus begins the Sermon on the Mount with words of blessing that are actually words of congratulations from God to the followers of Jesus based on the development of God's character in each follower's life.*

Book: The development of God's character in the Christian's life is described by Jesus in the beatitudes. While we celebrate the congratulations that come from God when these traits are present, we must remember the starting place for each one. *(See the chapter for specific statements and illustrations.)*

- The poverty of spirit is formed out of personal honesty before a holy God.
- The sorrow at seeing sin rises out of the contrast of our world against God's perfection.
- The control of human strength acknowledges our place before a powerful God.
- The hunger for God's presence recognizes God as the only source of satisfaction.
- The practice of mercy is the extension of God's mercy through us to a lost world.
- The purity of heart removes all barriers between a holy God and us.
- The practice of peace is the fulfillment of God's relational reconciliation with us in Christ.
- The persecution that results from living out God's character points to the on-going enmity between God and a lost world.

Going Deeper: Beatitudes for the 21st Century (another activity for the "Book" section)

How would Jesus state the beatitudes for the 21st-century person? Would He use different words or phrases? What words would you use to make Jesus' blessings more meaningful for today's audience? Have some members of your class take the challenge to paraphrase the beatitudes so that they can be shared at your next time together.

Transition Sentence: God is just waiting for us to open up our lives through the development of His character in our daily walk. This opening releases His pleasure with us—a pleasure that is experienced through His blessings.

Look: While it may be exciting to know about God's promised blessings, the personal issue that faces us every day is, "Are there any personal barriers that keep us from the establishment and development of these characteristics in our life?" Let's go back through the list of character traits that Jesus identifies in the beatitudes and identify what kinds of wrong thinking or actions could keep us from developing God's character on a personal basis. *(This is a good activity for small groups, but you will need to move through it quickly in order to revisit all of the beatitudes again. You should be prepared to offer ideas of your own in order to conclude this activity effectively.)*

Transition Sentence: Jesus left us with a tall challenge when He described the godly character traits that should be in our lives—however, we must remember the desired goal: the presence of a personal God's character in our life.

Took: Jesus knew that a list like this would overwhelm us. He also knew that it is man's desire to be congratulated and blessed. So, just as it is with any other big project, the best approach to the growth of the beatitudes in our life is to take one step at a time. Which trait would you choose to see develop in your life this week? What plan would you put in place to promote the growth of this trait? Let's take a few minutes to individually select one trait, and then create a plan that will encourage its growth. *(You may want to have note cards or outline worksheets ready for your students to use as a reminder of the choice they made during the lesson. Be sure to close this personal time with prayer.)*

Lesson #3: THE INVASION
OF THE DIFFERENCE MAKERS
Text: Matthew 5:13-16

Key Issue: How do we make a difference in the world?
Key Verse: Matthew 5:16

Hook: The presence of light is assumed in the world today. In fact, we are so used to light that we are startled more by darkness than by light. This was not the case in Jesus' day—there was so little man-made light that the darkness of night was deep and difficult to penetrate. Have you ever been in a place that was truly dark? Let's try an experiment with darkness. *(Have a blindfold ready that creates total darkness when put on by a volunteer. Have this volunteer stand and try to accomplish tasks with the blindfold on. Ask the person to describe the sensations they experience in total darkness—for example, do they experience disorientation, insecurity, or awkwardness?)*

Light was never taken for granted in Jesus' day. Light was so valuable that Jesus could say, "Neither do people light a lamp and put it under a bowl" (5:15a)—light was too badly needed to hide it. The same was true for salt—there was no way to preserve and season without salt.

Transition Sentence: *Through the Sermon on the Mount Jesus is introducing a change in people's thinking that will bring a change in their actions, but intertwined in both of those areas is Jesus' call to make a difference as God's people in a lost world.*

Book: Jesus illustrates the potential influence of God's followers with two simple, but meaningful object lessons: salt and light. Both of these objects penetrate and change the things around them. *(See the chapter for specific statements and illustrations.)*

- Salt penetrates the setting in which it is placed. Salt has three forms of influence: it is an essential element for life, it preserves things in storage, and it flavors the things around it.
- Light penetrates darkness because it is dynamic. Light has three forms of influence: it is essential for protection, it leads to safety, and it extends the day.
- Both salt and light lose their influence and become useless if they are not allowed to work—salt can experience chemical breakdown and light can be covered over or put out.

Jesus wants the followers of God to be like effective salt and light—to influence the context in which they find themselves and bring a change that is positive. Thus, He gives the command, "Let your light shine before men, that they may see your good deeds and praise your Father in heaven." In this context, making a difference has a purpose: God's people are to bring glory to God so that others will join in praise to Him!

Transition Sentence: Jesus wants His followers to make a difference in their world by attracting others to the great God in heaven, but how is that done? How is influence exerted in a way that glorifies God?

Look: To make a difference is to bring change to a situation. According to Jesus' teaching, that change should reflect God's beauty to those around us in a way that influences our culture for what is truly good. This change should penetrate thinking and actions—like the penetration of salt into food. This change should be clearly measurable—like the difference between light and darkness. So, how would you make a difference in the following settings? How would you advise the people involved? *(Divide the class into six small groups and assign each group one of the following settings. Ask each group to develop some ideas for influencing the setting with the values of God and have them report back to the rest of the class after a period of discussion.)*

- You are a teacher in a school where you are not allowed to talk about God.
- You are a youth sponsor with teenagers who do not seem to care about how they live.
- You are a state legislator in a state that supports abortion.
- You are a business person in an office where there are no ethics being practiced.
- You are a member of a church that has no outreach to the community.
- You are a nurse to the terminally ill.

Going Deeper: Are there specific places in your community in need of Christian influence? (another activity for the "Look" section)
Invite a leader from your community to speak to your class on this topic: "What parts of our community are the most in need of a positive influence?" Encourage this speaker to be very specific—to not only explain the need, but also suggest ways in which a difference can be made. Follow this presentation with a discussion about ways your group could develop a project to meet one of these needs.

Transition Sentence: Jesus assumed that each follower would be salt and light, beginning in the home and extending throughout the community. Where will you begin?

Took: It is one thing to talk about making a difference and another to actually take action to make a difference. Where will you begin? Here are some ideas. I am going to ask you to select one and, in a few minutes, share with your neighbor here in class how you will begin to make a difference in the setting you selected. *(Provide the following list to the class and give the students a couple of minutes to consider their choice. Then give them a few* *minutes to share their choice and their plan with the person sitting next to them. Encourage them to close in prayer for each other.)*

Where will you make a difference this week?

- In your neighborhood
- At your workplace
- At your local school
- In your community volunteer group
- In your church

Lesson #4: PERSONAL RIGHTEOUSNESS
Text: Matthew 5:17-20

Key Issue: How do I develop Jesus' kind of righteousness in my life?
Key Verse: Matthew 5:20

Hook: Each of us makes dozens of decisions daily. Many of these are moral decisions based on our interpretation of what is right or wrong. What standards do we use to make these decisions? Is it the law of the land, personal opinion, or an ethical system?

Here is an example: A student is provided the opportunity to cheat on a major test. What steps of thinking does the student go through in making that choice? What is the difference between the student who chooses to cheat and the one who does not? *(This situation could be role played by two or more class members with observations made by the class at the end.)*

Transition Sentence: For Jesus, doing right is built on an outlook found in a right relationship with God, not in the empty practice of rules. This is the core issue of the Sermon on the Mount, and we will see Jesus break down the practice of rules at every step.

Book: Jesus was speaking to a group of people who had lived with a strict legal structure for generations. They saw right living as a checklist of good things done or wrong things avoided. Jesus came to put right living back into the context God had hoped for when He gave the law to Moses. That context says that living by God's standards is based on the character of God and His desire for mankind to enjoy the benefits of living out His character on earth. Jesus expands on this distinction in the Sermon on the Mount by identifying the difference between true righteousness (God's) and false righteousness (man's). *(See the chapter for specific statements and illustrations.)*

- True righteousness is right behavior (godly living) based on the right goal (honoring God).
- False righteousness is seemingly right behavior (following the law) based on the wrong goal (honoring self).

These two outlooks form the basis for Jesus' teaching in the next sections where He says, "You have heard it said . . . but I say to you. . . ." Righteousness, Jesus teaches, is not something we do, but is something we desire—it is not something we find in ourselves, but something we gain from a personal relationship with God.

Transition Sentence: It is human nature to act out of false righteousness because it is so easily defined. If that is the case, then how do we avoid the trap and make true righteousness a part of our life?

Look: Jesus used Himself as the perfect example when He said, "Do not think I have come to destroy the Law or Prophets; for I have not come to destroy, but to fulfill" (5:17). In His life He demonstrated how to live with true righteousness in the heart—here are some examples:

- The healing of a man on the Sabbath (Matt. 12:9-14)
- The feeding of the 4,000 (Matt. 15:29-38)
- The story of the unforgiving servant (Matt. 18:21-35)
- The story of Jesus' anointing by a woman (Matt. 26:6-13)

In each of these cases, Jesus described and followed a choice that was based on fulfilling God's character on earth. What is it in these stories that makes this clear to us? *(This question can be answered in a large group setting by using one or two of the passages or in small group discussions with one passage assigned to each group.)*

Going Deeper: Another Example of Righteous Living—Abraham (another activity for the "Look" section)
We know the biblical Abraham as a man of faith, but the Bible tells us that his faith was "credited to him as righteousness" (Gen. 15:6). In a character study from Genesis 12-15, describe the traits of Abraham's life that opened the door for righteousness to develop. *(This study can be done individually or in groups, during class or as a follow-up assignment from class. Be sure to ask for reports when this research is finished.)*

Transition Sentence: True righteousness begins with a personal relationship with the one righteous God, so Jesus calls us to seek Him first instead of basing our spiritual life on a list of right actions.

Took: We are faced with the challenge of building a relationship with a personal God who we cannot see or touch. So, how do we reach the goal of righteous living by intensifying our relationship with God? Let's develop some strategic ideas for drawing near to God in a 21st-century culture. *(This list can be generated by the group. There may be some in the group who have ideas to share from actual experience. The goal is to mutually encourage one another in avenues of knowing God so that His righteousness will develop in us.)*

Lesson #5: MANAGING ANGER
Text: Matthew 5:21-26

Key Issue: How do I avoid the pitfalls of anger?
Key Verse: Matthew 5:22b

Hook: Anger is something seen throughout our society today—on the sidelines of ballgames, on the highways, in shopping lines, and on television shows. A prominent example highlighted by the media in recent years is in the overreaction of parents during children's ballgames, sometimes leading to open violence. Let's analyze this situation. *(Write the group's answers to the following questions on a chalkboard or newspaper pad for later reference):*
- Why do parents get angry at ballgames?
- How do parents express their anger in these situations?
- What affect do these outbursts have on the umpires/referees? On the coaches? On the children?
- Do you believe this affect is lasting?

Transition Sentence: The demonstrations of anger in our culture are a growing concern because they are leading to increasingly ugly results. In His first application of righteous living, Jesus confronts anger and the damage it leaves not on others, but on us.

Book: There seems to be a tension between good anger and bad anger. What is the difference? *(See the chapter for specific statements and illustrations.)*
1) Good anger can preserve personal worth, essential needs, and basic convictions.
   a) God displayed anger with the Israelites because of their idolatry (Exod. 32:1-14).
   b) Jesus displayed anger with the Pharisees at their practices on the Sabbath (Mark 3:1-6).
   c) The Holy Spirit displayed anger at the lies of Ananias and Sapphira (Acts 5:1-11).
2) Jesus is teaching that bad anger is destructive both toward others and ourselves.
   a) Externally it leads to the destruction of another person.
   b) Internally it leads to a destructive hatred of others.
3) In describing this bad anger, Jesus applies it to three problems that lead to progressive damage in the heart and in relationships:
   a) Anger with someone even though words are not spoken.
   b) Anger with someone that leads to disrespect.
   c) Anger with someone that condemns another.

Transition Sentence: Regardless of the time or the culture, almost every

*group of people in history has had a law against murder, but Jesus raises
the bar from the codebook of the law to the workings of the heart and ties
the problem to anger.*

Look: With this teaching Jesus provides illustrative examples to help us
with the application. How would you apply Jesus' warnings about anger
in these contemporary forms of Jesus' examples? *(This discussion can
be carried out in one large group or two small groups. It could also be
role played, using Jesus' illustrations as the background for the characters involved.)*

- Setting #1: You are in the worship service and about to participate
  in the offering when you remember that a friend is carrying a
  grudge against you. Jesus tells us to take care of this problem
  quickly. How would you do that? What are the possible results to
  you and your friend if you don't?
- Setting #2: An adversary is taking you to court. Jesus tells us to
  settle the disagreement before you get to court. How would you
  do that? What are the possible results for you and your adversary
  if you don't?

Going Deeper: *Five Ways to Handle Anger (another activity for the
"Look" section)*
The following are five choices for handling anger. As you review these
options, discuss the possible results of each one. Are any of them choices the Christian can make? Discuss why each option is or is not a good
choice. *(This study can be done in a large group or be assigned in parts
to small groups.)*
- a) Suppress anger: Hold anger in so that you do not appear rattled
  or weak.
- b) Express open aggression: Express anger at someone else's
  expense.
- c) Express passive aggression: Express anger behind the scenes,
  still at someone else's expense.
- d) Express anger in reconciliatory ways: Express anger in a way
  that seeks to resolve the problem so that the needs and feelings
  of others are considered.
- e) Drop anger: Recognize your personal limits and choose to forgive in the context of kindness.

Transition Sentence: *Jesus teaches that anger can be controlled so that
our relationships reflect God's influence.*

Took: Anger is not something any of us are willing to admit, but it is a
common problem in our self-centered society. Jesus makes it clear that
anger is a problem of the heart. Are there steps we can take to avoid the

development of anger and its relatives (e.g., resentment and grudges) in our heart? Is there something we can put in anger's place in order to keep it from growing? *(Have your class develop these ideas in pairs. Have each pair share their conclusions before leaving class. Close the study with directed prayer that seeks God's help with the anger problems we face.)*

Lesson #6: ADULTERY
Text: Matthew 5:27-30

Key Issue: How do I resist temptation with purity of thought?
Key Verse: Matthew 5:28

Hook: While campaigning for President in 1976, Jimmy Carter admitted in an interview that he had lusted after women and committed adultery in his heart. His campaign immediately lost the momentum he had built over President Gerald Ford. Let's consider why the American people responded this way to Carter's admission. *(Assign each of the following questions to a small group and have them report their answers after just a few minutes of discussion):*
- What do you think was the definition of lust that President Carter was assuming in his admission?
- Why do you think the American people found it offensive for a presidential candidate to admit this level of passion?
- Do you think the reaction of the people is in contradiction to current attitudes about lust in the American culture? Why or why not?
- Would Americans react differently today than they did in 1976? Why or why not?

Transition Sentence: *The prominence of sex continues to grow in the American culture through sources such as television, movies, magazines, and the Internet. How would Jesus help us deal with the temptations that accompany this proliferation?*

Book: In the previous section, Jesus confronted the difference between external and internal acts of hate—now He moves to the difference between external and internal acts of sexual lust. In doing so, He provides a new warning for those who would feast on sexual lust. *(See the chapter for specific statements and illustrations.)*
1) Sexual Perversion: The Bible is not prudish or pornographic when it speaks of God's design for sexual expression and enjoyment, but makes clear that sex is a divine gift with a strict prohibition.
   - Sexual perversion is any kind of illegitimate sexual intercourse or relationship.
   - Sexual purity builds on external and internal conformity to God's standard of sexual behavior.
2) Sexual Passion: God designed both sexual purity and sexual passion and so, Jesus is not prohibiting the sexual instinct, but making it clear that adultery takes place when the "look" turns into lust.
   - Sexual passion is out of control when the look turns to lust and the look accompanies the desire to engage in sexual activity (real or imagined).

- Sexual purity requires a continual cleansing of the heart and control of the eyes in order to obey our Father's commandments—sometimes radical "surgery" is involved to reach the goal.

Transition Sentence: In applying this text, Christians are called to an authentic appraisal of sexual thoughts in a world that seems to consider little else.

Look: When our thoughts are sexually immoral we must identify the cause. There must be no compromise, no accommodation, no concession or negotiation, only confrontation of contaminants that lead to sexually immoral thoughts. Yet, the presence of tempting sexual thoughts are all around us.

- Consider John MacArthur's description of our culture's fantasy with sex: *"Ours is a day of unbridled indulgence in sexual passion. People propagate, promote, and exploit it through the most powerful and pervasive media ever known to man." (See the chapter for the full quote.)*
- Understanding that we are faced with this attitude every day, how are we to apply Jesus' teaching to avoid being drawn into lust by the world around us? What forms of control can we put in place to fight off the temptations that come through today's media? How radical do you believe we must be as Christians in this fight? *(Divide the class into groups and assign each group one of the following sources of media: a) television, b) movies, c) Internet, d) books, and e) magazines. Have the groups create a proposal that will help Christians avoid the "look" that turns to "lust" as fed by the specific media source.)*

Going Deeper: How bad is it really out there? (another activity for the "Look" section)
Invite a Christian leader from the community to describe the level of sexual activity among teenagers in the current culture. This might be a Christian counselor or one of the area youth ministers. You should encourage this speaker to be frank about the impact that the actions of contemporary leaders and heroes have had on our children. Be sure to allow enough time for the class to ask questions of this person.

Transition Sentence: We are surrounded by the promotion of sexual activity without any moral compass. At what point will each of us draw the line to protect ourselves and our families from falling into the trap of lust?

Took: The issue of impure thoughts and actions is intensely private, but as we can see in our culture, high profile involvement in sexual immorality has had significant impact on adults and teens alike. Jesus believed it was possible to keep this from happening. Where will you draw the line in your life? How will you protect those around you by drawing the line on "looks?" *(Give each person a 3x5 card and urge them to write down one definitive step that they will take to protect themselves and those around them from sexual temptation. Close with prayer directed toward finding the strength to follow through.)*

Lesson #7: DIVORCE
Text: Matthew 5:31-32

Key Issue: Is divorce and remarriage in conflict with the biblical view of marriage?
Key Verses: Matthew 19:4-6

Hook: The Barna Research Group (Ventura, CA) found that 27% of born again Christians are currently divorced or have been divorced. This compares with the following statistics:
- 11% of the American population is currently divorced
- 25% of all adults have experienced at least one divorce
- 24% of adults who are not born again have been divorced
- 21% of atheists and agnostics have experienced divorce
- 21% of Catholics and Lutherans have experienced divorce
- 29% of Baptists have experienced divorce
- 30% of Jews have experienced divorce
- 15% of Protestant senior pastors have experienced divorce

What surprises you about these statistics? Why do you think the statistics are not that different for born again Christians from the rest of the American populace? *(Write the ideas suggested by the group on a board or piece of paper so that they can be referred to later.)*

Transition Sentence*: Jesus was concerned about the impact of divorce among believers and so His teachings contained warnings about the source and impact of divorce.*

Book: The Bible is not silent on divorce. For background study read Gen. 2:18-24; Deut. 24:1-4; and Mal. 2:8-17. Also see Jesus' teaching on the subject in Matt. 5:31-32; Matt. 19:3-12; Mark 10:2-12; and Luke 16:18 along with Paul's teaching in 1 Cor. 7:1-40. *(You may want to provide this information to your class in a pre-printed outline.)*

What Jesus says about divorce can only be understood in the context of a biblical view of marriage (i.e., one woman and one man committed to each other for life in a permanent relationship, a harmonious partnership, and a spiritual companionship). His intent is that a Christian's attitude toward marriage and divorce will be different from that of both the Jews and the Gentiles of His day. His teaching was needed because of the first century culture's view of divorce. *(See the chapter for specific statements and illustrations.)*

Going Deeper: *Is there a tie between lust and divorce? (another activity for the "Book" section)*
It is not accidental that Jesus' teaching regarding divorce follows His teaching regarding lust and adultery. In fact, it is important to note that the issue of adultery appears in both of these texts. In a class discussion, ask your students to analyze the impact of lust and adultery on marriage. Consider these questions: How do lusting and adultery affect the person initiating it? How do lusting and adultery by one partner affect the other? Why would these actions lead to divorce? Can they be overcome in a marriage after the damage is done?

Transition Sentence: *God's standard for marriage is one woman and one man for life, but that seems to be a major hurdle in the world today.*

Look: Christian couples are faced with a number of challenges and tensions in their marriages just like those who are not believers. However, Jesus implies that the followers of God should be different. How can they be? Are there alternatives to divorce for Christian couples? Here are some possible choices:
- Working it out vs. walking out
- Practicing servanthood vs. demanding rights
- Striving for holiness vs. seeking happiness
- Legal separation vs. finalized divorce
- Reconciliation vs. remarriage

(Assign each of these alternatives to a small group in your class. Have each group prepare an explanation of ways to hold a marriage together by following the positive outlook in each choice. Have the small group assume that they must present this explanation to a couple about to chose the dissolution of their marriage.)

Transition Sentence: *Protecting a marriage in a world full of temptations and choices is not easy, but it is vital to the Christian and his or her family.*

Took: What could you do to protect your marriage or that of someone close to you? Depending on your current status, complete the following statements:
- If you are married, renew your vows so that . . .
- If you are single, commit yourself to . . .
- If you are divorced, clear your mind of . . .
- If you are a parent of a teenager or unmarried adult, determine to . . .

(Provide each person with a sheet of paper that has the above statements written on it. Conclude the lesson by leading the group in a prayer that asks for God's help in maintaining strong marriages.)

Lesson #8: TRUTH
Text: Matthew 5:33-37

Key Issue: Why is telling the truth imperative for the kingdom person?
Key Verse: Matthew 5:37

Hook: Do you remember the last time someone lied to you? How did you feel? What was the result of that lie in your relationship with that person? *(Have the class divide into pairs and answer these questions. Encourage them to compare their experiences and feelings when lied to. At the end of a brief period, have some of the pairs share their observations about the impact of lying.)*

Transition Sentence: Telling the truth has almost become a game in our media-driven society—we want to be told the truth, but it is evident that many are not willing to tell the truth until forced to do so or until it becomes convenient.

Book: Jesus was confronting the perversion of the law by the religious leaders of the day (e.g., Pharisees, scribes, and priests). Another of the perversions being taught by these men was the acceptability of adding oaths to statements in order to make those statements acceptable or believable to others. In other words, they were providing a formula by which someone could appear to be telling the truth by adding a phrase that appealed to the power of God, the earth, or some other authoritative object. This would be similar to our phrase, "I swear on a stack of Bibles"—as if that guarantees the truthfulness of our claim.

Whether we should participate in an oath (as in a promise) is not the issue. In fact, the Bible has several examples of oaths:

- Abraham claims an oath with God (Gen. 14:22-24).
- David swore an oath to his friend, Jonathan (1 Sam. 20:16).
- Ruth made a promise to Naomi (Ruth 1:16-18).
- Even God established oaths (to Abraham, Gen. 22:16-17, and to Israel, Jer. 11:3-5).

The problem was using something outside the honesty of a person's own word to establish the truthfulness of a statement. *(See the chapter for specific statements and illustrations.)*

Transition Sentence: Jesus cut to the heart of the matter by telling His followers to speak the truth so that their words would be accepted as valid without any additions or appeals.

Look: In Jesus' day, telling the truth had become an art form, not a part of living an honest life. Jesus says that the real formula for telling the truth was to simply offer a "yes" or "no" that represents the core of the matter—

there should be nothing needed beyond this. Jesus wants our speech to be truthful, believable, and direct.

However, there are many today who would suggest that telling the truth is not always in our best interest or that of others. How do we reconcile Jesus' call to be truthful with the conflict over telling the truth that we see in our culture today? Here are some illustrations—how would you apply Jesus' teaching in each case?

- A bold face lie: A co-worker tells you that his or her report is accurate when you know that it is not, but confronting that co-worker will get others involved and implicate you in the inaccuracy of the report.
- A little white lie: Someone calls you, but you don't want to talk to him or her, so you tell the person answering the phone to say that you "are not available" even though you are.
- Embellishing the truth: A fellow member on a non-profit board underreports a problem situation that could impact the organization's function and position in the community.

(Have three people prepared to role play these situations by telling a story based on these backgrounds, but not offering a solution. Have the class, either as a whole or in small groups, provide possible solutions based on Jesus' call for telling the truth.)

Going Deeper: *Examples for measuring truth? (another activity for the "Look" section)*

The American court system focuses on finding the truth behind every case heard before the bench. Have a lawyer visit your class and define the legal measure for telling the truth. Then have him or her explain the importance and implications of telling the "whole truth and nothing but the truth" in a court case. Have the class compare this situation with Jesus' teaching.

Transition Sentence: *Jesus teaches that the truth should be told without appeal to someone or something else—our words should be authentic and acceptable in all cases.*

Took: We must make every effort to be people of the truth. Our entire persona must be that of truthfulness. We must make every effort to be filled with the truth and then allow that truth to flow forth in every word we speak and action we perform. How can we build standards for ourselves to make sure this happens? Try this quiz:

- Do I have a good working definition of the difference between truth and falsehood?
- Do I always seek out the truth of a matter before speaking or acting upon it?
- Do I first measure my words or my actions against the truth to make sure I am in line with it?

- Do I keep my life open to others as a way of being accountable for truthfulness?
- If I find that I have not been truthful, do I go to those involved, seeking to both apologize for the error and to correct it?

(Provide this checklist to the class and allow your students some time to answer the questions and consider options for resolving any problems. Close the class time with prayer, asking for God's help in making us people of the truth.)

Lesson #9: DEALING WITH AN ENEMY
Text: Matthew 5:38-42

Key Issue: How do I resist evil and respond positively to those who would bring evil to me?
Key Verse: Matthew 5:39

Hook: Long after World War II was over and after she had been released from a Nazi prison camp, Corrie ten Boom was faced by one of her captors at the end of a church meeting. As he approached her and she recognized who he was, she was forced to make a decision about confronting her enemy. What were her choices? What motives would drive these choices? *(As your class mentions the possible choices, list them on a board or sheet of paper. Then list next to these choices the motives that go with each choice. Ask the class to consider what Jesus would have done in that situation and why he would have done it.)*

The story goes on to tell how Corrie ten Boom met the man, extended forgiveness to him, and was freed from the hatred that had burned inside her for years.

Transition Sentence: *Americans are taught the merit of revenge from the time they are children, but Jesus has a different idea about meeting any evil done to us.*

Book: Just as the Jewish leaders had justified anger, lust, and lies (Matt. 5:21-37), they had justified revenge against those bringing evil upon the individual. But, just as He did with all the other rationalizations, Jesus turns this one inside out and teaches that His disciples are to treat all adversaries with caring consideration. In fact, they are to go the second mile. On what basis? On the basis of God's intent that we offer more than anyone might expect of us, even under threatening circumstances—a pattern that is totally opposite of the self-absorbed, postmodern Western culture.

Jesus illustrates His point with four examples:
- When struck by words or insults, the disciple is to turn the other cheek (submission).
- When sued for material items, give the opposition more than they seek (compassion).
- When pressed into service, go over and above what is demanded (sacrifice).
- When relentlessly pursued for donations, give more than is asked (generosity).

(See the chapter for specific statements and illustrations.)

Transition Sentence: *In contrast to those who wish evil upon us, Jesus' disciples are to turn the threat into an opportunity just as He did when He willingly died at the hands of evildoers.*

Look: The whole notion that Jesus' followers should offer more than is expected or required to Christ-less opponents is preposterous by modern standards. But it happens to be Jesus' own way and we should find ways to bring this courage and witness into the 21st century. Using Jesus' four examples, let's identify modern day parallel situations and suggest solutions:

- How would injury and insult come to today's Christian? How would he or she turn the other cheek?
- How would someone seek to sue us today? How would we go about offering more than the opposition might seek?
- How would a Christian be pressed into service against his or her will? How would that same Christian go over and above what is demanded?
- How would a person be relentlessly pursued for a donation today? How would Jesus' disciple respond by giving generously?

Going Deeper: A visible example of giving to the evil person (another activity for the "Look" section)
Announce a movie night and invite your class to watch *The Hiding Place* (produced by Billy Graham's Worldwide Pictures). This is the story of Corrie ten Boom and how she learned to trust God while not returning evil for evil in the face of threats and shame. Make time at the end to analyze how Corrie ten Boom reacted to what she experienced. Can your group identify all of Jesus' illustrations in Corrie ten Boom's life?

Transition Sentence: Jesus' words in the Sermon on the Mount may seem to us like far-fetched idealism, but His life tells another story—the story of going the "second mile" to a Roman cross on Calvary.

Took: During the riots that followed the Rodney King verdict several years ago, a man named Reginald Denny was dragged from his semi and cruelly beaten while the world watched in horror. At one point, someone threw a brick at his head and Denny lay motionless, apparently dead. After an extended and painful recovery, Reginald Denny met his attackers face to face, shook their hands, and forgave them. Would we do the same?

Is there someone in your life you consider to be an enemy who threatens you? Take a few minutes to evaluate what you are doing in response to this person? Are you turning the other cheek or going the second mile in order to show God's compassion to this person? What would it take for you to do so? What one part of Jesus' example could you use to confront this person in a godly way? *(Give the class some quiet time to consider these questions. There may be some individuals who are willing to share, but do not force sharing unless it comes naturally within the group. Conclude the time with prayer.)*

Lesson #10: LOVING THE ENEMY
Text: Matthew 5:43-48

Key Issue: How do we love an enemy?
Key Verses: Matthew 5:44-45a

Hook: All of us have heard excuses for getting even with someone. As an example, you should find it easy to complete the following statements *(Have the class finish the following statements and list similar statements they have heard.)*:

- Get him before he _____.
- Turn about is _____.
- Well, she did it _____.
- It isn't fair, she _____.
- What goes around, _____.

Why do people think this way? Do we actually feel better when we get even with someone who has treated us badly? *(Encourage the class to identify the motives behind the desire to get even. Be sure to have them consider what they believe is the source of this kind of thinking.)*

Transition Sentence: *There is something about human nature that makes us believe that one bad deed deserves another, but Jesus does not want us to think that way.*

Book: The Jewish culture had become an exclusive "club" that viewed all outsiders and outcasts as potential enemies. The reasons were myriad: race, religion, politics, and socio-economic status were just a few of the bases for this prejudice. Jesus, however, taught and lived a different way of thinking and so, opened His life to individuals and groups that no other Jew would consider for a personal relationship. Jesus made it clear that the foundation of this receptive thinking was in the very law that the Jews used as a dividing line for their relationships. *(See the chapter for specific statements and illustrations):*

- *Jesus knew that Leviticus 19:18 did not include "hating your enemy."*
- *Jesus knew that Jewish teaching, in fact, encouraged assisting foreigners and enemies.*
- *Jesus knew that God cared for all people and did not discriminate.*
- *Jesus knew that God's perfect love could only be lived out when we eliminate discrimination from our outlook.*

In summary form, Jesus' teaching about our relationship with our enemies is built on the compassionate character of God—something He expects to see develop in the life of His children.

Transition Sentence*: The way of man is to create prejudicial barriers between him and others who are different—the way of God is to treat all individuals in a loving way without discrimination.*

Look: To be like Jesus and His heavenly Father, we are to practice a love that is complete and rounded, not one-sided or partial. This kind of thinking is challenged in our lives every day because, at some point in the day, each one of us is confronted by a person who is very different from us. Perhaps it is a matter of dress or culture. Maybe it is political or religious views. It may be someone at work that appears to be out for our job. How can we be as perfect in our love toward that person as Jesus was?

Here is a problem to solve: You work in a small office of eight people. Of the eight, you have seniority, but you are not the leader of the office. One person on the team has made it very clear that she does not like the way you do your job and seems to go out of her way to make your work difficult. She has suggested to others that you should be replaced. At times she has even made fun of your Christian faith and practice. What should you do? Here are four possible solutions. *(Present this situation to your group or class, then divide into small groups and assign one of the possible solutions to each group. After a few minutes, each group is to present and defend its assigned solution as an avenue to express God's love for this person.)*

- Possible solution #1: Resign from the job.
- Possible solution #2: Meet with the office manager.
- Possible solution #3: Meet with the opposing person.
- Possible solution #4: Seek an indirect way to resolve the problem.

Going Deeper*: How do we express God's love to those who are opposed to Christianity? (another activity for the "Look" section)*
Tolerance has become the watchword in a highly pluralistic 21st-century America. Tolerance is defined as an atmosphere in which all faiths are acceptable and of equal merit. In this context, no one is allowed to criticize or denigrate another person's position(s), but is expected to support their right to express their faith in any possible manner. How do we fulfill the teaching of Jesus in 5:44-45a in this cultural setting? What responses should we be practicing when we meet or work around these people? *(This activity may be substituted for the activity above or used as a special project outside of your study time.)*

Transition Sentence*: Jesus portrays God's love as consistent and caring in a way that puts all other relational approaches to shame. Is it possible for us to put this kind of love into practice?*

Took: An honest inventory of our personal life probably reveals at least one relationship in which we feel opposed. Our normal instinct is to avoid interaction with that person, but chances are that avoidance cannot be permanently maintained. Have you considered an alternative? Jesus has offered one for us—love and pray. This would be a good time for each of us to consider the one relationship that causes us the most fear and consider a plan for demonstrating consistent love to the person involved. *(Allow the group some personal time to write down some ideas that can be used to change personal attitudes and actions in a setting like this. Close with a prayer time that seeks God's help to take action as early as the next morning.)*

Lesson #11: GIVING
Text: Matthew 6:1-4

Key Issue: What kind of giving acknowledges God's character and compassion?

Key Verses: Matthew 6:3-4

Hook: Many churches in the Democratic Republic of the Congo have a tradition in which members make their financial contributions using only their right hand. They hide the money by rolling it tightly and making a fist to cover it. Accompanied by rhythm instruments, they form a line and do a dance as they make their way to the offering basket. These cheerful givers each place their hand deep into the basket before releasing the money, ensuring that no one else knows how much was given.

    While the common American custom encourages the secrecy of giving through the use of envelopes, do you find other parts of the Congolese custom helpful for a Christian trying to improve his or her focus on giving? *(Have your group identify the various elements of the Congolese practice illustrated here and suggest how they might be adapted to the American practice of giving. Encourage the people in you group to look behind the physical elements and consider the attitudes these elements represent.)*

Transition Sentence: *Strange as the Congolese custom may seem, it is based in part on Jesus' teaching about giving found in Matthew 6.*

Book: Charitable giving is an important part of the Christian life. In our text Jesus assumes that believers will give and describes giving as an "act of righteousness" (the term righteousness meaning an "upright and God-centered life"). Jesus makes the following points about giving *(see the chapter for specific statements and illustrations)*:

- God is not pleased if charitable giving is done for the wrong reason and in the wrong manner. Jesus condemns those who seek the honor of men by attracting attention to themselves when they give.
- God sees and rewards charitable giving when it is done for His glory. There is to be no secret pride, but rather a sincere desire to honor God and help others.
- God sees and rewards purity of motive when these factors are a part of our giving: 1) we seek God's pleasure in giving, 2) we understand that reward is given by God's grace, and 3) we remember that reward comes out of the loving Father/child relationship God has with us.

Transition Sentence: *Understanding that charitable giving rises out of our relationship with God and a desire to please Him may challenge and change how we approach our giving today.*

Look: Our society has created an entire culture of giving based on the growing needs of non-profits in America and around the world. Most Americans are bombarded by "asks" from dozens of charitable organizations, so how does Jesus' warning to avoid giving for the wrong reason or in the wrong manner guide our responses to the needs of these organizations? How would you respond to the following requests for donations? *(Assign each of the following illustrations to a small group in the class. Have these groups identify the motive being used to encourage a gift. Have each group propose an alternative that would allow the giver to participate in a way that matches Jesus' teaching about giving. Each group should share their conclusions to the rest of the class.)*

- Your church is in a capital campaign for a new building and the campaign committee has designated certain levels at which donors will be listed and honored publicly. You had already determined your gift to the campaign, but now are considering a larger gift based on this recognition system.
- At the end of the calendar year you plan to give a large gift for a worthy cause and you are trying to decide whether to give to your church, an inner city ministry, or an overseas missionary. You know that at least one of these organizations will publish your name because of the size of the gift.
- You have been asked to give a donation to the organization on whose board you serve. The leadership's intention is to recognize board members individually for their charitable giving, but you are not in a position to give the size of gift requested.
- You regularly donate to a non-profit organization in your community. This organization recently announced that it is creating a donor recognition wall in the foyer of its office building. Your name will be added to that listing.

Going Deeper: *How do we give to the poor today? (another activity for the "Look" section)*
Providing for the poor continues to be a growing problem in America. A number of organizations now serve needy people and must find ways to obtain significant contributions in order to continue their services. Invite the leader of one of these service ministries to your class and ask him or her to explain how they seek contributions. Have your class discuss with this leader ways by which Jesus' teaching about giving can be fulfilled through a cooperative effort between the organization and its donors.

Transition Sentence: *Jesus teaches that we are to give out of a sincere desire to help others and bring glory to our Father in heaven, but how does that desire translate into our giving plans?*

Took: Jesus was the champion of the downtrodden and established an example in His concern and care for those with needs. Have you considered your personal motives and standards for giving? How would you put Jesus' teaching from the Sermon on the Mount to work in your own life? *(Have class members brainstorm practical standards they think each Christian should have in place when making a decision about his or her giving plans. Perhaps some will want to research ways by which the class can participate in meeting the needs of the poor in your area.)*

Lesson #12: PRAYER
Text: Matthew 6:5-8

Key Issue: What kind of attitude in prayer acknowledges our relationship with God?

Key Verse: Matthew 6:6

Hook: We are overwhelmed by communication sources every day. From the radio and the television to pagers and cell phones, we are seldom out of touch with those who want our attention. These devices are a constant interruption. The result is that most of us have very little quiet, reflective time in our daily routine. Let's take a moment to analyze our own experience with the "communication explosion." *(Provide each member of your group with the following list and ask them to identify how communication sources are impacting possible quiet times during the day. After a few minutes of personal reflection, ask the group if any have observations to share about this problem.)*

1) How many communication sources do you have around you every day? (Count phones, pagers, computers, radios, televisions, etc.)
2) How many hours a day are these sources on and available to you?
3) What kind of information do you obtain from these sources?
4) What percentage of this information do you find personally helpful for work or personal life?
5) In contrast, how much quiet time do you have when these sources are off and not available to you? What are you doing during that quiet time?

Transition Sentence: *Jesus assumed that all believers would spend personal time in prayer, but the setting He had in mind was totally different than the prayer habits of His day.*

Book: When Jesus thought of prayer, He thought of relationship over mechanics and semantics. Just as He taught that giving is rooted in our relationship with God, He taught that prayer is a primary link in that same relationship. So, His teaching about prayer breaks into two parts—what should I be doing when I pray (5:5-8) and what should I pray about (5:9-15)? In this study, we are focusing on the first part where Jesus taught the foundations for meaningful prayer. *(See the chapter for specific statements and illustrations.)* He said:

- Our prayers should be authentic and represent our true personality.
- Before we pray, we should assess the purpose of our prayer, particularly for public prayer.
- Prayer is a petition to God from whom we are seeking eternal rewards.

- Private prayer allows us to confide totally in God without compromise.
- Prayer that adores God helps us acknowledge His true attributes.
- God knows our motivations and actions long before we present them to Him.

Transition Sentence*: Jesus made it very clear that prayer is our primary opportunity to communicate with a personal God who knows us well and that we should give this communication our full attention.*

Look: The key to Jesus' teaching about prayer is the concept of a personal God who desires to relate intimately with us. What if there were no barriers and you could actually sit down with God to talk with Him face to face? Are there things you would share with Him that you haven't? Are there things that you would not share with Him that you should? What would make the difference in how you share with Him?

Imagine what it would be like to actually sit down with God in person and talk with Him about your deepest needs? The following sentences are designed to help you imagine a personal encounter like that. *(Divide your class into groups of no more than four people. Ask them to complete the following sentences with a focus on experiencing a totally open relationship with our heavenly Father.)*

- If I could sit down with God today I would feel

  _____.

- If I could sit down with God today He would

  _____.

- If I could sit down with God today I would tell Him

  _____.

- If I could sit down with God today I would ask Him

  _____.

- If I could sit down with God today He would say to me

  _____.

(After the groups complete this activity, ask them to answer one last question: "What is it that keeps us from actually talking like this with God now?")

Going Deeper*: What can we learn about prayer from others? (another activity for the "Look" section)*
The books about knowing God and prayer would fill a small library. There are classics such as *The Pursuit of God* by A.W. Tozer and *Knowing God* by J.I. Packer, and then there are the more contemporary studies such as *The Prayer of Jabez* by Bruce Wilkinson. There are probably people in your group who have read these books. Ask them to report what these men would encourage us to do in our personal prayer lives.

Transition Sentence*: God is waiting for us—He wants a personal relationship with us, so what is keeping us from this relationship?*

Took: God wants our complete focus when we seek a relationship with Him. Most of us claim that we have a schedule problem when it comes to time with God, but Jesus would not accept that answer. He would say it is an issue of priorities. Is there one thing we could change in our personal schedule that would allow us to make time alone with God a priority? Consider the following points in your daily schedule to see if there is one point you could regularly dedicate as a quiet time with God:

- Morning time before or after preparing to start the day.
- A mid-day break after eating lunch.
- Evening time just before or after supper.
- Late evening time just before retiring.

(Encourage your group to consider one of these options for a quiet time with God and develop a plan for pursuing this time. Remind them of Jesus' points regarding the format of that time. Challenge them to try a quiet time during the upcoming week and consider sharing their experience the next time you meet.)

Lesson #13: THE MODEL PRAYER
Text: Matthew 6:9-15

Key Issue: What are the appropriate issues for our prayer time with God?
Key Verses: Matthew 6:10-12

Hook: You probably remember some people you have heard offer wonderful prayers. These people may have been ministers or church leaders. They may have been family members or close friends. There was just something about their prayers that stand out in your memory. In fact, you may have picked up some of their phrasing in your own prayers. What were the characteristics of these prayers that made them so special? *(Have your class or group share about individuals they remember whose prayers were particularly outstanding. As people share, create a list that describes what the group believes are the important elements in dynamic prayers. You will be able to use this as a comparison with Jesus' model prayer later in the lesson.)*

Transition Sentence: *Prayer is our communication link with God and it requires true focus in what we share with Him.*

Book: Jesus knew that the true prayer link with God had been lost by the people of His day, so He provided a model for communicating with the heavenly Father. This model presents both a simple and comprehensive basis for communicating with God. *(See the chapter for specific statements and illustrations.)*
  - It has seven components: God's name, God's kingdom, God's will, our needs, our sins, our protection from temptation, and our deliverance from evil.
  - It has two objectives: divine intervention and the meeting of human needs.
  - It is sustained by two concerns: our concern for the prevailing of God's kingdom and our concern that forgiveness be the overwhelming ethic in that kingdom.

Going Deeper: *How do other Bible prayers compare? (another activity for the "Book" section)*
There are a number of prayers recorded for us in the Bible. Have some of your group members research how the following prayers compare with the model prayer Jesus gives in the Sermon on the Mount. Are there similar elements? Are there significant differences?
  - The prayer of David—2 Sam. 7:18-29
  - The prayer of Solomon—1 Kgs. 8:22-30
  - The prayer of Daniel—Dan. 9:5-15
  - The prayer of Nehemiah—Neh. 1:5-11

Transition Sentence: *It is God's desire for us to talk with Him in an open and honest way, so how do we make sure we are communicating in that manner?*

Look: We can assume that Jesus' model prayer focuses on the most important elements of life and should be used as an outline, regardless of the era in which we live. With that in mind, we should be able to transpose Jesus' outline into contemporary terms. Using Jesus' model, we can work together to identify specific issues on which the 21st-century Christian should focus his or her prayer life. *(Divide into seven small groups and have each take a section of the model prayer. Ask the groups to design a specific focus that will help a Christian build his or her communication with God in terms of this century. When finished, ask each group to share their proposals. Post them for all to see so that they can be reviewed in comparison to what Jesus stated in His model and to the other examples you have discussed.)*

1) Focus on the holiness of God
2) Focus on the impact of God's kingdom on earth
3) Focus on the completion of God's will
4) Focus on man's true needs
5) Focus on man's need for forgiveness
6) Focus on the protection man needs from temptation
7) Focus on the deliverance man needs from evil

Transition Sentence: *It is clear that Jesus intended our prayer life to be personal and intentional—it may require some practice to develop our prayer life at that level.*

Took: We have studied Jesus' model prayer and transported that prayer into today's terms. Now the question is, "How will we apply this personally?" To begin the search for this answer, let's have a shared prayer time, using the outline just developed in class to structure our conversation with God. *(Break this prayer time into seven sections, using the terms just developed in class as the heading of each section. Give the terms to the class one section at a time, allowing them a few moments to consider the focus and talk to the Lord about it. While a time of spoken prayer might be helpful, there may be several in the group who have never prayed in public, so the teacher should be sensitive their concerns and fears.)*

Lesson #14: FASTING
Text: Matthew 6:16-18

Key Issue: Why should the Christian fast?
Key Verses: Matthew 6:17-18

Hook: Many of us have had to fast for medical tests. The doctor's orders for a fast are usually very clear: "No food or drink other than water" for a specified period of time. Why does a doctor want us to fast before these medical tests? How does a fast enhance a medical test? Did you find fasting difficult to do? *(Have your group respond randomly to these questions.)*

During the last part of the 20th century a number of people fasted as a protest against something they thought was wrong or as a way to draw attention to an issue. What is different between this kind of fast and a medical fast? What are the elements that make a protest fast possible? *(Again, have the members in your group respond randomly, but list their answers on a chart for later reference.)*

Transition Sentence: *Fasting was another spiritual activity that religious leaders were using to prove their religious superiority, but Jesus taught that there was a deeper benefit to fasting than they were seeking.*

Book: The definition of fasting is to "go without food" for a specific purpose—in the case of our study that purpose is spiritual. However, the spiritual leaders of Jesus' day had turned fasting into a symbol of religious arrogance by making a show out of their actions. They were practicing the wrong kind of fast and Jesus called His followers to practice the right kind of fast in contrast to what they were seeing. What was the difference? The wrong kind of fast sought to attract man's attention—the right kind of fast sought to attract God's attention. The question is, "Why seek God's attention this way?" Here are some reasons *(see the chapter for specific statements and illustrations)*:

- Fasting helps us keep our relationship to God in perspective and helps us open our hearts to Him.
- Fasting removes other distractions so that we can focus totally on God's will.
- Fasting empowers us to follow God's will in service.

Obviously, there are significant reasons for us to fast!

Going Deeper*: Examples of fasting in the Bible (another activity for the "Book" section)*
There are a surprising number of fasts recorded in the Bible. Have some of your group members research the following examples from Bible people to determine the purpose and impact of fasting in their lives.

- Jehoshaphat—2 Chr. 20:2-30
- Esther—Esth. 4:12-5:5
- Daniel—Dan. 9:2-21
- Anna the prophetess—Luke 2:36-38
- The early church—Acts 13:1-3

Transition Sentence*: Jesus taught that the right approach to fasting allows us to draw closer to God, improving our understanding of God's work in the world and in us.*

Look: In the Sermon on the Mount Jesus describes the wrong kind of fast, the right kind of fast, and the reward of the fast. His teaching reflects the words of Isaiah as the prophet describes God's reaction to the fasting of His people (Isa. 58). There is something for us to learn from God's evaluation and its parallels to Jesus' teaching in Matthew 6—let's compare the two sections:

- The wrong kind of fast (Isa. 58:2-5)
- The right kind of fast (Isa. 58:6-7)
- The reward of the fast (Isa. 58:8-11)

(Divide your group into three equal parts and assign each group one of the above topics. Ask these small groups to review and discuss what Isaiah is saying about fasting. Have each group prepare to explain how Isaiah's teaching affects our view of fasting. This should be a persuasive presentation that offers ideas and challenges for fasting as a discipline for today's Christians.)

Transition Sentence*: In a culture that celebrates eating, fasting is a difficult challenge for us today—still Jesus teaches that it is important.*

Took: If you have ever had to fast, you know it is possible, but is it a probable activity in our spiritual walk? Can we focus so intensely on God that we are willing to forgo eating and other distractions in order to know Him better? *(Using the same three groups as before, have each group develop ideas that would encourage and assist a believer to practice fasting as a spiritual discipline. Encourage the groups to suggest ways to overcome the assumption and fascination with eating so prevalent in today's culture. Allow enough time for each group to share at the end of class.)*

Lesson #15: TREASURES
Text: Matthew 6:19-24

Key Issue: Where are your real treasures?
Key Verse: Matthew 6:20-21

Hook: When someone mentions "valuables" our first thought is often about the kinds of things that we put in safe places (e.g., stocks, jewelry, cash, etc.). There is a scene in the movie *Richie Rich* where the crooks finally break into the family vault only to find it full of keepsakes that have no earthly value. When questioned, Richie's father explains, "The stocks and bonds are in the bank, but these are the things that mean the most to us." If someone broke into your vault or safety deposit box, what would they find? What would these items tell them about what is most valuable to you? Do these items reflect anything about your relationship with God? *(Provide a piece of paper on which each group member can list what he or she considers his or her most valuable possession. After they have had time to make the list, ask them to explain to a neighbor why these items are most important to them.)*

Transition Sentence: Jesus moves from the things that enhance our personal relationship with God to the issue of the most important items in our life—the things on which we really focus day after day.

Book: In this section of the Sermon on the Mount, Jesus not only defines treasures for the kingdom person, but describes the obstacles to keeping our focus on those treasures. *(See the chapter for specific statements and illustrations.)*
- Jesus begins by describing what happens to treasures stored up on earth—they are ruined, making them unavailable for God's use.
- He then describes what happens to treasures stored up in heaven—they are preserved and available for God's use.

We should not make any assumptions about what these treasures are! *(Ask the class to help you create a list of earthly treasures and heavenly treasures. Ask each person to explain how he or she chose the item listed. After developing the list, have your class members answer this question: "Is it possible that some obvious earthly treasures can be transformed into heavenly treasures? How?")*

Transition Sentence: Christians are faced with the challenge of keeping their focus in heaven while facing the demands of earthly living.

Look: Jesus says that there is a distinct difference between what man sees and what God sees. We want to delineate that difference in our study today.
- Man sees earthly things and gives his loyalty to them.

- God sees heavenly things and builds His ministry to man around them.

What is the difference between these two views? What can we do to make sure our view is the same as God's? *(Bring several different items to class that represent daily living [for example, you might bring a checkbook, some food, a piece of clothing, and a collectable]. Create two columns on a board or a large piece of paper—one side for man's view and the other for God's view. Ask the class to provide descriptions of each sample item from the two views, man's and God's.)*

Jesus did not say that earthly things were bad—He said that focusing on earthly things alone had no future. Having considered the contrasts between man's view and God's view, it is obvious that there is more purpose and significance in taking God's view. Whether or not we hold that view is determined by the focus of our eyes and the loyalty of our hearts. When we focus on God's will, we bring all thoughts and decisions under His purposes. When we give Him our total loyalty, worldly possessions are no longer a priority.

Going Deeper*: How does a true steward invest in heavenly treasures? (another activity for the "Look" section)*

The story of the talents (Matt. 25:14-30) shows how three men responded to taking responsibility for their master's riches. Two of them successfully interpreted their master's goals and invested wisely—the third did not. Ask a local stockbroker or investor to speak to the class and describe his or her responsibility for investing other people's money. Ask this person to explain how focus and goals determine how funds are invested. Consider how this outlook fits with Jesus' teaching about treasures.

Transition Sentence*: In several other places in the Gospels Jesus teaches the difference between God's ownership and our stewardship—a central factor to our outlook regarding treasures.*

Took: If you could transfer the ownership of all you owned to God, how do you think He would manage it? If you could actually do this, how would it change your outlook regarding your valuables? *(Have your class create a description of God's management of treasures.)* With this in mind, how would you manage your treasures differently? Is there something you could do as early as this week?

Lesson #16: WORRY
Text: Matthew 6:25-34

Key Issue: Is there any reason for a Christian to worry?
Key Verse: Matthew 6:33

Hook: It would take several pages to list all the things that people worry about in the American culture. With pressures from job and family, few of us are exempt from this issue. But have you ever considered why we worry? What is it that causes us to be concerned about our lives and the things around us? Let's try to put this in perspective by creating a "worry" chart. *(On a board or large piece of paper draw a line that starts at one of the low corners and moves up toward the other corner—it should go diagonally across the surface. The low point would be less worry—the high point would represent a lot of worry.)*

To begin, let's list items that may be troublesome, but about which we really don't worry a lot. *(As you write these items on the chart ask the group to categorize them by the amount of worry they might cause—spread these items along the lower part of the line.)* Now, we will add things that cause us a lot of worry. *(Write these items at the upper end of the line, spreading them out as the class categorizes them.)* What causes us to worry about these things and why are some more troublesome than others?

Transition Sentence: Jesus taught that worry does not accomplish anything and, in this section, He gives us help in confronting worry.

Book: There are increasing pressures on all of us and these pressures create concern, but how do we handle these concerns so that they do not dominate our life as worry? Jesus has some suggestions *(see the chapter for specific statements and illustrations):*

- There is nothing productive about worry—it does not make anything better in our lives.
- Worry is unhealthy—it causes a number of physical problems.
- Worry is unnecessary—if God is truly omnipotent, He is capable of resolving all problems.
- Worry is unspiritual—it focuses on things that are not eternal.

The opposite of worry is trusting God, but how do we work this out in our lives?

Transition Sentence: Jesus paints a picture of a God who cares for all things, so the question is, why don't we trust Him to take care of us?

Look: Jesus gives us two specific reasons to trust God: 1) God cares for us because we are more important than animals, and 2) God knows what we need and has proven that He can care for His creation.

Jesus goes on to say that the problem is not God's ability to provide, but our ability to seek His will above all and in all areas of life. How do we do that? Here are some specific areas in life that seem to provide significant cause for worry in our culture. Let's see if there are ways that we can overcome these issues by focusing on God's kingdom. *(Divide the class into six different groups and assign them one of the statements below. Ask them to apply the points of Jesus' teaching, as listed above, to their assigned topic and to develop advice for the person so that there is balance between personal responsibility and trusting God.)*

- I have not had a raise in three years, yet the cost to provide for my family continues to increase.
- I have three children, the first of which will enter college in four years.
- My employer does not provide health insurance and I have two young children.
- I am self-employed and have found it very difficult to set aside funds for my retirement.
- I have a family member with significant health issues and this person may have to live with me.
- We are a newly married couple and want to buy a home soon.

Going Deeper*: How does a true steward plan for the future? (another activity for the "Look" section)*

It is extremely difficult to determine how we should plan for the future without becoming overly concerned about things like finances, insurance, investments, etc. Ask a trusted financial planner to visit your group to explain the best way to make plans for the future without worrying about it. Preferably this person is a Christian who understands the biblical principles involved in planning for life while trusting God in all ways.

Transition Sentence*: God does not want us to dwell on earthly things, but to bring our priorities in line with the plan for His kingdom.*

Took: Have you identified the true priorities in your life? What really is the most important part of your life—the part that dominates your thinking and effort? It may or may not be a wrong thing—the issue is whether you are trusting God in this area or not. We are going to take a few minutes to measure our priorities against this teaching of Jesus: "Seek first his kingdom and his righteousness, and all these things will be given to you as well." We will do this in stages *(provide paper and have your group follow step-by-step)*:

1) List the things that are truly most important in your life.
2) Ask this question about each item: "Have I submitted this area of my life to God's rule?"
3) If the answer is "yes," make sure you know how you are fulfilling God's plan in the area.

4) If the answer is "no," consider options for fulfilling God's plan in this portion of your life.

(Close with prayer that seeks God's intervention in the lives of your group members as they sort out the priorities and submit them to God.)

Lesson #17: JUDGING JUSTLY
Text: Matthew 7:1-6

Key Issue: How do we relate to others' errors?
Key Verse: Matthew 7:2

Hook: What happens when you get something in your eye? The normal reaction is for us to try to get it out by ourselves first. But there are times when we need someone else's help to get a small object out of our eye. How do you prepare to get an object out of someone else's eye? What does it require for the person who is offering the help? *(Have the group brainstorm about how they would prepare to help another person get something out of his or her eye.)*

Above all else, the person trying to get a speck out of someone else's eye must have clarity of sight! His or her own ability to see must be unimpeded in order to find the speck and remove it.

Transition Sentence*: According to Jesus, the same is true when we are trying to deal with a character flaw or problem in a fellow believer's life.*

Book: Attitudes have been a recurring theme in our study of the Sermon on the Mount. In this section Jesus confronts one of the most destructive attitude issues in the church—that of judging one another in a critical way. We should not hide behind any excuses—this is not a performance evaluation or act of discernment! Jesus is addressing the person who has an ongoing critical attitude that condemns the people around him or her rather than finding ways to encourage them. This is a dangerous trap, so how do we avoid it? Jesus has some answers. *(See the chapter for specific statements and illustrations.)*

- We should watch our attitude because it will come back to us.
- We should watch out for our own blind spots.
- We should watch out for a wasted effort.

God has the responsibility for judgment—our job is to help others grow as one fellow struggler helps another along a difficult path. We are to approach this responsibility with personal insight into our own status so that we have clear discernment regarding the status of those we want to help.

Transition Sentence*: While Jesus often spoke directly and bluntly to His listeners, He established an atmosphere of service among His disciples so that their relationships and care for each other would be built upon a caring attitude.*

Look: The Scriptures have a lot to say about the relationships within the Christian community. Jesus set the tone for this portrayal in His teachings and then Paul wrote much about Christian relationships in his letters. These teachings are helpful in expanding on the attitude of service that Jesus exemplified. Some of these passages will help us consider the necessary attitude regarding any judgment directed to a brother or sister in Christ. Here are some references from Paul that are directed to this end:

- "Accept one another . . ." (Rom. 5:7)
- ". . . instruct one another" (Rom. 5:14)
- ". . . serve one another in love" (Gal. 5:13)
- "Submit to one another . . ." (Eph. 5:21)
- "Encourage one another and build each other up . . ." (1 Thess. 5:11)

How do the attitudes behind these actions help us avoid the trap of being judgmental as we work with our brothers and sisters in Christ? *(Divide your class into five small groups, with each assigned one of these passages. Ask the groups to: 1) determine what each passage means [based on the word used for ministry to one another], 2) describe the attitude behind this ministry, and 3) explain how this approach would help us avoid a critical attitude when ministry to each other's faults.)*

Going Deeper: *How do we create an atmosphere of encouragement in our church? (another activity for the "Look" section)*
It is a significant challenge to confront someone without appearing to be judgmental, but the attitudinal perspective of the church can set the tone for this kind of ministry. Perhaps your church has someone on staff or in leadership that deals with this issue through counseling, mentoring, or supervising others. Ask this person to come to your class to share suggestions for setting a positive tone of service within your group or in the church at large. Ask them to explain what they believe is the right way for ministering to a fellow Christian in a way that allows for helpful correction.

Transition Sentence: *Jesus is clear that ministry to others begins with our own heart.*

Took: We certainly appreciate the fact that all of us have blind spots that need attention. Perhaps you have a lost relationship with someone because of a bad attitude on your part or a poor response on the part of your friend or family member. Examine your life to see if the right attitudes discussed earlier are in place. If not, consider which of these attitudes needs the most attention at the moment. *(This is a reflective exercise that cannot be easily shared with others. Lead the class in some personal prayer time and ask each person to target an area in which he or she can improve his or her attitude toward someone else.)*

Lesson #18: ASK, SEEK, AND KNOCK
Text: Matthew 7:7-12

Key Issue: Seeking answers from God
Key Verse: Matthew 7:7

Hook: Have you ever really wanted something so badly that there was nothing else you could think about? This desire probably dominated every waking moment and you let everyone know that this was the case. However, the key question is, "Did you have a plan for making this dream come true?" (*Ask your group to think of one time in their lives when this was the case. It may be something they wanted to own, or a special event they wanted to attend, or something special they wanted to achieve. Do not have them share their thoughts at this point.*)

Jesus portrays God as a parent in the section of Matthew we are studying today. Before we look at this section, let's role-play a couple of the incidents you were thinking of. (*This activity assumes that the members of the group have been thinking of something from their childhood. Ask one of your group members to role-play a parent who would listen and respond like God would. Then ask two of your group members to role-play themselves, one-at-a-time, making the request for their dream to come true.*)

Transition Sentence: *We know God is a loving God and we know that He cares deeply about His children, but how does God respond to our requests of Him?*

Book: In these verses, Jesus portrays God as a listening, loving God who responds to His children when they ask. This personal God is available and open to our persistent requests. Does this character of God guarantee the answers we want? Maybe not. (*See the chapter for specific statements and illustrations.*)

- There are times we ask the wrong way and God does not answer at all.
- There are times we ask for the wrong reason and God does not give us the answer we sought.
- There are times we ask for the wrong things and God does not answer as we would expect.

Whatever the case, how God answers our prayers does not change His character and so, Jesus calls us to model God's love in our relationships just as He has done in answering our requests. This teaching is the heart of the "Golden Rule" because God has treated us as He would have us treat Him. This means that we need to let the love of God rule in our lives in order to help us love others. Of course, if the Jews truly knew the law, they would have known that this was the background of what God desired when He first established the law with Israel, thus the "Golden Rule" truly "sums up the Law and the Prophets."

Going Deeper: *How does God respond to our persistence? (another activity for the "Book" section)*
In Luke 11:5-8, a parable is added to this same teaching about asking, seeking, and knocking. The portrayal is of a man who responds to his neighbor's need only after the neighbor persistently keeps asking for help. What does this parable add to our understanding about God in reference to our prayers? Does it change any of the conclusions we have drawn about God and how He responds to us? What does it tell us about our approach to God? *(Be sure to research the background of this parable before discussing it with your class.)*

Transition Sentence: *It seems obvious that prayer is the primary application of this teaching about asking, seeking, and knocking, but what are the attitudes we develop about prayer that extend this teaching into our personal lives?*

Look: James talks about prayer and God's character at several different points in his letter. Many of the teachings from James apply to today's study—for example:

- The contrast between faith and doubt is introduced in James 1:5-7.
- The goodness of God's provision for us is presented in James 1:16-17.
- The issue of motives behind our prayers is addressed in James 4:2b-3.
- The specific example of praying for the sick is discussed in James 5:13-16.

All of these instructions can be applied to asking, seeking, and knocking before God. *(Divide your group into four parts, assigning one section from James to each of the groups. Ask the groups to create an illustration based on the teaching found in their assigned portion. This real-life illustration should demonstrate how we approach God and what answer we should expect from Him. Have each group share after a time of discussion.)*

Transition Sentence: *Jesus wants us to understand that God is our Father and that He longs to hear from us about our needs.*

Took: There may be something on your heart right now about which you urgently want God's answer. What have you learned from today's study that would help you in your approach to God? *(Take a few minutes with the group to list things they have learned about God's love. Ask them how these characteristics affect our approach to Him in prayer.)* Now, the question comes, what will you do today when you talk to God about this issue? *(In closing, lead the group in a personal prayer time during which they consider the issue of greatest concern to them and how they will present this issue to the Lord.)*

Lesson #19: CHOICES
Text: Matthew 7:13-14

Key Issue: How will you choose between the earthly way and the heavenly way?

Key Verse: Matthew 7:14

Hook: Game shows are famous for the choices they require people to make. At one time there was a show that featured the "doors of destiny." There was a different item or opportunity behind each door, but only one of these items was a really wonderful prize. The participants in the show had to make blind choices in order to advance toward a higher prize, sometimes giving up what they have in hand. Let's consider this illustration for a few minutes:

- What is it that people are always looking for in a game show like this?
- What motivates them to give up one prize for another they cannot see?
- Do you think there are any similarities between these choices and the spiritual choices Jesus asks us to make?

(Let your group discuss these questions for a few minutes, but urge the participants to analyze human nature as the discussion develops. The goal is to contrast these choices with the choice that Jesus presents in this section of Scripture.)

Transition Sentence: In our study today, Jesus says that there are only two choices in life—both of which have present and eternal consequences.

Book: Jesus is coming to His conclusion in the Sermon on the Mount. Like all good preachers, He is getting ready to ask His hearers to make a choice: follow Me or follow anything else but Me. A clear choice, but Jesus goes on to describe some implications about choosing the narrow gate *(see the chapter for specific statements and illustrations):*

- There is only one entrance that takes us to God—the narrow gate.
- This entrance to God is narrow because we must deny self to get through it.
- Only few find this entrance because it requires difficult, life changing decisions.
- Choosing the narrow gate gives us the greatest opportunity to deal with life successfully.

In contrast, there are also implications from choosing the wide gate:

- By human standards it is the most appealing, but it is also the least revealing.
- The wide gate is the most comfortable where you go in, but offers the least success for life.

Transition Sentence*: While the choice between the two gates appears to be a no-brainer, it must not be because so many people struggle with this choice.*

Look: Jesus implies some truths about the wide and narrow ways that are not directly spoken in our study. These truths relate to what it is like to walk the two different roads. One, Jesus says, is a road of destruction—that would imply that the other is a road to perfection. How do we describe these roads to the people around us? Could you expand on and explain what it means to walk the two different paths to someone who was just getting to know Jesus? *(Have two long pieces of butcher paper available with the title "Narrow Way" on one and "Wide Way" on the other. If your group is small, divide into two equally sized groups—if not, you may want to duplicate this activity in order to increase participation. Have the groups decorate each "way" with the experiences they think fit Jesus' description. For example, the "narrow way" may have lots of prayer, Bible study, and service opportunities on it while the "wide way" has items that are selfish and destructive. When the groups are finished, have them describe their poster just as they would to someone new to Christ.)*

Going Deeper*: The illustration of* Pilgrim's Progress *(another activity for the "Look" section)*
One of the greatest illustrations of Matthew 7:13-14 is John Bunyan's classic, *Pilgrim's Progress*. Throughout this book, the main character struggles to stay on the way to God. Have different people in your group read different chapters in the book and bring back to class a summary of Bunyan's description of the ways his character struggles to stay on it.

Transition Sentence*: It is one thing to describe the two paths that Jesus describes in this text, and it is another to follow it.*

Took: Most of the people in our group have chosen to follow Christ, but it is possible that some have not. However, it is certain that everyone in the group knows someone who has not made this choice. Our study today is built around the truth that Jesus is the only access to eternity and the way of blessing that God provides. So, how would you introduce a friend to this way? Why would this be so important? *(Close this study by asking some of your class members to describe the narrow way in a manner that would appeal to someone outside of Christ. Allow the group to respond to the descriptions in order to help clarify the opportunity given by Christ for eternity through the narrow way. As you conclude, ask each person to think of one friend they know who is outside of Christ. Ask them to make this person a matter of prayer and preparation with the hope of sharing what they learned today.)*

Lesson #20: WARNINGS
Text: Matthew 7:15-23

Key Issue: How do we identify false teachers?
Key Verse: Matthew 7:21

Hook: Identifying and rewarding productive people in our society has become a science. There are many theories about evaluating people so that strengths are recognized and weaknesses are confronted. Some have tried to apply these theories within the church. After our study of the Sermon on the Mount, how would you evaluate a productive Christian? What would you say are the most important factors in identifying Christians who are truly making a difference? *(Divide your class into groups of four or five. Tell each group that they are to identify the most productive person in the church. Before beginning the task, they must create a grid against which they can measure Christian productivity. This grid is to be based on Jesus' teachings in the Sermon on the Mount. After giving the groups a few minutes, ask them to present their work to the rest of the class.)*

Transition Sentence: *Jesus knew that there would be people who tried to look like His followers, but whose lives would not bear the markings of a true relationship with God.*

Book: History tells us that it did not take long for false teachers to start moving about in the early church. Jesus knew this invasion was coming and would be dangerous for the young believers. In the conclusion of His teachings, Jesus gave His followers tools with which to separate true teachers from false teachers. First, He says, false teachers are really "wolves in sheep's clothing" who care for nothing but their own purposes *(see the chapter for specific statements and illustrations):*
- False teachers will claim to speak for God, but their actions will reveal their true loyalty.
- False teachers will gain a hearing among those who only want to hear flattering instruction.
- False teachers will actually attack and destroy the sheep in God's flock.
- False teachers will build loyalty to themselves instead of to God.

Often these characteristics are hidden so that hearers do not know the intentions of a false teacher, but Jesus said they would ultimately be identified in the results of their work? At this point Jesus changed His metaphor from wolves to fruit trees in order to describe these results:
- Their false intentions will be seen in a character that is driven by fleshly desires.
- Their false teachings will be found in conflicts with the truth of Jesus' teachings.

- Their false influence will be measured in followers who are self-absorbed and self-indulgent.

In this description Jesus puts all of us on the lookout for those who would abuse the opportunity to serve the Lord.

Transition Sentence*: As Jesus concludes the Sermon on the Mount, He makes it very clear that there should be a consistency between a believer's internal thinking and his external actions—a lesson that applies to all believers.*

Look: There is a danger in thinking that the description of false teachers only applies to a group of outsiders that we have never met. The kind of thinking behind false teachers is insidious and can quietly influence all of us whether we are leaders in the church or not. Paul gives a lengthy description of those who are ready for true leadership in 1 Timothy 3. We might consider this to be the positive contrast to Jesus' negative description of false teachers. *(As you lead your class through this study, you should create a list on a board or large piece of paper that describes the false teacher. At this point, have the class turn to 1 Timothy 3:1-13 [this is a description of lifestyle qualities expected of elders and deacons]. Assign one characteristic from this list to each class member and ask him or her to state the characteristic in contrast to the negative descriptions found in today's study. Be sure to point out the implied intentions and results assumed by Paul in his descriptions of good leaders.)*

Going Deeper*: What are today's false teachers like? (another activity for the "Look" section)*

The most obvious false teachers in today's world would be the pseudo-Christian cults that have grown rapidly in recent years. There are a number of resources available for the study of the cults including study guides and videotape series. There may even be a specialist in this field who could come and speak to your group. In either case, the focus of this special activity is to identify the characteristics of false teachers in groups that exist today in parallel to Jesus' description in Matthew 7. This would be a good opportunity for another extra learning and fellowship time with your class or group.

Transition Sentence*: These issues are not limited to false teachers or leaders, but to anyone who claims to follow Christ and does not show that loyalty in the fruit of his or her life.*

Took: As we reflect on today's discussion, the issue of our own relationship with the Lord must be considered. While we know that we enjoy this relationship simply by God's grace, it is obvious that we hold responsibility for living out that relationship in our thinking and our actions. One of the most dynamic portions of Scripture for measuring the fruit of our own life is found in Galatians 5:22-23, called the "fruit of the Spirit." Reviewing this list is one way of asking, "Is God at work in my life in a measurable way?" *(There will not be time to study the "fruit of the Spirit" during this session, but there should be time for each person to reflect on the production of godly fruit in his or her own life. This should be a quiet time, closed with directed prayer.)*

Lesson #21: OBEDIENCE
Text: Matthew 7:24-27

Key Issue: How do I make sure obedience to Christ is a part of my life?
Key Verse: Matthew 7:24

Hook: We normally do not see the foundations of a house or a building—since they are functional and not attractive, they are buried in the ground. However, we know these foundations must be there. In fact, they are so important that there are very specific regulations for the building of foundations so that there is no danger to those who eventually inhabit the structure that sits upon them. *(Ask a contractor to visit your class for this lesson and to speak to the importance of foundations in construction work. Ask him to explain how the specifications for foundations must match the buildings that will rise on them.)*

Transition Sentence: *Jesus concluded His sermon with a vivid illustration about foundations, and He applied that illustration to each one of us.*

Book: Jesus begins His conclusion by saying, "Therefore, everyone who hears these words of mine and puts them into practice is like a wise man who built his house on the rock" (7:24). There are four important points made in this simple verse *(see the chapter for specific statements and illustrations)*:
- The words of Jesus were designed to call for action.
- The words of Jesus were designed to call for a decision.
- The words of Jesus were designed to call for an application of God's will.
- The words of Jesus were designed to call for a careful choice.

Jesus intended for His hearers to be doers, but He didn't want them to just run out and do anything. His desire was for them to make careful choices so that His words were a solid foundation for daily life. To make His point, Jesus added a description of two builders to His call in verse 24—one wise and one foolish. What was the difference between the two? What was it about the foundation that made one house solid and the other weak in the face of storms? *(Ask the class to work through this comparison with you.)*

Going Deeper: *How did others listen to Jesus and respond? (another activity for the "Book" section)*
The Sermon on the Mount is followed by several encounters between Jesus and the people who came to hear Him. As a group, review the incidents found in Matthew 8–9 and list the responses of the people to Jesus. Did some act upon His words? Did some not act upon what they heard? What was the difference in the results as seen in their lives?

Transition Sentence: The picture of building our lives on Jesus is vivid, but the decisions that follow that choice are not always simple.

Look: The following are key teachings in the Sermon on the Mount. Let's consider how these teachings are foundational for Christian living and what actions should come out of them:

- "Let your light shine before men, that they may see your good deeds and praise your Father in heaven" (5:16).
- "Be careful not to do your 'acts of righteousness' before men, to be seen by them" (6:1).
- "Store up for yourselves treasures in heaven, where moth and rust do not destroy, and where thieves do not break in and steal" (6:20).
- "Do not worry about your life, what you will eat or drink; or about your body, what you will wear" (6:25).
- "Ask and it will be given to you; seek and you will find; knock and the door will be opened to you" (7:7).
- "Enter through the narrow gate" (7:13).

(This activity can be done in small groups. You may want to let each group choose its own verse from the Sermon on the Mount or assign verses that received particular attention during your study. The point of the discussion should be focused on what Jesus would expect us to do with these teachings in everyday life.)

Transition Sentence: As a good preacher, Jesus calls His audience to make a decision after hearing His sermon—what will you choose?

Took: It is one thing to hear Jesus' words and quite another to act upon them daily. In his commentary, *The Parables of Jesus*, Neil Lightfoot asked this question, "How is it that we can hear and not obey?" Here are the three answers he suggested:

- Sometimes we choose not to act when we should.
- Sometimes we do not want to be inconvenienced.
- Sometimes we do not look ahead.

Are you struggling with any these problems? Is there a way to head them off in order to be a wise builder? Is there a storm headed your way that may expose a weakness in your walk with God? *(Ask the individuals in your group to choose a statement from Lightfoot that best describes their current situation. Give them a few minutes to consider this evaluation and what they will do to remedy the problem. Close with a personal prayer time.)*

Lesson #22: CONCLUSION TO
THE SERMON ON THE MOUNT
Text: Matthew 7:28-29

Key Issue: Has the authority of Jesus made a difference in how I live my life?
Key Verse: 7:29

Hook: Ask your class the following questions—What do you think of when you hear the word "authority"? Do you think of a person (such as a policeman, boss, parent, etc.) or do you think of something more abstract (such as laws, position, or power)? Does this word have a positive or negative connotation to you? How do you think it is seen in our culture today? *(Make a list on a board or piece of paper as the class describes their thoughts regarding authority.)*

Transition Sentence: *These ideas represent the forms of authority that we think of today—the people of Jesus' day probably had the same images, but when they heard Jesus speak, they knew He had an authority that was far different than anything they had ever witnessed.*

Book: This chapter explains that Jesus' teaching was different because of His authority, authority based in the person of Christ. The following are points from the chapter that support the source of Jesus' authority. *(See the chapter for specific statements and illustrations.)*
   4) He spoke as the Son of God.
   5) He spoke from His own authority, not from the authority of others.
   6) He spoke with a call for His hearers to change what they were doing.
   7) He spoke and His authority was recognized.
Oswald Chambers wrote: *"Beware of placing our Lord as a Teacher first. If Jesus Christ is a teacher only, then all He can do is tantalize me by erecting a standard I cannot attain. . . . I must know Jesus Christ as Savior before His teaching has any meaning for me other than that of an ideal which leads to despair. But when I am born again of the Spirit of God, I know that Jesus Christ did not come to teach only: He came to make me what He teaches I should be."* What is Chambers saying about Jesus' authority?

Going Deeper: *A Gentile meets Jesus' authority (another activity for the "Book" section)*
In Matthew 8:5-13, a Roman centurion comes to Jesus requesting healing for a trusted servant. Much of the conversation Jesus has with this man relates to authority. What does the centurion understand about authority? How does he apply this understanding to Jesus? What should we understand about Jesus' authority from this encounter?

Transition Sentence*: Jesus carried the authority of God Himself in His person and those who heard Him recognized it in His teaching.*

Look: The chapter provides twenty questions that help us evaluate the impact of Jesus' authority on our lives. How would you answer these questions? *(Depending on the size of your class, select one to five questions and assign them to small groups for discussion. Ask the class to consider two points about the assigned question: 1) What does Jesus' authority have to do with the area of life involved with this question? 2) What would be possible answers to the question if Jesus' authority is fully applied?)*

Transition Sentence*: Jesus is the same today as He was when He presented the Sermon on the Mount—His words have not changed, neither has His authority. How will that authority from Jesus Christ change you?*

Took: If your students could change one thing about their relationship with Jesus what would it be? *(Make a handout of the twenty questions offered in this chapter and provide it to all of your students. Encourage each of them to choose one question to ponder this week. Ask them to consider what differences Jesus' authority would make in that area of their life. Give them a few moments to consider what they will do this week to allow the authority of Jesus to work in their life. Close with the challenge of words on Patrick's breastplate [quoted at the end of the chapter].)*

Works Cited

Aland, Barbara, et al., eds. *The Greek New Testament*. 4th Rev. ed. New York: UBS, 1994.

Albright, W.F. and C.S. Mann. *Matthew: Introduction; Translation and Notes*. The Anchor Bible. Garden City: Doubleday, 1971.

Allen, Lloyd. "The Sermon on the Mount in the History of the Church." *Review and Expositor* 90 (1992).

Anonymous. *A Little Book of Irish Verse*. Trans. Kuno Meyer. San Francisco: Chronicle Books, 1991.

Augsburger, Myron S. *Matthew*. The Communicator's Commentary. Vol. 1. Waco: Word, 1982.

———. *Mastering the New Testament: Matthew*. Gen. ed. Lloyd Ogilvie. Waco: Word, 1982.

Bailey, J.L. "Sermon on the Mount: Model for Christianity." *Currents in Theology and Missions* 20 (1993).

Bailey, J.L. and S.P. Saunders. "God's Merciful Community." *Currents in Theology and Missions* 14 (1987).

Balz, Horst and Gerhard Schneider, eds. *Exegetical Dictionary of the New Testament*. Vol. 1. Grand Rapids: Eerdmans, 1990.

Barclay, William. *The Gospel of Matthew*. The Daily Study Bible Series. Vol. 1. Philadelphia: Westminster, 1975.

Barna, George. "Christians Are More Likely to Experience Divorce Than Are Non-Christians." Barna Update. December 21, 1999 <http://www.barna.org>.

Barth, Karl. *The Doctrine of the Word of God: Prolegomena to Church Dogmatics*. Vol I. 2. Trans. G.T. Thompson and Harold Knight. Edinburgh: T & T Clark, 1956.

———. *The Doctrine of God: Church Dogmatics*. Vol. ll. 2. Eds. G.W. Bromiley and T.F. Torrance. Trans. G.W. Bromiley, et al. Edinburgh: T & T Clark, 1958.

Batey, Richard A. "Jesus and the Theater." *New Testament Studies* 30 (1984).

Bauer, Walter, F. Wilbur Gingrich, and Frederick Danker. *A Greek-English Lexicon of the New Testament and Other Early Christian Literature*. Chicago: Univ. of Chicago Press, 1979 (Logos).

Bauman, Clarence. *The Sermon on the Mount. The Modern Quest for its Meaning*. Macon, GA: Mercer, 1985.

Betz, H.D. *The Sermon on the Mount: A Commentary on the Sermon on the Mount, including the Sermon on the Plain*. Minneapolis: Fortress, 1995.

Bilodeau, Lorrainne. *The Anger Workbook*. Center City, MN: Hazelden Foundation, 1994.

Blomberg, Craig L. *Matthew*. The New American Commentary. Nashville: Broadman, 1992.

Boring, M. Eugene. *The Gospel of Matthew*. Nashville: Abingdon, 1995.

Bright, Bill. *The Coming Revival*. Orlando: New Life, 1995.

Briscoe, Stuart. *The Sermon on the Mount: Daring to be Different*. Wheaton: Harold

Shaw, 1995.

Bromiley, Geoffrey W., ed. *Theological Dictionary of the New Testament.* Eds. G. Kittel and G. Friedrich. Trans. G.W. Bromiley. Grand Rapids: Eerdmans, 1985.

Brown, Colin. ed. *The New International Dictionary of New Testament Theology.* Vol. 2. Reprint. Grand Rapids: Zondervan, 1979.

Bruce, A.B. *The Synoptic Gospels.* The Expositor's Greek Testament. Vol. I. Ed. by W. Robertson Nicoll. Grand Rapids: Eerdmans, 1961.

Bruner, Frederick Dale. *Matthew: A Commentary.* Vol.1. Dallas: Word, 1987.

Bullock, C. Hassell. *Encountering the Book of Psalms.* Grand Rapids: Baker, 2001.

Carson, D.A. *God with Us.* Ventura, CA: Regal, 1985.

———. *Matthew, Mark, Luke.* Vol. 8. The Expositor's Bible Commentary. Ed. Frank E. Gaebelein. Grand Rapids: Zondervan, 1984.

———. *The Sermon on the Mount: An Evangelical Exposition of Matthew 5-7.* Grand Rapids: Baker, 1978.

Carter, Les and Frank Minirth. *The Anger Workbook.* Nashville: Thomas Nelson, 1993.

Chambers, Oswald. *The Complete Works of Oswald Chambers.* Grand Rapids: Discovery, 2000.

Chouinard, Larry. *Matthew.* College Press NIV Commentary. Joplin: College Press, 1997.

Clapp, Philip S., Barbara Friberg, and Timothy Friberg, eds. *Analytical Greek Concordance of the Greek New Testament,* Vol. 1. Grand Rapids: Baker, 1991.

———. *Lexical Focus.* Grand Rapids: Baker, 1991.

Colson, Charles. *How Now Shall We Live.* Wheaton: Tyndale, 1999.

Connick, C.M. *Jesus: The Man, the Mission, and the Message.* 2nd ed. Englewood Cliffs, NJ: Prentice-Hall, 1974.

Crossan, John Dominic. "Divine Immediacy and Human Immediacy: Towards a New First Principle in Historical Jesus Research." *Semeia* 44 (1998).

Danby, Herbert. *The Mishnah.* London: Oxford Univ. Press, 1977.

Danker, Frederick W. *A Greek-English Lexicon of the New Testament and Other Early Christian Literature.* 3rd ed. Chicago: Univ. of Chicago Press, 2000.

Davies, W.D. *The Setting of the Sermon on the Mount.* Cambridge: Univ. Press, 1964.

Davies, W.D. and Dale C. Allison. "Introduction and Commentary on Matthew I-VII." *The Gospel According to Saint Matthew.* The International Critical Commentary. Vol. 1. Edinburgh: T & T Clark, 1988.

Dawson, George and Richard Glaubman. *Life is So Good.* New York: Penguin USA, 2001.

Deming, Will. "Mark 9. 42-10:12, Matthew 5.27-32, and B.Nid.13b: a first century discussion of male sexuality." *New Testament Studies* 36 (1990) 130-141.

Dibelius, Martin. *The Sermon on the Mount.* New York: Scribners, 1940.

Dockery, D.S. and D.E. Garland. *Seeking the Kingdom: The Sermon on the Mount Made Practical.* Wheaton: Harold Shaw, 1992.

Donelson, L.R. "The Sermon on the Mount: the Stripping of Ideology." *Insights.* 110 (1995).

Dumais, M. "The Sermon on the Mount. An Unattainable Way of Life?" *Chicago Studies* 37 (1998).

Duty, Guy. *Divorce and Remarriage—A Christian View.* Minneapolis: Bethany Fellowship, 1968.

Ebeling, Gerhard. *Our Prayer: The Lord's Prayer in Today's World.* Philadelphia: Fortress, 1966.

Filson, Floyd V. *The Gospel According to St. Matthew.* Black's New Testament Commentaries. 2nd ed. London: A. & C. Black, 1971.

———. *A Commentary on the Gospel According to St. Matthew.* New York: Harper, 1960.

Fisher, Fred L. *The Sermon on the Mount.* Nashville: Broadman, 1976.

Foster, Richard. *Celebration of Discipline.* San Francisco: Harper, 1988.

———. *Money, Sex and Power.* San Francisco: Harper, 1985.

Fowler, Harold. *The Gospel of Matthew.* Bible Study Textbook Series. Vol. 1. Joplin: College Press, 1968.

France, R.T. *The Gospel According to Matthew.* Tyndale New Testament Commentaries. Vol. 1. Grand Rapids: Eerdmans, 1985.

Frew, Robert, ed. *Barnes Notes on the New Testament.* Grand Rapids: Baker, 1949.

Goetchius, Eugene van Ness. *The Language of the New Testament.* New York: Charles Scribner's Sons, 1965.

Green, H. Benedict. *The Gospel According to Matthew.* London: Oxford Univ. Press, 1975.

Green, Michael. *Matthew for Today.* Dallas: Word, 1988.

———. *The Message of Matthew.* Downers Grove: IVP, 2001.

Greenfield, G. "The Ethics of the Sermon on the Mount." *Southwestern Journal of Theology* 35 (1992).

Guelich, Robert A. *The Sermon on the Mount: A Foundation for Understanding.* Waco: Word, 1982.

Gundry, Robert H. *Matthew: A Commentary on His Handbook for a Mixed Church under Persecution.* 2nd ed. Grand Rapids: Eerdmans, 1994.

Hagner, Donald A. *Matthew 1-13.* Word Biblical Commentary. 33A. Dallas: Word, 1993.

Han, Nathan. *A Parsing Guide to the Greek New Testament.* Scottsdale, PA: Herald, 1971.

Hare, Douglas R.A. *Matthew.* Interpretation. Louisville: John Knox, 1993.

Harner, Philip B. *Understanding the Lord's Prayer.* Philadelphia: Fortress, 1975.

Harris, Ralph, Exec. ed. *Matthew.* The New Testament Study Bible. Springfield, MO: The Complete Biblical Library, 1989.

Hawthorne, Gerald F. "Marriage and Divorce, Adultery and Incest." *Dictionary of Paul and His Letters.* Eds. Gerald F. Hawthorne, Ralph P. Martin, and Daniel G. Reid. Downers Grove: IVP, 1993.

Hayford, Jack. *Hayford's Bible Handbook.* Nashville: Thomas Nelson, 1995.

Henderson, Marion. "Life of Christ." Syllabus. Course taught at Lincoln Christian College, Lincoln, IL, 2002.

Hendricks, Herman. *The Sermon on the Mount.* London: Geoffrey Chapman, 1979.

Henry, Matthew. *Matthew Henry's Commentary on the Bible.* Peabody, MA: Hendrickson, 1960.

Hill, David. *The Gospel of Matthew.* Grand Rapids: Eerdmans, 1972.

———. *The Gospel of Matthew.* Greenwood, IN: The Attic Press, 1975.

Holmes, Michael. *The Apostolic Fathers: Greek Texts and English Translations.* 2nd ed. Grand Rapids: Baker, 1999.

Horsley, Richard A. "Ethics and Exegesis: 'Love Your Enemies' and the Doctrine of Non-Violence." *Journal of the American Academy of Religion* 54 (1986).

House, H. Wayne, ed. *Divorce and Remarriage, Four Christian Views.* Downers Grove: IVP, 1990.

Hultgren, Arland J. *The Parables of Jesus: A Commentary.* Grand Rapids: Eerdmans, 2000.

Hunter, A.M. *A Pattern for Life: An Exposition of the Sermon on the Mount.* Philadelphia: Westminster, 1965.

Instone-Brewer, David. *Divorce and Remarriage in the Bible: The Social and Literary Context.* Grand Rapids: Eerdmans, 2002.

Jeremias, Joachim. *Jerusalem in the Time of Jesus.* Trans. F.H. and C.H. Cave. Philadelphia: Fortress, 1969.

———. *The Sermon on the Mount.* Trans. Norman Perrin. Philadelphia: Fortress, 1963.

Jones, D. Martyn-Lloyd. *Studies of the Sermon on the Mount,* 2 vols. Grand Rapids: Eerdmans, 1971.

Keener, Craig S. *Matthew.* IVP New Testament Commentary Series. Downers Grove: IVP, 1997.

———. *The IVP Bible Background Commentary: New Testament.* Downer's Grove: IVP, 1993.

Lambrecht, Jan. *The Sermon on the Mount: Proclamation and Exhortation.* Wilmington, DE: Michael Glazier, 1985.

Law, William. *A Serious Call to a Devout and Holy Life.* Philadelphia: Westminster, 1955.

Lawson, Leroy. *Matthew. Unlocking the Scriptures for You.* Cincinnati: Standard, 1986.

Lenski, R.C.H. *The Interpretation of St. Matthew's Gospel.* Minneapolis: Augsburg, 1943.

Lewis, C.S. *The Weight of Glory and Other Addresses.* Grand Rapids: Eerdmans, 1965.

———. *The Last Battle.* New York: Collier Books, 1956.

———. *Reflections on the Psalms.* New York: Harcourt, Brace, and World, 1958.

Lightfoot, Neil R. *Lessons from the Parables.* Grand Rapids: Baker, 1965.

Lischer, R. "The Sermon on the Mount as Radical Pastoral Care." *Interpretation* 41 (1987).

Lloyd-Jones, D. Martyn. *Studies in the Sermon on the Mount.* Reprint. Grand Rapids: Eerdmans, 1981.

Lochman, Jan Milic. *The Lord's Prayer.* Trans. Geoffrey W. Bromiley. Grand Rapids: Eerdmans, 1990.

Long, Thomas G. *Matthew.* Westminster Bible Companion. Louisville: Westminster/John Knox, 1997.

Lucado, Max. *The Applause of Heaven.* Dallas: Word, 1990.

MacArthur, John. *Matthew 1-7.* The MacArthur New Testament Commentary. Chicago: Moody, 1985.

Manson, T. W. *The Sayings of Jesus.* London: SCM, 1957.

"Marriage." *Dictionary of Biblical Imagery.* Ed. Leland Ryken, James C. Wilhoit and Tremper Longmann III. Downers Grove: IVP, 1998.

Marshall, I. Howard. The *Work of Christ.* Grand Rapids: Zondervan, 1969.

May, Rollo. The *Meaning of Anxiety.* New York: W.W. Norton & Co., 1996.

Mays, James Luther, ed. *Harper's Bible Commentary.* New York: Harper, 1988.

McClain, Aloa J. The *Greatness of the Kingdom.* Winona Lake, IN: BMH Books, 1980.

McKenzie, John L. The *Gospel According to Matthew.* Vol. 2. Englewood Cliffs, NJ: Prentice-Hall, 1968.

McNeile, Alan Hugh. The *Gospel According to Matthew.* Grand Rapids: Baker, 1980.

McReynolds, Paul. *Word Study Greek-English New Testament.* Wheaton: Tyndale, 1999.

Metzger, Bruce M. A *Textual Commentary on the Greek New Testament.* 2nd ed. New York: UBS, 1971.

Moore, Mark. *The Chronological Life of Christ,* Vol. 1. Joplin: College Press, 1996.

Morgan, G. Campbell. The *Gospel According to Matthew.* New York: Fleming H. Revell, 1929.

———. The *Gospel According to Matthew.* New York: Fleming H. Revell, 1959.

Morris, Leon. The *Gospel According to Matthew.* Grand Rapids: Eerdmans, 1992.

Moulton, J.H. and G. Milligan. *The Vocabulary of the Greek Testament Illustrated from the Papyri and Other Non-Literary Sources.* Grand Rapids: Eerdmans, 1930.

Mounce, Robert H. *Matthew.* Peabody, MA: Hendrickson, 1991.

Murray, John. *Divorce.* Philadelphia: Committee on Christian Education, Orthodox Presbyterian Church, 1953.

Neil, William. The *Life and Teaching of Jesus.* Philadelphia: J.B. Lippincott, 1965.

Origen, "Origen's Commentary on Matthew." *Ante Nicene Fathers.* Ed. Allen Menzies. Trans. John Patrick, Vol. X. Grand Rapids: Eerdmans, 1951.

Orr, James. *The Christian View of God and the World as Centering in the Incarnation.* Kerr Lectures 1890-91. Grand Rapids: Eerdmans, 1948.

Owens, Virginia Stem. *Looking for Jesus.* Louisville: Westminster/John Knox Press, 1999.

Peterson, Eugene. *The Message.* Colorado Springs: NavPress, 1993.

Piper, John. *Let the Nations Be Glad! The Supremacy of God in Missions.* Grand Rapids: Baker, 1993.

Pippert, Rebecca Manley. *Out of the Saltshaker and Into the World.* Rev. ed. Downers Grove: IVP, 1999.

Plummer, Alfred. *An Exegetical Commentary on the Gospel According to St. Matthew.* Grand Rapids: Eerdmans, 1960.

Powers, Ward. *Learn to Read the Greek New Testament.* Grand Rapids: Eerdmans, 1982.

Pritchard, James B., ed. *Ancient Near Eastern Texts Relating to the Old Testament.* 3rd ed. Princeton: Princeton Univ. Press, 1969.

Rausch, Jerome William. "The Principle of Nonresistance and Love of Enemy in Matt. 5:38-48." *Catholic Biblical Quarterly* 28, 1 (1996).

Riga, P. "The Challenge of the Sermon on the Mount." *Emmanuel* 106 (2000).

Schuller, Robert. *The Be (Happy) Attitudes.* Waco: Word Books, 1985.

Scott, E.F. *The Lord's Prayer.* New York: Scribners, 1957.

Selye, Hans. *The Stress of Life.* New York: McGraw-Hill, 1978.

Shepard, J.W. *The Christ of the Gospels: An Exegetical Study.* Grand Rapids: Eerdmans, 1939.

Sheppard, Sandy. "What Would Jesus Do?" *Christian Reader* May/June (1998).

Smith, David R. *Fasting: A Neglected Discipline.* Fort Washington, PA: Christian Literature Crusade, 1969.

Spicq, C. *Agape in the New Testament.* Vol. I. Trans. by M.A. McNamara and M.H. Richter. St. Louis: B. Herder Book Co., 1963.

Spurgeon, C.H. *The Gospel of the Kingdom.* Pasadena: Penguin, 1974.

Stassen, Glen H. "A New, Transformative Peacemaking Ethic." *Review and Expositor* 82 (1985).

Staton, Knofel. "Divorce the Divider" (Five-Part Series), *The Lookout.* Cincinnati: Standard, April 8, 15, 22, 29, May 6, 1979.

———. *Meet Jesus.* 1980. Eugene, OR: Wipf and Stock, 2000.

Stein, R.H. "Divorce." *Dictionary of Jesus and the Gospels.* Eds. Joel B. Green and Scot McKnight. Downers Grove: IVP, 1992.

Stott, John R.W. *Christian Counter-Culture: The Message of the Sermon on the Mount.* Downers Grove: IVP, 1978.

Strecker, Georg. *The Sermon on the Mount: An Exegetical Commentary.* Trans. O.C. Dean Jr. Nashville: Abingdon, 1988.

Tasker, R.V.G. *Matthew: An Introduction and Commentary.* Grand Rapids: Eerdmans, 1983.

Tenney, Merrill C., ed. *The Zondervan Pictorial Encyclopedia of the Bible.* 5 Vols. Grand Rapids: Zondervan, 1975.

The NIV Study Bible: New International Version. Grand Rapids: Zondervan, 1985.

Thielicki, Helmut. *Life Can Begin Again.* Philadelphia: Fortress, 1963.

Thurneysen, Eduard. *The Sermon on the Mount.* Trans. William James Robinson. Richmond: John Knox Press, 1964.

Vine, W.E. *Vine's Expository Dictionary of Old and New Testament Words.* Grand Rapids: Fleming H. Revell, 1981.

Wallace, Dan. *Greek Grammar Beyond the Basics: An Exegetical Syntax of the New Testament.* Grand Rapids: Zondervan, 1996.

White, Mel. *Deceived.* Old Tappan: Fleming H. Revell, 1979.

White, R.E.O. *The Mind of Matthew: Unique Insights for Living Today.* Philadelphia: Westminster, 1979.

Willard, Dallas. *The Divine Conspiracy: Rediscovering Our Hidden Life in God.* San Francisco: Harper, 1998.

———. *Renovation of the Heart: Putting on the Character of Christ.* Colorado Springs: NavPress, 2002.

Williams, J.G. "The Sermon on the Mount as a Christian Basis of Altruism." *Humboldt Journal of Social Relations* 13 (1985;1986).

Windisch, Hans. The *Meaning of the Sermon on the Mount: A Contribution to the Historical Understanding of the Gospels and to the Problem of Their True Exegesis.* Trans. S. Maclean Gilmore. Philadelphia: Westminster, 1951.

Wink, Walter. "Beyond Just War and Pacifism: Jesus' Nonviolent Way." *Review and Expositor* 89 (1992).

Wright, D.F. "Sexuality, Sexual Ethics." *Dictionary of Paul and His Letters.* Eds. Gerald F. Hawthorne, Ralph P. Martin, and Daniel G. Reid. Downers Grove: IVP, 1993.

Yancey, Philip. *Soul Survivor.* Grand Rapids: Zondervan, 2001.

Yoder, J.H. *The Politics of Jesus.* Grand Rapids: Eerdmans, 1972.

Zerwick, M. *Jerome Bible Commentary.* Rome: Graecitas Biblica, 1960.